David Pichaske

Poland in Transition: 1989-1991

Poland in Transition: 1989-1991

David R. Pichaske

Ellis Press, 1994

Other Books by David R. Pichaske

Beowulf to Beatles: Approaches to Poetry
Beowulf to Beatles and Beyond: The Varieties of Poetry
A Generation in Motion: Popular Music and Culture in the Sixties
The Jubilee Diary: April 10, 1980-April 19, 1981
The Poetry of Rock
Visiting the Father and Other Poems
Late Harvest: Recent Rural American Writing

Cover design and photographs by David R. Pichaske.

ISBN: 0-944024-27-0

Poland in Transition, 1989-1991

Acknowledgments

Some of these essays previously appeared in very different form in the Marshall (Minnesota) *Independent* and the Peoria (Illinois) *Journal-Star*; and I am grateful to the editors of those two newspapers for allowing me to work out ideas in print. "Upon Awakening from a Dream of Poland" appeared first in *Eureka Literary Magazine*. Southwest State University saw fit to underwrite this project with a research grant, as the International Research and Exchanges Board did not. I am grateful to individuals who have read this manuscript in whole or in parts at various stages in its development: Ms. Ewa Bednarowicz, Ms. Anna Kępa, Ms. Iwona Kozlowiec, Dr. Agnieszka Salska, Bill Holm, Leo Dangel. I appreciate their contributions and corrections, and add that all errors are mine alone. Thanks also to my wife Michelle, who shared the adventure with me, took some of the photographs for this book, and did the darkroom work on others, improving as best she could the natural fog of East Bloc Orwo film. Thanks also to Tom and June Carmichael, Elizabeth Corwin, Ned Conway, Steve Nagle and Sara Sanders, Ken Luebbering and Robyn Burnett, Muriel Joffe, Brother Milton and Brother Leo Ryan, Gabriele Jones, Łukasz Salski, Krystyna and Olaf Krzemiński and their parents, Dr. Krzysztof Andrzejczak, Dr. Barbara Lewandowska-Tomaszczyk, Neil, William, Christine, Anna, Agnieszkas Leńko, Tynecka and Jabłońska. Thanks to Norbert Blei, whose *Chi Town, Door Way*, and *Neighborhood* provided a model of sorts for this book. Finally and most importantly, I want to thank the Fulbright Commission and Southwest State University for the fellowships and the sabbatical leave which made my years in Poland—and this book—possible.

for Dr. John Nemo (1942-1993)
The Dean Himself

Upon Awakening from a Dream of Poland

Walk with this woman at your own risk.
The touch alone of her hand on your arm
will drive you deep into yourself.
Lose whole afternoons in baroque cathedrals.
Wander confused down cobblestone alleys,
through forests of birch and pine,
across fields golden with shocked grain.
Grow inexplicably fond of beet-root soup.
Beware the power of strong music;
fear evenings in the darkened opera,
night walks in Market Place Square.
She has style, she has grace.
She wears blue eye shadow.
Bring her silver. Bring her amber,
bugs suspended in frozen honey.
Dance with this woman just one night,
and walk your remaining years with a limp.

A Brief Preface

"I got a Nikon camera,
I love to take photographs. . . ."
—Paul Simon

The following essays were written at various moments during my two-year stay in Poland as a Fulbright lecturer in American culture at the University of Łódź. They were prompted on the one hand by my need to fix that remarkable adventure on paper, to explore the political and social landscape, my own reaction to that landscape, and my own self in the landscape . . . and on the other hand by American curiosity about life in Eastern Europe. Over the past three years that curiosity has shifted eastward to Russia, but Poland is still news, and people seem as fascinated as ever by details of my stay there.

1989 to 1991 brought dramatic changes in Eastern Europe, in Poland, and in Łódź, Poland's second-largest city. Through the eyes of Polish television, I saw the dissolution of the Polish Communist Party, the opening of the Berlin Wall and the subsequent unification of Germany, and (Christmas of 1989, replayed incessantly in private homes, in public offices, on monitor screens in Warszawa Centralna Train Station) the execution of Rumanian dictator Nikolai Ceausescu. With my own eyes I saw the arrival in Polish stores of sugar, toilet paper, bananas, cans of diet Coke, copies of the *International Herald Tribune*, boxes of Fruit Loops cereal, genuine Levi jeans and Benetton sweaters; the inflation of bus and tram tickets from 30 to 1800 złotych; the opening of dozens of private shops along Piotrkowska in Łódź and in cities all across the country, and the closing of most Pewex hard currency shops which sold, in fall of 1989, almost all luxury items available in Poland; trains packed with Polish peddlers headed for Berlin, Prague, and Budapest (and, one gray day in August, 1991, lines of grim-faced Soviet peddlers rushing home to a nation whose president was under house arrest, in jail, or possibly dead). I saw the names of communist heroes purged from parks and boulevards, Stalinist memorials hoisted from their pedestals and trucked off to the junkyard of history. By summer, 1991, I saw Fiats, Mercedes, VWs and Ladas jamming the hopelessly inadequate road system

1

of a city where, in fall of 1989, I could have walked in absolute safety, at any time of day or night, down the center of any city avenue or boulevard.

Sometimes I think each of these pieces should bear its own date: year, month, even week and day. Each time I thought I'd figured Poland out, Poland was no longer as I had it figured. The country seemed to reconfigure itself every three months, and looking around me now, I scarcely recognize the landscape to which I came. Of course my status as an outsider and my perspective on events (from the street up) only obfuscated matters, but possibly confusion itself is the constant, the essence of country and people. Does anyone really know what's going on in Poland? Ask three Poles, the saying goes, and get four opinions. A phrase I heard from natives and foreigners alike—"one of those Polish deals"—is no joke. When I read that the Polish Beer Party elected sixteen members to the Sejm, that a "Party of the Bald" "and a "Congress of Polish Eskimos" registered for the 1993 elections, that in May, 1992 Prime Minister Hanna Suchocka failed a vote of confidence by a single vote because one supporter overslept, I couldn't help thinking to myself, "Poland is ever and always Poland."

Rereading these pieces, I find impatience mingled with affection. They contain much criticism, but I hope readers, especially Polish readers, find tenderness in the honesty. My affection is genuine, something both Michelle and I felt from our first moments in Poland; much of the impatience, I have come to believe, is projected: less a dissatisfaction with Poland than a fear of what I see America becoming, the land of Mediocrity empowered and enthroned.

2

The American phone system(s) work not much better these days than the Polish phone system; compared to bureaucrats at U.S. Immigrations—hostile, incompetent, arrogant, lazy—Polish civil servants are models of civil service. Free speech, privacy, and pursuit of happiness are a hundred times more threatened by American Neo-Puritans masquerading as political correctivists than by anything I encountered in Poland. At least once a week some news item sets me to thinking, "This country has become a speech, glance and thought police state. Laws are in the book. We are East Bloc, 1989."

Part of Poland's attraction for me was in fact the opportunity to live among real people confronting real problems: scrounging food, housing, clothing, gasoline, good medical care, even warmth and clean air and potable water in a land where all were scarce; keeping a job in a nation without unemployment insurance; sustaining one's modest hopes and visions through complex and dangerous economic and political reconstructions. In contrast, American problems—at least those most attended by media and courts—seemed the trivial complaints of middle class victim princesses bruised by a pea, a case of Solutions in Search of Problems. Who really cares whether Clarence Thomas discussed porno flicks with Anita Hill, what Marge Schott said on the telephone, or what Woody Allen's heart desires? Even those Americans who battle daily hardships akin to what I saw in Poland are fewer in number, and their position certainly less desperate: it is to the U.S. that Poles come, desperate for illegal, exploitive, low-paying employment. And it is from the U.S. they depart two or three years later . . . with $75,000 in their pockets.

3

If my view of Poland was distorted by projected anxieties and romantic adventuring, it was not clarified by increasing familiarity. The closer I looked, the more I saw . . . and the less—not the more—I thought I understood. Another two years in Poland and I would have been as unable to interpret Poland as I am able to explain America. ("You've been talking about the American Dream for the past three days," one student told a 1990 panel of Fulbright lecturers in American Culture, "and not one of you has defined the term." "Well, well, well," we all said; "America is complicated and 'American Dream' is difficult to define." "Not at all," she replied: "the American Dream is driving your truck 200 kilometers per hour down an empty road, the tapedeck playing at top volume, throwing empty beer cans out the window behind you.")

If I couldn't always interpret events, I could speculate. And I can report what I saw. The words and images of this adventure ride on their own detail.

I can't say I have the story right. There seem to be so many stories. Some may be fables, although they had the ring of truth and are stories worth retelling. Perhaps, Poland being still *in medias res*, there is no complete story yet, just a series of images, many a little blurred. It was a quick trip, really, and people were on their best behavior around Americans. I traveled at dusk. Much of the country was closed for renovation. Our plans changed quickly and without notice. Trees sometimes blocked my view.

But I can tell you now what I saw: she was very beautiful, graceful as a willow and fine-featured, stylishly dressed in black and white. She smiled when I waved, but turned her back quickly as I raised my camera. Then she disappeared into a blok of flats.

Urban Landscape with Student Party

It is early evening, and Michelle and I are crossing the traffic circle where Nowotki Street intersects Żrodłowa and Strykowska, on our way to a party hosted by Violetta Chląd, one of the fourth-year students. Classes are done for the year, the weather is warm and clear, and the American literature exam is still two weeks away, so I'm in a mellow mood. Besides, Jacek Szymanski says Violetta throws a good party. We have brought the last of the Russian champagne purchased in November for $1.80 a bottle, and six red roses purchased from a sidewalk vendor for twenty cents each.

In the field adjacent to the circle, in the lengthening shadow of a smoke-smudged factory wall, stands a horse-drawn hay rick. A farmer and his family are loading grass they cut, to judge from the unevenness of the stubble, with hand scythes, commonly used implements even in 1990. Using wood-toothed haying rakes and a wooden haying fork, they gather the ragged rows of sweet grass into small piles, which are pitched one after the other onto the rick. The adolescent son rakes, his father pitches, and his mother, in a printed cotton skirt and a dark, dirty sweater, stands atop the rick, treading each forkful onto the cart, building gradually up and out, so the top of the load overhangs the cart. Periodically the farmer borrows his son's rake to trim overhanging shag, gather it in another small pile, and toss it up to his wife. When not drawing the wagon from one stack to another, the horse grazes absent-mindedly on stubble. A Dalmatian chases insects kicked up by the raking. Though the grass has been curing for a couple of days, all this raking and tossing fills the air with the country smell of fresh-cut hay. The long, low light of late afternoon washes the scene in the warmth peculiar to that time of day, and for a second I think I've wandered into some nineteenth century landscape . . . or one of those village scenes, painted just last year in the style of the Old Masters, sold in Łódź art galleries for $20.

In fact, many components in this scene could easily have come from a Constable painting. The rake handle is not the smooth lathed dowel found on American garden tools, not any machine-made form at all, but the stripped trunk of some young pine, full of knots and bumps, hand-polished with grease and dirt and sweat to a soft yellow. The fork is hand-crafted. The wagon, all wooden and

5

ramshackle, must be a century old . . . except for the automobile tires which have replaced the Old Masters' heavy wooden wheels. This too is common in Poland: in the Stary Rynek of more elegant cities like Warsaw and Kraków, you often see horse-drawn carriages for hire to western tourists, their drivers spiffed, their carriages spit shined, their horses dressed and groomed, the way it's done in Vienna or New York. Tthen you notice those four balding automobile tires and think to yourself, as you often do in Poland, "Well, that's the general idea. . . ."

Every component of this scene is in fact quite familiar to me, fragments of various half-remembered landscapes brought into jarring juxtaposition in the middle of Poland's second largest city. The horse I have seen before, and perhaps the wagon as well, filled with turnips and cabbage in early fall, loaded with coal in late October, hauling paving stones up Żrodłowa earlier this spring. The owner lives in Bałuty, north and east of my flat, a very old section of Łódź. He lives in a one-story wooden building on ulica Sporna, a house with green shutters, no paint, a tar roof, and red geraniums in the windows. He gets his water from a backyard well, which is something else you often see in Poland: weathered wooden single-family dwellings still without municipal water service hunkering atavistically among the blocks of encroaching six- and seven-story high-rises. "The buildings will be demolished next year anyway," conventional wisdom goes, "so why bother with city water?" And next year comes and next year goes in this country always in some stage of incompletion, and the wooden buildings remain, with their well and sewage trench running to a gutter in the street. Where this man farms, I can't imagine, unless it's well out of the city; excepting a few parks and a section of those small family garden plots found in all European cities, Bałuty is all flats and shops built on ghetto rubble. Maybe this is why he cuts hay in the field beside the traffic circle in the middle of Łódź.

I have seen haying before, of course, along the ditches of rural Minnesota roads and on ranches in the Dakotas, and haying is familiar to me from Hamlin Garland's descriptions of nineteenth-century haying in *A Son of the Middle Border,* and Donald Hall's description of early twentieth-century haying in *String too Short to Be Saved,* and Verlin Klinkenborg's fascinating account of later twentieth-century haying in *Making Hay.* Lately I've seen Polish haying in front of my flat, where every afternoon a man has come to scythe a swath of lawn and carry a wicker basket full of clippings to his garden patch across the street.

This spring I observed through the windows of passing trains the gathering of first-cutting hay in the Polish countryside, as last fall I watched the final cutting: the interplay of man and animal (seldom man and machine), the simple wooden contrivances (often broken and often mended) commended by neo-agrarians like Wendell Berry. The potato-shaped, earth-encrusted men and women. The long, ragged lines of raked grass. The careful mounds of gathered hay running the length of a narrow field, shoulder high to a short man. The hand-bound sheaves of grain, shocked as in a Currier and Ives print. The patient

6

horses and the wooden carts come to gather grain and grass. The hay stacks themselves, pitched around a central pole pointing twelve, fifteen feet into the air, rounded loaves of matted vegetation like loaves of brown *chleb,* or the huts of some South Sea Islanders, or the stacks Monet painted again and again for sale to the wives of new-made Chicago millionaires.

No Pole, I am sure, gives a second's thought to the curious scene in front of University Church at the traffic circle: horse and rick, cars and trucks, the farmer and his family, Dalmatian, trams 6 and 17 and 23 clattering north and south, buses 57 and 51 and 80 east and west. The gray cement walls and dirty glass windows of six-story apartments at Nowotki, the shops, the street venders, the University dormitories looming obscurely in the background.

I too am quick to transcend the moment, intent as I am on Violetta's party, and on the larger student celebration, Juvenalia, held annually between the end of classes and the beginning of exams: three days of party to cap a semester of parties before three weeks of serious studenting. Previously festivities were underwritten by the Party's Youth Club, but the Party is not as flush this year as of old, so students must provide for themselves. Still, every lounge on every floor of every dorm is booked for one "occasion" or another, streets are awash with beer and vodka, and students in wild costumes prowl the alleys. The dorm quadrangle rings with jazz, blues, and rock-n-roll. "You should have been here yesterday," somebody tells me; "Janusz is in a band, and he was playing blues."

7

Violetta's party is deluxe by Polish standards. Of course she and her friends have prepared several trays of *kanapki,* slabs of brown *chleb* covered with thin slices of cheese, boiled egg, cucumber, kiełbasa, lettuce, tomato, pickle. She has stocked the standard Pepsi Cola, Polish vodka and Bulgarian red wine. But somewhere in Łódź this spring of 1990 she has found wines from Hungary, France and West Germany. And American gin. And three different kinds of Polish beer, including Żywiec beer, Poland's best, brewed in the south, not easily found in Łódź. Her Panasonic boombox plays up-to-date Western music, mostly disco, including Top Forty tunes like "Lambada" and "La Bamba," and Tina Turner, who is very hot in Poland right now. Music ricochets off plaster walls and ceiling, Sławek Wiesławski's tripped-out dachshund skitters around the room, and the students dance, dance, dance: jitterbug, versions of the bump, a tamed down lambada. Their dancing is excellent, certainly to the standards of Band Stand of the 1950s and early 60's, when Dick Clark transformed dozens of South and West Philadelphia high school juniors into American teen stars.

In fact, this affair strikes me as a very American kind of party. Conversation drifts from one Western cocktail topic to another. One student wants to know the relative prestige of Pulitzer and Nobel prizes. Another inquires about the status of Bellow, Roth, Vonnegut and Updike, the four contemporary American authors most taught at the Institute of English Philology. (Although their thesis year is upon them, these students have yet to enter the '80s, or even the '70s in working familiarity with U.S. writers. I suggest Kerouac, Kesey, and Bly among the older males, then tick off a list of women writers from Ursula LeGuin and Annie Dillard to Leslie Silko and Toni Morrison. They have not heard of a one.)

Inevitably talk turns to politics, to the New Poland, to the recent railroad strike in the northwest, to Lech Wałęsa's as yet unannounced run for the presidency. "He does not speak very good Polish," I am told. Speaking good Polish is apparently an important skill in anyone aspiring to the Polish presidency, although nobody has ever complained about the Polish of current President General Wojciech Jaruzelski. Prime Minister Tadeusz Mazowiecki, a Catholic intellectual, speaks very good Polish, and most of these students, like most of their teachers, support the Prime Minister. But I have come to sense a genuine class distinction between student-teacher intellectuals on the one hand and shipyard workers on the other, so I play the devil's advocate.

"Never trust an intellectual to get the job done," I advise. "Look at recent American presidents—while some have hired intellectuals to work for them, effective presidents have not themselves been intellectuals."

"What would a Western leader think, talking to Wałęsa? This fat, rumpled worker. . . ."

"What do you think fat, rumpled Helmut Kohl would think of fat, rumpled Lech Wałęsa? He is respected. Westerners see Wałęsa as the man who took direct action in a moment of crisis."

"But he has no ideas, no plans. . . ."

"How many boxes of bananas did the intellectuals bring into this country?" Michelle asks, shifting the focus of conversation from laborers to peddlers, a class despised by students and laborers alike. "Not a single banana, I can promise you that."

"Bananas are not what New Poland is all about."

"Bananas are exactly what New Poland is all about," she responds. "I watched the New Poland being born, and I saw very plainly what people want: consumer goods on an open market. When the country opened up, that was the first thing Poles went for. You had peddlers hawking bananas on every street corner. Every trash can in Łódź was filled to overflowing with banana peels."

"Bananas contain everything necessary to sustain human life," Ewa Bednarowicz observes; "I personally have lived on nothing but bananas for days."

"In Western democracies, people vote against intellectuals every time," I continue; "even in France, and especially in America and Britain. I don't know but that they're right. Poland doesn't need ideas, Poland needs . . ."

". . . to Just Do It," Ewa Ziołańska interjects as she dances by, echoing the slogan that has become something of an Institute motto ever since I wore a Nike T-shirt to American Culture lectures.

The soundtrack of *The Blues Brothers* blasts from the tapedeck. "Hash Music!" somebody shouts. "The Rolling Stones! Janis Joplin! The Doors! This is the greatest music ever made!"

Violetta swirls sensuously by, eyes glittering, hips swaying, a kind of manic intensity to her being, a bacchante, a maenad, the spirit of the wind.

"I have seven different recordings of 'Minnie the Moocher,'" Sławek tells me, apropos of nothing in particular.

"Leonard Cohen visited Poland several years ago," somebody else says. "He was not well known, but people understood that he was popular in the West, so his concerts became a very big thing. The price of tickets rose from maybe 500 złotych to 10,000, which at that time was astronomical. You could not buy them. Only Party members and their fat wives attended the concerts. They did not know the songs, and they could not understand English, of course, but this was the right place to be. They applauded like crazy. I know a man who wrote his magister thesis on Cohen, and he could not even get into a concert.

"Then Cohen was interviewed for three hours on the radio by somebody who had never listened to his music, who knew nothing about him. Cohen was polite, but the man kept asking questions like 'What do you think of Britain's economic sanctions against Poland because of martial law?' He didn't even realize that Cohen was Canadian. It was very embarrassing."

In spring 1990, Cohen bootlegs sell on Polish streets for about a dollar.

Sławek waits for a break in the music, moves to the center of the room calling for attention. "Please do not give the dog any more vodka," he requests; "he's had enough already. Thank you."

9

My hostess invites me to dance, but I beg off. "I'm not a good dancer," I apologize. "Americans like to do only what they can do well, and you are all much better dancers than I. This is why my Polish has remained so bad, I guess: I am too embarrassed to practice."

"The Japanese are like that," she muses. "An Italian . . . an Italian will learn a few words and phrases and fumble along, always making mistakes, ignoring grammar, but somehow managing to make himself understood. The Japanese and the Americans are always so cautious. And the *British* . . . !"

I tell my story about the wife of the Poznań consul who mispronounced the Polish word for "pollution" into the Polish word for "wet dream," complaining at great length about the "terrible wet dream problem in Poland."

"How could you grow up in America and not know how to dance?" Violetta demands.

"I led a sheltered youth," I tell her. "My father is a Lutheran minister. Instead of dancing to rock-n-roll, I played Beethoven and Mozart on the piano. Dancing did not interest me until the high sixties. And by then, dancing was not . . . a necessary preliminary."

"That's a good story," she says dismissively.

We finish our wine, make our excuses, leave before midnight, before this party has even cranked up. Some couples have disappeared into dorm rooms, and reappeared from dorm rooms. One reveler has stripped to her slip. Violetta is dancing the lambada. Outside of Dom Studentcki 2 somebody sings Bob Dylan songs. The accent needs work, but he has a good nasal whine on the

10

refrain: "Hey, Meeester Tamboureeeen Mon. . . ."

We should have been around last night: Janusz was playing blues.

Juvenalia has spilled onto Nowotki, watched by three-man patrols of jealous *milicja* (newly rebaptized into *policja* by the simple expedient of painting a *po* over the *mi* on their automobiles). A number 6 tram grinds toward me, but it is a ghost headed somewhere for cleaning or repair. Service ended an hour ago. We walk home, thinking that we have seen our students, finally, at their best, in a setting that gives free reign to their mad Slavic souls and the strengths of their character: improvisation, intensity, animation, emotion. How easily they wear the West, how kinetic they make it seem, how much like the sixties (a good time, which, I have come to understand, was not at all the West). If these people control the fate of the New Poland, the country will not only survive, it will flourish.

On the wall of an old factory not far from the dorms, I notice a bit of graffiti: a caricature of General Jaruzelski, the man who imposed martial law on Poland, the man in the black glasses, the President, the man also caricatured on Orange Alternative posters over the caption "Wanted Dead or Alive." Here the General looks out a window beside a pot of geraniums, above the phrase "Love Me Tender."

When we cross the traffic circle, the horse, the cart, the farmer and his Dalmatian are long gone.

Seasons in a Half-Remembered Landscape

Whatever this curious synthesis is, it will not last long: the paradoxical cohabitation of managed economy and free-market capitalism; of militant Catholicism and, still, a lot of communist mental references; of cheap tram service to the edge of the countryside and shiny metallic-blue VWs, silver-gray BMWs and bright yellow Mercedes; of horse-drawn hay ricks and satellite dishes pirating Sky TV; of All Saints Day cemetery vigils and visa-free travel to Germany and beyond; of traditional street markets and smart private shops; of street workers sweeping sidewalks and streets and even the lawn itself with their twig brooms and the influx of expensive Western goods prized by Poles.

And since it is impossible to imagine this country slipping backwards further into the nineteenth century, and given Poland's historic attraction to the West (previously France, now "America," which in glazed Polish eyes does no wrong), and since the West is the land of all things new, I conclude it will be the old elements of present Polish life that will disappear, precisely those things that most stir my imagination: steam locomotives and wicker shopping baskets filled with eggs or garden produce; clean-up crews with their two-wheeled, hand-pushed carts hauling cardboard boxes down the center of Kościuszki Street to the recycling center off of Zachodnia; flower venders sitting on stools and crates behind plastic buckets filled with pink gerbers and red roses at every busy corner of Łódź; tin dinner pails in the hands of workers on their way home from small factories to country houses; vest-pocket specialty shops for meat and bread, ma-and-pa groceries 200 steps from each flat, and corner venders of fresh vegetables in late summer and early fall; glass bottles of unpasteurized milk; butchers hacking away with black mediaevel curt axes at the corpses of freshly slaughtered pigs, head and feet in full view and for sale on the table in front of them; the wooden sleds that appear each winter, bolted together, rusting steel blades covering each runner, pulled on twine ropes and carrying, always, some ruddy-cheeked, heavily bundled youngster of two, strapped bolt upright into his seat; the open air markets where you can buy a bundle of fresh twigs for your broom, or a wicker shopping basket, or pickles from the barrel, kraut from the crock, cheese from the wheel.

13

Aluminum milk cans lining village streets in the early morning, one or two per home, awaiting pickup by a man on a heavy Ursus tractor or a horse-drawn cart. The fur hats of red, gray, silver, white, black, brown that appear the first really cold day of winter, turning a bouncing bus into a sea of rippling fox, rabbit, wolf, mink. The old cobblestone walks, and the paved-over streets, cheap macadam bearing the imprint of automobile tires, red paving stones showing through holes in the crumbling asphalt. Even the drab, dull cement walls of buildings, chipped and scaling, red brick beneath flaking cement, buttressed (I have seen this) with pine trunks or steel girders wedged at an angle between sagging wall and earth.

The trams, their worn wooden seats a yellow luster in the night, radiating a soft warmth as they clatter through empty streets. The bent women in faded floral dresses, graying sweaters, and black coats, on their way to market. The rose gardens in front of each apartment, so carefully tended.

It is not fair to love a country because it appears to be backward—although I could name half a dozen towns in Western nations that make handsome currency off their refusal to enter the twentieth century—but that's not exactly what I was saying. If Poles love the West because to them it represents a Future in which they believe as fervently as Jay Gatsby believed in the green light at the end of Daisy's dock, I treasure in Poland an Old which is hard to come by in the West, especially in the America where I live. This nation goes back centuries, and despite fifty years of communist reconstruction and centuries of floating borders, outcroppings of these old deposits show in every aspect of

14

Polish life. Writing in the *New York Review of Books,* Neal Acherson once observed, "Poland is full of time zones, constantly crossed by people who seem to be migrating from the eighteenth century, or even further back, toward the present—some completing the journey, many disembarking in the landscape of the 1830's Romanticism, other preferring the Positivism of the late nineteenth century, others again alighting after 1900. . . . It is seamed by broken and faulted zones of locality." Poland's attraction for me has been the way various components of its landscape call to sympathetic elements in my own fifty-year-old self. Some zones speak to a personal history, to memories of my childhood; others touch something more communal, something deeper, more mysterious, more hidden: tales my parents told me, stories of their parents before them, a life I have learned from books and old magazines.

On the simplest level, Poland in 1990 represented what in my naivete I thought Europe always was and always should be: comfortably cheap, a little broken, vastly rich in monuments, scenery, and smelly restrooms guarded by little old lady attendants. I am a prisoner here of my own experience, having grown up with a post-War Europe a good deal more cheap and broken than Paris and Berlin, Vienna and London have historically been. Today those cities—each substantially more expensive than New York or Chicago, and more vibrant at least than New York—are closer to the historical norm than the London, Paris, Berlin I visited as a wide-eyed youth three decades ago. Who can afford them today? And why shell out that kind of money for an upscale parody of what you left behind?

Poland in 1989 was still the old story: rich in history, relatively untouristed (even Kraków, Warsaw and Gdańsk), mostly pristine (yes, there has been restoration, but it's careful restoration which the patina of Polish pollution has rendered antique as ever), still plenty of broken, and still plenty cheap. Łódż of 1990 is Berlin of 1952, when first my parents visited a war-devastated Germany. Gabriele Jones, a Berliner fully cognizant of all the usual German-Polish distinctions, took one look at Jan Filipski's Łódż landscapes hanging on my living room walls and choked with emotion: "This is my childhood," she said, agitated. "Every afternoon when I came home from school, my mother would give me my piece of bread smeared with lard or jam, and sit me on my little chair in front of the window, and I would eat my bread looking out the glass at these same crumbling cement walls, these same red bricks, these same broken fences."

The Polish landscape recalls as well images from family photographs of post-War Berlin and little Rhenish villages, and scenes from my own brown memories of summer loading boxcars in a German factory, 1966. And images drawn second-hand from other sources: classic texts of American and European history, historical novels, *National Geographic* magazines stored in cardboard boxes in the attic of my boyhood home, with their black-and-white photos of exotic market places—Brussels, Mexico City, Istanbul—not too different from the markets of this city; films set in pre- and post-War Europe, *The Blue Angel, All Quiet on the Western Front, Sophie's Choice*; the novels even of Dickens and Balzac, the short stories of Bernard Malamud and Isaac Bashevis Singer; World War I and II television documentaries; visits to reconstructed enclaves of the American past like Sturbridge Village, Massachusetts or Pioneer Village, South Dakota, to abandoned farm sites in southwestern Minnesota, to ghost towns in Wyoming, to decaying miners' dwellings in West Virginia and Kentucky, the weathered boards, the cracked plaster, the broken fences, the chimney stones in a heap in the cellar, the rusted tin pans and rotting leather harnesses and broken shards of glass in gray window casements. From childhood fairy tales, legends, old myths, from the depths of dreams and the dark recesses of my own subconsciousness, images leap out, drawn by some psychic charge in the Łódż landscape.

I do not board a Polish tram without once again boarding the old Suburban Trolley which ran from Media, Pennsylvania to 69th Street, Philadelphia during my high school years.

I do not see a worker shoveling coal into a Łódż cellar that I do not think instantly of the coal cellar where Billy Allison and I played ourselves black in Buffalo, New York, 1953; and of the converted coal cellar of my old Peoria house, where I built my son's box-hockey game, and my daughter's doll house.

The typewriter on which I write this manuscript is the very image of the typewriter my father used at Muhlenberg College in the thirties, and passed to his son when I left Philadelphia for Wittenberg, three decades ago: a black

16

manual portable with no key for open and close parentheses, and if you make a mistake, it's reach for a pencil with an eraser.

The roundhouse at Skierniewice is home to half a dozen black steam engines, and in every Polish railroad station you'll see at least one water tower at which an old engine can belly up. In 1990, steam locomotives were still used for occasional yard work in Białystok and Kutno.

The brooms used by Polish streetworkers are precisely the brooms ridden by black witches silhouetted against orange moons on American Halloween decorations, the kind of brooms you can't find in America, that disappeared from Western Europe two decades ago.

Whenever I see a merchant weighing carrots or apples or live chickens in his iron balance scales, carrots in one tray, iron weights (or makeshift equivalents) of .5K, 1K, 2K, in the other, I think of the antique balance scale on my father's family room shelf in New Market, Virginia. Every wooden implement in daily Polish use belongs in the collection of old wooden farm tools bought at Virginia auctions and hung on his family room walls. And when Tom Bednarowicz announced happily that he finally found a good, heavy duty aluminum kettle for his folks, something they'd been wanting for a year, I told him that I'd seen one sell for $18 at a farm auction just before I left the States. As an antique.

Entering the Institute of English Philology and looking toward the ceiling light fixtures (concentric circles of cream colored plastic), I gaze directly, again, at the ceiling of Herbert Hoover Elementary School, Kenmore, New York, erected in 1952.

I cannot see a child run up to touch a chimney sweep from behind without being transported instantly into *Mary Poppins*. And in Poland, chimney sweeps are nearly as common as nuns, priests, and monks . . . young nuns, priests and monks.

In his beat-up Syrena, Łukasz Salski reminds me ever and anon of Dean Moriarty and his 1949 Hudson, for a Syrena looks exactly like a 1/3 scale model of a Hudson, inside and out, steering wheel and dashboard. (And about 1/3 the Hudson's horsepower as well.)

Nowhere in America are chimney sweeps and twig brooms, iron balance scales and wood-seated trams, wicker baby carriages and 1949 Hudsons integral components of daily life. Poland is the chance of a lifetime for a Westerner to come home . . . or it was when I was there.

Poland whispers as well to a human history which comes locked in recessive genes, in dusty atoms on distant branches of the DNA molecule, a history which is not mine personally but could have been. I know this history from books, fairy tales, dreams and Jungian psychology.

On the streets of Łódź troops first fired on factory workers demanding work and bread in 1905.

In Łódź you can still see *gypsies* . . . .

And old *babcie* in the market seated behind their baskets of eggs, or leading a cow down some country road on its way, perhaps, to market. (Finally the day came when there was no food at all in the cupboard, and no money in the teapot. 'Jack' the boy's mother said to him, 'you must take the old cow to market'. . . .")

Every journey was an exploration of some great archetypal landscape, urban or rural: figures bent and twisted, a dead drunk at our very tram stop, storks in their nests atop barns and telephone poles, an old horse-drawn Black Maria clattering through the cobblestoned backroad of a remote village, the thatched roof on a farm outbuilding.

In Bałuty, the old Łódź ghetto, 200,000 Jews produced 5,000 German uniforms a week. They all died. Rumkowski, the Eldest of the Jews, selected "volunteers" for "relocation." They all died. Rumkowski himself rode the last train to the extermination camp. This brick rubble we kick up when we scrape the earth with our bootheel is the siftings of people's lives.

Here unspeakable things happened, things out of your worst nightmare. "The reason there are no apartments on this strip of ground," a friend says matter-of-factly as we round a corner a hundred yards from my apartment," is that the building across the street is the old police station, and it's believed that bodies may lie buried underneath those trees. . . ."

Finally there is the intangible of Slavic soul, that great underground reservoir of suffering and vitality, described by Miłosz in *Native Realm* as "a sudden ebb or flow of inner chaos." Like Afro-American soul, Native American soul, Latin-American soul, Slavic soul is difficult to define, impossible to impersonate, but you know it and love it when you feel it. To a base of mystery and remove add traces of ecstasy and terror, fervor and indifference, generosity and cruelty, light and dark. Don't be afraid of too much dark. Here is the Eastern "right brain" to the Western "left brain": spontaneity to Western structure, intuition to the Western reason, the collective to Western individualism, emotion to Western restraint. In the land between Berlin and Moscow a Westerner enters, with a curious feelings of déjà vu, the long-lost Other. And as he struggles to comprehend this half-remembered landscape, a long-repressed secret self emerges, something dark and moist and messy, vaguely out of control, oddly comfortable.

Call it the dark side. Call it the Id. Call it Slavic soul.

This rational Westerner calls it home.

Street Markets

The big story in Poland 1989-91 was economic, and that story was bipartite. Inflation, as everyone remembers, was horrendous, despite self-serving claims by the new government and American economic advisor Geoffrey Sachs that economic "shock treatment" stopped inflation dead in its tracks during the first quarter of 1990. No such thing: all prices rose continuously through 1990, except the price of the U.S. dollar, which, through some monetary hocus pocus, held steady at about 9,500 złotych throughout the year, down from 11,000 or 12,000 on the street in August of 1989. Tram and bus tickets, to take a more or less random example, shot from 30 złotych in August, 1989, to 60 in September, to 120 in early 1990, then to 360, then to 400 by August of that same year, to 700 in December, and to 1200 by early 1991. Whenever people ask about inflation, I pull out my Łódź bus-and-tram pass, a small document with photograph and number, validated by affixing a small stamp purchased each month at the Rectorat. The price of the stamp for 11/89, I show them, was 7,000 złotych. The stamp for 1/90 bears a price of 14,000. The stamp for 3/90, 24,000; that for 5/90, 45,000; that for 1/91, 70,000. The stamp for 4/91 cost 100,000 Polish złotych, substantially more than Tom Bednarowicz's parents paid for their summer cottage slightly more than a decade ago.

"How did Poles cope with that kind of inflation?" people ask me. "The way you might expect," I tell them. They printed more money, introducing first a 50,000-złotych note, then a 100,000 note, then a 500,000 note, and finally,

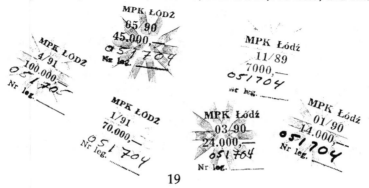

19

yes, a 1,000,000-złotych note. When we collected our monthly pay at the University bursar's office, the serial numbers of our crisp new bills were always in sequence. Most Polish salaries also inflated during this period, from an average of 200,000 per month in fall, 1989, to an average around 2,000,000 per month in spring, 1991. People who lost their jobs suffered economically. Everyone suffered vertigo.

The other side of the Polish economic story, the up side of inflation (coupled with the stable foreign exchange), was increased supplies of every conceivable consumer product and service, to the point that in summer of 1991, you could buy anything you wanted, in any quantity you wanted, on the streets of Poland. Westerners will find no surprise here: increased prices mean increased goods. Remember the gasoline shortages of the 1970's, and the gasoline glut that followed, once prices ballooned from 29 cents a gallon to over a dollar? We have been there before, you and I.

Poles, however, had lived their lives, and their parents' lives as well, in a world of controlled production and more or less controlled distribution. An aircraft-carried sized building in Warsaw decided what would be produced, and where it would be shipped. "Look how huge," a taxi driver exclaimed in English, pointing to the great block of cement and glass; "and look what all their decisions brought us!" Goods did not appear, and what was not available, people could not buy. Or goods did appear, and if what appeared was not what they wanted, they bought anyway, because there was nothing else on which to spend their money. I remember heavy-duty chain hoists, the sort used to derrick automobile engines out of cars, appearing one week in a shop on Piotrkowska in the fall of 1989. They were cheap, maybe fifteen dollars. The shop was full of them, and people were buying them. In a month, the supply was exhausted, and I doubt they've been available since.

Precisely because goods might not reappear for quite some while, people usually bought two or three—even refrigerators and television sets. Or they converted their złotych into dollars, which they stuffed in a mattress. Food especially was stockpiled. When I complained early on about shops running short of rice, one colleague said, only half-jokingly, "Any Pole would have a six-months' supply."

In fall of 1989, people were mostly not buying, although the situation had improved from the famous "peas and vinegar" days when only those commodities could be found on most state store shelves, and Polish women spent their time in queues exchanging new recipes for preparing peas in vinegar. Sugar had been unavailable for months (although bakeries and restaurants were kept supplied, and the Pepsi Cola bottling plant), and colleagues left work without censure or pangs of conscience on the mere rumor of sugar in this store or that, to wait long hours in long lines in hopes of buying the two-bag limit. I once witnessed a near riot triggered by the mere mention of sugar: a stout middle-aged women in a gray coat at the head of the line made the pro forma

20

inquiry, rather too loudly, "Do you have any sugar?" She received the usual "no," but the answer was too quiet to be heard. Then she bought two bags of something that looked a lot like sugar—probably flour, although a number of commodities were sold in those plain brown bags—and one woman well back in line got the notion that those were bags of sugar. "You've got sugar??!!" she shouted in great hope and enthusiasm, which brought everyone running, pushing, jostling, until the clerk climbed on the counter and barked impatiently, "No, I do not have sugar today!"

Customers pilfered sugar from restaurants, a few teaspoonfuls folded in a napkin and tucked in the pocket, until managers removed sugar cups from the tables. At the Embassy commissary, granulated sugar—trucked in from Berlin—disappeared upon arrival, as Americans bought for themselves and for Polish colleagues. Michelle and I contented ourselves with sugar cubes, counting ourselves lucky and pulverizing whatever we needed for baking.

Toilet paper was also a problem, and remained a problem long after the 1989 sugar beet crop had been harvested, refined, and distributed. You could not get TP anywhere, not even at the private markets. I once saw a fellow bring a pushcart of toilet paper out of a doorway on Piotrkowska; he wasn't a hundred yards down the street before it was sold. In mid-December the University distributed rolls of toilet paper to all its faculty as a very welcomed Christmas present. This odd year-end bonus (and two 8-roll packages of paper brought from

21

the States) saved us from having to follow the lead of other Poles and shred newspaper or magazines (but not the Sears catalog, a much-prized item in Poland). In better hotels, you could buy a few sheets from the WC attendant for 200 zł, but most of the time there, as on the trains and in underground conveniences, and even at the University, you found shredded dailies, if you found anything at all.

There were other shortages: clothing, food, toys. Everything except bread, milk, jam and cheese. I remember long lines in the Central Department Store, waiting five minutes to get on the escalator to the second floor, then finding in the shoe department perhaps three pair of shoes, in the toy department maybe a couple of heavy Russian bicycles. I remember once being absolutely unable to find pork anywhere in the city of Łódź, population 900,000. When we couldn't find drinking glasses, a young medical student who took private English lessons from Michelle promised, "Don't worry, my mother will get you some." But Rafał's mother couldn't buy drinking glasses either, and after a three-week search donated six of the family's own to redeem her son's promise.

A rule obtained in those days, which foreigners learned quickly: if you see it, and you or a friend might need it, buy two. Much of every Pole's cache came from the black market or the private market (which I saw only in vestigial operation), which is why people had warned us on entering Poland, "Don't try to go it alone. You need a network of Polish connections—or a friend who has a network of connections." Part of every Pole's life's work was the cultivation of such a network to supply coffee, sugar, car parts. (One student entertained Michelle and me in a house her father had built for absolutely nothing, trading with his network for all necessary materials, labor, permits, furnishings.) The Fulbright Commission directed host institutions to provide visiting scholars with "shepherds," who could provide networks into whom they could plug.

Networks are no longer necessary in Poland—not when it comes to buying sugar or toilet paper, and not even for tricky operations like obtaining official export documents for works of art, or buying special car insurance for trips to Austria or Germany. Nor is it necessary to spend hours in a queue, or to hire others (as did some of my American friends) to queue for you . . . or to boast (as did other American colleagues), "I do not queue," putting, always, a little spin on the *not*. The black market became the street market, and inflation brought an avalanche of consumer goods, even luxury items like olives, peanuts, diet cola, Polish ham, coffee, soy sauce, Heinz catsup. Foreigners who had not kept abreast of the emerging Poland could be embarrassed: one Austrian arrived in spring, 1991, with a small suitcase full of coffee. He'd been told coffee would make handsome gifts for his hosts . . . and at one time it would have. Chocolate and coffee: two staple gifts in the East. But by spring, 1991, chocolate and coffee were available everywhere west of the Soviet border. "I can't give this to anyone," he confided in me; "I would embarrass them and myself. Do you have any use for it?"

In spring, 1990 prices rose so high, and stock piles of consumer goods were so great, and Poles were so suddenly cautious, that the unimaginable actually happened: supply exceeded demand. Discounts appeared, and sales on all sorts of items, up to fifty percent off, even on the pirated "designer" clothing with Gucci and Benetton embroidered across the front. "Okazja!!!" the hand-written signs announced. Sales! In Poland. Who would have thought it?

We were witnessing in Poland the construction of a private market out of elements of the old black market, the underground network of hidden suppliers and consumers, and what remained of the merchant class. That construction crossed a great distance in a very short time, bounding from one phase to the next in a matter of weeks or months. First the black market emerged from the closet as a public but carefully monitored hodgepodge of bazaars and street markets, some in traditional market areas (the market by Centrum, for example, and the market in Bałuty), some in non-traditional but strategic central Łódź locations (in front of the Opera, or in the Central Department Store parking lot), some in fields on the outskirts of town. In early 1990, private peddling exploded all over the streets—again with official sanction—before stabilizing later in the year into individually owned private shops, some along the city's major boulevards, some hidden in back courtyards and secondary streets, some in rented kiosks: corrugated steel over two-by-four frames, or molded plastic, factory-produced, trucked in, and deposited at key intersections around Łódź. (This was about the same time that currency exchanges became legal, moving off the street corners and into private shops. One is no longer pestered in Poland by greasy thugs whispering "Change money? Change money?") Inevitably some private shops failed; a few shops expanded into chains. Then wholesalers appeared (they sold both retail and wholesale): by fall, 1991, everyone with a free-standing house on the edge of Łódź seemed to operate a *hurtownia* of one sort or another.

Shopping in Poland was an exercise in hanging loose: just when you developed a feel for the system, it changed. You had no sooner structured your Saturdays to include a weekly visit to the Super Bazaar at Kaliska Station, than you realized there really wasn't much shaking at Kaliska last week . . . or the week before that either, come to think of it. Where did everyone go? Or one day you hiked over to the Central Department Store parking lot, intent on buying maybe a kilo of pork from one of the truck-butchers, and the whole operation had disappeared—not a truck or table anywhere. Or suddenly shops were staying open evenings, or weekends, or even 24 hours a day—first just the Stanley shop on Piotrkowska, then many, if not most retail stores.

Or suddenly Kilińskiego Street had blossomed with all kinds of spiffy new shops, with colored awnings, plate glass windows, and a fresh coat of paint (not an entire building, mind you—just on street level, and only as far as the shop extended). Argentum, that new jeweler next to Hortex, was accepting Master Charge, Visa, American Express (although it took nearly an hour to clear your card number with Warsaw). A new Julius Meinl shop—Austrian chain—had opened on Piotrkowska, up the street from the "House of Beer" and the shop that sells leaded glass lamps for $800. The news stand on Narutowicza had installed a 1-hour film processing machines (within a month, six other such machines appeared elsewhere in Łódź, including in the Polish craft shop, "Cepelia," by the English Institute.)

Street markets played an important role in the emerging free Polish economy, and even today Agnieszka and Grzegorz Siewko, who run a small dress-making business, sell more at a street market than in private shops, identical prices both locations. For at least a century there has been an active street market in Łódź, as in all major European cities, the vendors an odd mix of professional middlemen and farmer-producers. Prices have always been low, and commodities traditionally basic. In *Love and Exile,* Isaac Bashevis Singer remembered markets in Warsaw "where one could get black bread for half price. Peasant women brought cheese, mushrooms, groats and onions from the country that I could buy for next to nothing." Tuesday and Friday are traditional Polish market days, but in a city the size of Łódź activity continues every day, except for high holidays and Sunday. Some merchants set up inside wooden sheds about the size of a modest garden house, or in a booth inside the actual market building (new to Łódź in fall, 1991; market halls were popular long before that in other cities like Wrocław and Gdańsk). Others spread their wares on wood or concrete tables provided by the city. Many bring a table or a folding cot. Some simply open their suitcases, or pile goods on newspaper spread on the street, on cardboard or cloth or just there in the mud or dust. Or they hold goods in their hands, dangle gold necklaces and bracelets from their fingers, wear fur or suede coats on their backs. The market is full of sheds, carts, cars, trucks, wooden crates, cots, planks, cardboard, tables, Poles, Ukrainians, gypsies, Russians, craftsmen, farmers, hucksters, hustlers. I have seen versions of the old shell game, complete with hired shills, and Boardwalk-style demonstrations of miracle kitchen gadgets guaranteed to slice, dice, cut and curl a wide assortment of vegetables with no effort at all, money back if you are not completely satisfied.

You're supposed to bargain, of course, but I rarely do. Prices seem surprisingly consistent, even on the flea market items, and they're low enough for me. 50,000 for a grey Russian fur cap? I'll take it! "You should have bargained with him," Ewa Ziołańska tells me.

"50,000 is cheap. What would we have got it for do you think?"

"40,000 probably, maybe 35,000."

"50,000; 40,000. What's 10,000 złotych?"

"10,000 is half a pizza. Do it twice, and you've got a free lunch."

In spring, 1991, the market by Centrum (the intersection of Pabianicka, Piotrkowska, and Rzgowska) is the liveliest in Łódź, especially on a Saturday morning: mushrooms, cut flowers and bedding plants, baskets for shopping and laundry-sized hampers, fruit (bananas, peaches, rhubarb, kiwi, oranges, cherries, strawberries at 20 cents a pound, lemons, apples as always) and vegetables (tomatoes, cucumbers, carrots, onions, cauliflower, lettuce, radishes, cabbage, potatoes as ever). There are straw hats, River Cola and German chocolate bars, coffee, peanuts, Turkish sweat- and T-shirts with the usual English slogans ("American Superbowl, Beverly Hills," "Navy Marine Seaporf," "Space Age: 21th Century," "West California State, Las Vegas, Nevada"), slippers and shoes, plastic shopping bags bearing the likeness of Michael Jackson or the Lucky Strike logo. There are vegetable peelers and kraut cutters, ladies' undergarments, umbrellas, racks and racks of the old East Bloc clothing so out of fashion even Central won't stock it. These beside pseudo-designer shirts bearing names like "Gucci" and "Chanel, Paris" and "Benetton." Peddlers offer pirated video tapes including *Dirty Dancing* and *Rambo,* Madras shirts from India and dress shirts purportedly from France and Italy, *Playboy* magazine, gold jewelry, fur coats and animal furs ready to be made into fur coats, seeds and bulbs sold bulk from cloth bags, flour and ground grains from larger plastic sacks, leather belts and watchbands, cosmetics, a Westa sewing machine and an "overedging sewing machine made in the People's Republic of China," a Soviet microscope for $35 and Soviet binoculars for the same price, Western telephones, Sharp and Goldstar VCRs, stamps and coins—including a Maria Theresa thaler and a 1922 U.S. silver dollar at $10—brooms with green leaves budding on the twigs, eggs, bolts of textile and bobbins of thread, vinyl floor covering, fresh fish and smoked eels, an unusual number of drafting sets and sets of drill bits, leather jackets without labels, live ducks and geese and bunnies. There are flea market items and military regalia, from Soviet army caps, belts, and medals to a Polish medal for service in the World War II underground. Even Nazi medals. It's not unusual

25

here to see customers strip to their BVDs, even in winter, trying on jeans between the wooden sheds along "clothing alley." Or in the spring to see peasants scoop great clouds of downy chicks or ducklings from one box to another, selling by the dozen, count 'em after they've been poured from seller's box to customer's.

This market has settled into zones, which are being made gradually more permanent by the construction of wooden or corrugated steel sheds and the raising of metal fences: food stuffs, electronic goods, fur and leather, cotton clothing, bikes, automobile parts, stamps and coins, watches, gold and jewelry, and meat (most butchers now being located inside the main market building). Furriers' row is particularly fascinating: you can buy coats—suede and fur—or pelts of any animal from skunk to silver fox. I once watched a peddler and customer haggle over six or seven magnificent white mink pelts. After a brief but intense discussion both nodded, and the customer stuffed those lovely white furs into his plastic shopping bag as casually as I would eat a French fry.

Toward the rear of the market, in the area of permanent structures where the old East Bloc fashions are sold, are the shops of several shoemakers: men fashioning footwear from scratch, to customers' specifications, tacking and sewing wooden heels, thick leather soles, and pieces of shoe leather cut from hides of various hues and textures. One man wanders through the crowd selling *Lody Bambino*—chocolate-covered ice cream on a stick—from a cardboard box. Girls in black and white dresses buy bright costume jewelry. The Old Ones hunch over their wares, selling, selling, selling. And always there are the

young, aggressive male Polish traders, eyes sharp for a sale, dangling wares from their hands, giving a slight jiggle to catch your eye, as you would lightly jerk a Little Cleo after casting it in front of some large-mouth bass.

Today dirt is heavy on the sidewalks, dusted by buses and cars over the kiełbasa and other sausage, over the lungs, chickens, tongue, liver, bacon, kidneys. Some meat is shaded by umbrellas, truck roofs, or other forms of covering, but most is not. One vendor swishes flies off his beef with the branch of a tree. Another butcher hacks away at the skull of a pig, splitting it in half for somebody who only wants a half a head of swine. At another stall, the skinned skull of a steer, picked nearly clean of flesh. Beneath another makeshift counter of crates and plank, a plastic basket full of plucked chicken heads.

The gold-sellers are out in force in one corner of the market, hands in the air, half a dozen rings on each finger, chains wrapped around their arms, broaches pinned to their blouses and jackets. The gold is a deep red color, either a copper alloy or very high karat, but the bands are thin, and what appears to be a large ring is surprisingly light. One expects deception, of course, even with jewelry smuggled out of gold-rich Russia, but not too much deception: a licensed jeweler has parked his camper nearby, and for 2,000 złotych he will test the ring you intend to buy. A scratch on a test plate, a drop of acid. Yes, this is genuine gold. How buyers can be sure this jeweler is not on the take, I can't say, but they seem to believe. Poles are clever tricksters on one hand, naive children on the other—something that will make an interesting and fair fight once Poland confronts unprincipled capitalism face to face. Anyway, this jeweler

has been here many months now, and, if he is indeed a scam, should have been detected long ago.

In front of Centrum stands the line of puppy merchants: boxes, suitcases, Big Shopper shopping bags wriggling with dog flesh, warm and soft-furred and puppy-breathed. Shepherds, Dalmations, mutts aplenty stuggle toward freedom, always to be pushed back into the bag. Usually a mother dog stands nearby, reassuring potential buyers with a nod of her head, "Yup, that's my baby. She's a Shepherd all right. Look just like me in a couple of years." Ewa says they are all diseased and will not live six months, but one is cuter than the other, and I have learned to keep Michelle far away from the puppy-peddlers. She alternates between one plan to "buy a pedigree Newfoundland here cheap, and fly him home while still a puppy; he can sleep in a basket on our lap," and another plan to buy every puppy in the place and give them away to good homes, thereby bringing joy to kids all over the city and saving the pups from certain drowning. "David," she will tell me earnestly, "somebody has to save these puppies!"

Many peddlers are Russians, Ukrainians, Central Asians come to Łódź to sell clothing, tools, matrioshka dolls and designer "perestroika" watches, vodka and Soviet champaign (now $5 a bottle), caviar ($6 a tin), and children's toys. Their "tour" buses are usually parked somewhere in the field along Rzgowska. But it is the Old Ones who most interest me: the old woman seated on an overturned plastic bucket, hands folded on her lap, on the ground in front of her five live rabbits in a cage, two dead chickens, a stack of eggs, a bag of salad lettuce, and a few bunches of radishes. The man selling the kraut cutter he obviously built himself. The weathered peasant standing patiently in front of an old balance scale, all he had left to peddle (I bought it for $10, and he packed it in a cloth bang, handed it to me, pocketed my money, and walked to the tram stop). The woman selling her old sewing machine. Or the other woman seated on a wooden crate, pouring cream (or borscht stock) through a funnel into empty vodka bottles. The liquid is so thick she has to pause every few seconds and shake it through the funnel neck into the bottles. These are the real stories of the street market.

I have taken from this market souvenirs aplenty (denim skirt for my daughter Kristin—"Pyramid Jeans: King of Desert, Best for You"—for $6.50; two old record albums, made in Poland, Buddy Holly and Billie Holiday, 35 cents each; three Polish fishing lures for Jack Hickerson—"If the walleyes won't take your Little Cleos, Jack old Buddy, whack 'em with some of these Polski spinners"), but I have precious few photographs of those remarkable old faces, the faces out of *National Geographic* or Singer stories. Some time I would love to spend ten hours in this market with a telephoto lens and a dozen rolls of film. Those photos might be the best buy in the place, the real treasure of the street market.

Most foreign goods come to Poland in brightly colored, soft-pack

plastic suitcases on trains, buses, cars hauled by a small army of private peddlers. Poland-Berlin, Poland-Budapest, Poland-Prague and Poland-Turkey were the most popular trading routes in late 1989, although Polish Peddlers were famous all over Europe: Michelle's friend Rafał Pniewski recalls being greeted upon arrival in Syria by an Arab inquiring in perfect Polish what he had to sell, and what he wanted to buy. A colleague recalls sitting in a Lot airplane on a flight returning from southern Ukraine, juice dripping on his shoulder from the bags of grapes stuffed into overhead compartments by his fellow passengers. Poles were in a specially favorable position to trade, because some quirk of the post-World War II settlement gave them visa-free access to West Bloc nations like Austria and West Berlin. The First Polish Peddlers Army operated in and around Berlin, the Second Army in Prague, the Third Army in Vienna. Stray battalions were scattered across the continent. Polish traders were, in fact, an international problem.

Unlike American salesmen on expense accounts, hard-core traders live as cheaply as possible while abroad. They sleep in tents or motor vehicles or sprawled on the grass. They bring their own food, living for weeks on boiled eggs, tea, *suchary* (thick, army-issue biscuits you have to karate chop to break), and tins of Mazowiecki paté (ground protein—and bone—with a hearty, dog foody aroma). Some even bring their own petrol. They undercut local merchants on what they sell, then bargain closely on what they buy. They thus produce minimal revenue for "host" countries. When they depart, they leave a mess. Germans and Czechs claim they steal everything too hot or heavy to haul away, although I have not known Poles to steal much from other nationals, except automobiles. The reason ordinary tourists can't purchase a train ticket for Berlin, Budapest or Prague earlier than thirty days before departure is that peddlers would, if allowed, buy out all seats months in advance; and the reason they have so much trouble getting a ticket to Budapest, Berlin and Prague later than twenty-nine days before departure is that peddlers have by then booked them out. (Perhaps it is for this reason that foreigners are sent to Orbis, but Orbis never, not once, produced a train ticket for me.) On trains the peddlers cause headaches for conductors and customs people, who naturally become cynical, careless, contemptuous and corrupt. The border between Czechoslovakia and Poland was a case study in mutual ill will, much of it the result of Polish traders. In late May of 1991, truckers blocked the German-Polish border crossing at Frankfurt am Oder, claiming they were being extorted by customs agents turned venal after dealing with too many Polish traders.

Peddlers are held in contempt by most Poles, who consider trading too undignified of a member of the lower nobility, too dirty for intellectuals, too suspect for peasants . . . although the greater community envies their wealth and has no qualms about consuming the goodies they bring into Poland.

Whatever difficulties Polish traders have caused for the heads of other governments, who must protect their various populaces, and for heads of their own government, who must negotiate visa treaties with Austria, Hungary, and the United Germany, they clearly constitute a re-emerging middle class. Professional peddlers piled up a good amount of money, and more is being made as prices rise even higher and a system of wholesaling develops. That this new wealth is not effectively taxed is the government's fault, not the peddlers'. Who volunteers taxes he is not required to pay? The fact is, it's the people who run risks—who in Gatsby's words "see an opportunity and take it," who spend the time in automobile lines at border crossings and the long hours riding train all over Central Europe—that reap rewards. And their rewards will increase. And their example will become an example to the Soviets in their tortured road to a free market economy. And, gradually, to Poles themselves, who must cease looking to America as a place where dreams can come true, and begin looking at Poland as the land of opportunity.

The Jewish Cemetery in Łódź

During official opening hours you can enter the Jewish Cemetery in Łódź through the main gate: trams 1, 15, or 19 to the Strykowska terminus, or the 51 bus in the direction of Wilanów. But the essence of this place is a growing horror which, like most nightmares, develops imperceptibly by degrees out of the most mundane scenes of daily life. It is better to use the back entrance.

Take bus 57 past the well tended and well attended Catholic Cemetery, past the Graphic Arts Institute, to where it turns down Wojska Polskiego. Get off at ulica Sporna and walk uphill through what was once the Łódź ghetto, past the Catholic Church, to a chain link fence around what appears to be a large meadow containing several groves of birch trees. If you look carefully in the far distance, you will notice a collection of gravestones. You will see a hole in the chain link fence, at the corner, with a path heading off into the field, toward the gravestones, through some raspberry bushes.

Climb through the hole in the fence.

At first you will think you are in a park, Hyde Park half a decade untended, unless it is winter or a recent arson has burned the grass to its roots. Foliage is high, litter is profuse, and trails radiate in several directions through the meadow and trees. Mind the dog droppings. Follow the paths toward the thicket of gravestones in the distance, or along the fence by the road.

Watch the earth.

Graves in this corner of the cemetery have been so obliterated that I might have trouble convincing you this is indeed a cemetery, but you will not have walked too far before noticing a broken brick or cement rectangle about the size of a coffin, or a fragment of marble or basalt lying in your path. You will see several tombstones of great size now three-quarters buried in the earth. The inscriptions are in Hebrew.

In early spring or winter, if there is no snow, you may notice fragments of bone, what looks to my untrained eye like bits of rib, or femur or ulna. I am not making this up.

So this is the cemetery, and you are in the southwest corner of a tract

31

that runs nearly a kilometer along the edge of Sporna-Zagajnikowa. In this corner, the story goes, Nazi barbarians began their systematic destruction of grave sites just before the liberation of Łódź by the Russians late in 1944. Working methodically up one row and down the other, smashing vaults, removing markers, stealing rings, teeth, jewelry—anything valuable—they wrecked the place so completely that it looks like a meadow, except for half-buried fragments of vaults or headstones. Even the CIA couldn't reconstruct the lives of people buried here.

The path which runs north, parallel to Sporna, will bring you past a great heap of grave markers, dumped together like the facing stone of some English monastery confiscated by Henry VIII, sold, and mined for some manor house that never got constructed. Perhaps these stones too were headed for a road paving or building construction project. They never arrived. Today they lie in a pile, trees growing out of the center.

As you move east from Sporna, toward the inner gate of the cemetery and the axial road that leads down the middle of the burial plots, vandalism becomes less thorough and the cemetery more recognizable: rows upon rows of graves, each three by six feet, one abutting flush with the other, except where a grid of roads and lanes offers access to most, but not all. At one end of each grave is—or was—a head-stone, in most cases facing the pre-burial hall outside the main gate. Some graves have—or had—stone or cement entablatures. A wrought iron railing or a low stone edging may have surrounded the grave. A low vault of brick or cement covered the grave proper. In almost all cases the vault is broken or gone, the headstone is fragmented or thrown down or both, and the iron railing is disrupted.

Moving due north and east, you enter a heavy wood sprung up over the past fifty years, as can be seen by counting the rings in those one or two recently felled trunks. In winter, 1939, existing trees in the cemetery were cut for fuel. The present crop grew haphazardly, in some cases directly out of graves. So a double forest: tombs and trees.

Near the main gate you enter a landscape of broken headstones, looted graves, overturned pillars, a forest of stone, the older graves of some of the richest people in turn-of-the-century Łódź: Polish and Swedish marbles, Czech and Hungarian granite, red sandstone, basalt, slate . . . all haphazard, topsy-turvy, overturned, displaced, thrown down, disrupted by human vandals, by weeds and bushes and the roots of trees which have, over four decades, shouldered even the most massive stone slabs to crazy angles, toppling headstones and Grecian columns and Egyptian ornaments into the dirt which rises to bury them. This place resembles some jungle archeological site in early stages of exploration . . . or the "Classical Antiquities" rooms of the British Museum, where servants of the crown have strewn carved stone fragments from all over the globe at odd angles across the floor. Or scenes which accompany those Museum marbles, showing fragments *in situ* before Captain Major Smith and his expedition brought them hither.

Or rather a pile of huge child's blocks, the remains of some kiddie edifice now toppled to a heap of cylinders, rectangles, squares and triangles.

The temples of the mightiest of the mighty have survived longer than those of the commoners: Poznański, Purssak, Jarociński, Konsztadt, Silberstein with his 50,000-ruble mausoleum of white Italian marble, a Corinthian temple with an Egyptian sarcophagus. Sumptuously carved stone *objets d'art* are stacked all over, some lying on their side, some leaning against each other, Grecian columns, basalt funereal vases, granite spheres, finials, fleches, obelisks, needles . . . a set from *Empire of the Sun*.

It is not the neglect of this place which so strikes the observer—we have all seen neglected cemeteries. Nor is it the eerie feeling of having entered someplace alien and forbidden, this place full of inscriptions in Hebrew and German and Russian, this place of strange symbols pregnant with hidden meaning—paired hands, their digits mysteriously separated between second and third finger; Stars of David; an oak tree with a broken branch; three- and seven-candle candelabra, sometimes with a broken center candle; tabernacles open to reveal two rows of books in various combinations, five over six, six over five, five over three, seven over five, six over six. Some stones retain traces of red, green, yellow, and black pigment. Some in the art nouveau style, others so standardized as to have been mass produced. What does all this *mean?*

No, it is not the mystery of the place that presses itself most upon a visitor. Nor is it even the vandalism, so gratuitous, so unrepaired, so contrastive

33

to the Catholic Cemetery on Strykowska (carefully tended, filled with votive candles), or the Evangelical Cemetery on Srebrzyńska (ignored, but not vandalized). It's the combination that oppresses: vandalism and mystery. And neglect: in the half century since World War II erupted, nobody has cared enough about this place to keep the trees from growing out of people's graves.

And danger. "Stay out," Poles tell me. "It is dangerous. A thirteen-year-old-boy was murdered there, his throat cut with a broken bottle. There are fires, lootings and vandalism still. It is a dangerous place, even in the day."

And the immensity of it all: a *lot* of people were buried here, many of them powerful people. An object lesson is what this place is, in the impossibility for even the mightiest among us to provide, provide:

> And on the pedestal these words appear:
> 'My name is Ozymandias, king of kings:
> Look on my works, ye Mighty, and despair!'
> Nothing beside remains. Round the decay
> Of that colossal wreck, boundless and bare
> The lone and level sands stretch far away.
>
> —Percy Shelley, "Ozymandias"

On one visit to this cemetery I met a guide, or caretaker, or self-appointed custodian of the land of the dead. He walked with the aid of a cane, his left leg lost or paralyzed. He asked me something in Polish, and I responded that I was an American. Did I speak Hebrew, he wanted to know. No. Russian then? German?

I told him I spoke a little German. What state did I come from, he wanted to know. Minnesota. Was I Jewish? Lutheran. He hesitated a moment, then directed me to the center of the cemetery, where the wealthiest of the wealthy of Łódź had built their final monuments, to the mausoleum of Israel Poznański. "Incontestably the wealthiest man in Poland," he told me. "His cloth was sold here to St. Petersburg. He once decided to pave his ballroom floor in golden rubles, you have seen his palace, it is now the city museum? And he would have done it, too, but first he asked the permission of his friend the czar. And the czar gave his friend Poznański permission, but asked that the rubles not be laid with his face up, because the czar did not want people dancing on his face. And that they not be laid face down, because he did not want his face to be turned down, to the earth. But if he were to set them on edge . . .

"Poznański was buried in a gold suit. On the ceiling of his mausoleum were golden tiles. It was done by an Italian firm, Andrea Salviatti."

I read the silhouette of letters long ago stolen—bronze? brass? a gold plate?—and note the fence that now surrounds the mausoleum. Come to this, the great Poznański, the czar's friend, the man who donated half the land for this cemetery, the man who was if not the richest man in Łódź a very definite second

(behind Karl Scheibler, whose neo-Gothic mausoleum in the Evangelical Cemetery looks like a small cathedral). And nobody to care? Astonishing.

My guide directed me toward the inner gate, to the cemetery wall. Three or four feet above ground level, the bricks have been blasted and broken by executioners' bullets.   In front of the wall, a row of shallow pits dug many years ago: graves of the executed, the last few dug but unfilled. The Russians were coming, and the ghetto had to be liquidated. On the wall itself, relatives of the deceased have placed memorial plaques in Polish, Hebrew, English and German. They do not mince words: "In Errinerung an meine lieben Eltern und Geschwister.   Chid Wolf Chaslowicz, Chaja Fajga Chaslowicz, Genia Chaslowicz, unbekommen durch die barbarische Nazi-Herrschaft in Polen." "This plague [sic] was laid in loving memory of my dear sister BLUMA, on 7 October 1980, who was shot dead by a German murderer without any reason in the ghetto Łódź, Poland." "In memory of all Kleinlehrer and Najman who were killed by the German beast in the Hlocaust [sic] from 1939-1945."

My guide departed abruptly, and I never saw him again—which is a shame because I have a dozen questions I would like to ask him. I would like to inquire about that heap of headstones. I have heard there is a gypsy section of this cemetery, but I have not found it. I have questions from my reading of *The Chronicle of the Łódź Ghetto*.

I have more questions, in fact, than I care to hear answered. The story of Nazi vandalism, for example, doesn't ring quite true. When did this vandalism take place? Immediately after the invasion of 1939, when troops were storming Russia in the east? Not likely, it seems to me, although the Łódź synagogue was burned on November 11, 1939. Torching a building is a one-night job; this methodical destruction took time.

After the ghetto was sealed in March 1940? Germans never entered the ghetto, having their dirty work done for them by insiders. After the liquidation of August 1944, with the Russians coming on hard, the Reich collapsing on itself? Possible, I suppose—Hitler was crazy enough to order the leveling of Warsaw, and his generals were crazy enough to obey. A start, perhaps, in the corner—but what about the other graves in this huge tract?

In spring, 1990, I voiced my reservations to an older Pole, one who lived through those years, a good friend to whom I could speak of such matters. Who? What? Why? When?

I was met by way of answer with what can only be called a profound silence. Then a clearing of his throat. Then an explanation of sorts: "You know, before the War, we knew nothing of them, really. It was like two separate nations on one land. Hundred of years they had lived among us, and most of them could not even speak decent Polish. We spoke no Hebrew. We read our newspapers; they read their newspapers. We went to our churches; they went to their synagogues. Their program of resistance was not our program of resistance, their program for the future was not ours. I would not call it anti-Semitism, really, I would call it a lack of knowing.

"Of course everyone thought they were all rich, and they must have been buried with plenty of money. There were stories, you know, of people buried in gold suits. The ceiling of Poznański's mausoleum was gold tiles, you could see that. People used to throw rocks up at the roof, trying to knock those tiles loose. Finally they put a fence around it. You have to understand; the times were very difficult. It is impossible to explain. . . ."

He did not continue, and I did not press him.

In *Leaves of Grass*, Walt Whitman writes of letting the grass cover all, atone for all, for all the sufferings and the deaths, here, everywhere. He had it right: earth finally reclaims its own stone, and grass covers everything. Sooner or later, it comes to this. We build our little houses in our little clearings in the woods, our little cities, our little lives, neatly structured in defiance of our own mortality. But in no way can we guarantee our immortality a few decades, a few short centuries at best. Chaos finally prevails. What desecrated these graves was Nature and human nature. Nature and human nature will desecrate, or forget, us as well. "Gritstone, a-crumble!"

The birds sing in the branches of these trees, and the bells of the Catholic church sing to the living. The earth rises to reclaim her own, and the grass, the grass, the grass—it covers everything.

Cityscape: Kraków

The essence of Kraków is Old: layers upon layers of Norman, Gothic, baroque, Renaissance, neoclassical, Victorian, art nouveau, renovation, decay, restoration, war, more decay, redecoration, vandalism, remodeling, additions, weatherings, losses, reclamations, now all cross-seasoned in one magnificent Polish bigos. Kraków is Old old enough to be just a little fallen, and thus not as full of itself as Warsaw, an easy city to live in and with. Kraków is Old old enough to be comfortable with itself, and thus graceful and unstrained, a self-assured and reassuring city. Kraków is Old old enough to have antiques behind the antiques: you can't exhaust this town, and Kraków doesn't have to throw what little it's got in your face, hustle you with façade. Kraków is old enough to have survived centuries before you happened along; if you don't care for this city, Kraków will get along for centuries without you.

Kraków is old enough to know quality when it sees it. Are you our sort of person?

Kraków is genuine Old: the Germans planned to destroy the city upon departure, as well you might expect, but liberating Soviet forces circled around the city and attacked unexpectedly from the west, while Polish agents within the city managed to disrupt explosives and detonating cables, sparing Kraków the horror which leveled the Warsaw Stare Miasto to a pencil line. Kraków is so full of Old that Old Town is under protection as part of the "World's Cultural Heritage," for whatever that's worth. This UNESCO seal of approval and a strong army might allow Kraków to survive the next global catastrophe. Or it might not. One rather hopes it does: Kraków is incontestably one of Europe's great cities. The powerful charge of planting one's feet on stones where, five centuries ago, princes robed themselves for coronation, and potentates decided the fate of the world is not to be found too many places on this globe.

This Kraków knows, as do increasing numbers of tourist bureaus. In summer Kraków is filled with foreign buses, multi-lingual guided tours, and horse-drawn carriages giving wealthy Westerners a clattering, jostling quicktrip around town. The inner side of the town wall by Floriańska Gate is plastered with paintings, some imitation Old Masters, some Kraków cityscapes, some

nude women, most of them tourist claptrap, all of them overpriced. Old Market Building is a warehouse of wood carvings, table cloths, chess sets, wall hangings, paintings and drawings, posters, books, pots, vases, T-shirts—the same kitsch you'll find in Paris, Munich or Rome, names and styles superficially changed to reflect Poland. You need reservations days in advance for dinner at the Wierzynek—Kraków's most elegant restaurant—or at the Kawiarnia Jama Machalika, a turn-of-the-century haunt for Krakówian theater types, now decorated in the main and entrance halls with cartoons, drawings, paintings, caricatures, costumes, puppets, and other theater memorabilia from that period. (More recently, the parking lot of the café was the scene of a genuine crime of passion, famous and jealous French singer rubbing out his wife's Polish lover.) On a winter evening, you can enjoy a delicious ice cream and hot tea on these plush red and black sofas and chair, but during high season you will have to fight off crowds of package tourists aggressively having the time of their lives, for which they worked so hard and saved so long.

You may even have trouble finding an empty table at the Balaton, a fine Hungarian restaurant on ulica Grodzka, identified by its sign of seven black frying pans, by the wine cask and goulash pot in the window, by the red and back tables below the low plastered vaults of the ceiling within. Or in getting tickets for the satirical theater Maszkaron, located in the basement of what used to be Old Town Hall, only a tower of which remains. Or, for that matter, just getting a drink at the Café/Bar Maszkaron during daytime hours, or when no production is in progress.

40

Probably you'd have better luck along the side streets, like the Kawiarnia u. Literacka, number 7 ulica Kanonicza, with its low, gray vaulted cellar, plaster walls, stone-cased windows, wood tables and beamed ceiling. (By the time you read this, the whole street may be a tangle of such pubs, cafés, and restaurants, no longer quiet, no longer mysterious, no longer out of the way. As I write, not a building in Old Kraków is not being renovated into some little shop for gold and silver, a currency exchange, a gift shop, a restaurant or a café. Catch Kraków while you can . . . or in the winter, when things quiet down. You'll think you're in Paris in 1958.)

Still Kraków contains Old enough for everyone, plenty of Old that package tourists will miss in the day and a half allotted to this city.

You must visit the Cathedral of St. Mary, with its two asymmetric twin towers, one resembling the crown of Heaven's Queen, gloomy Gothic interior still painted from base of nave piers to the top of its vaulted arches, and the famous altarpiece flush against the chancel wall, five enormous gold figures just behind the altar and three more carvings in each wing: gold flaming from all surfaces. There is the Jesuit church of St. Barbara's, adjacent to St. Mary's. There is old St. Peter's and St. Paul's, in the neoclassical style, with carvings of twelve apostles outside and restoration in progress inside. There is the old Norman church of St. Andrew the Apostle, renovated during the eighteenth century to mostly baroque, but still a fine Norman exterior, which sheltered some few Krakówians from the Tartar invasions of 1241 and 1259. There is the old Dominican basilica of the Holy Trinity, Gothic nave with blue ceiling, side altars in mostly nineteenth-century neo-Gothic, step down six steps from the

41

1990 street level to 1400 street level (entering St. Mary's, you step down three steps—we're talking Old here in Kraków), marble floor, stone piers. There is old St. Anna's, the University church, Poland's best example of high baroque, erected between 1689 and 1705.

If you're not keen on churches, take in the Old Market Building in the center of the town square, its low vaulted ceilings decorated with plaster city crests of famous Polish towns, Łódź included. Or walk the circumference of the old city wall, a wonderfully settling stroll for a couple in love or an individual in search of solitude. A wonderful idea too: the polluted, infected, stinking moat was filled with earth and planted into a tree-filled park which fully encircles the old town, dotted with dozens of ancient gates, each identified in a diagram on the reverse of Kraków city maps. One of life's finer moments is a night walk by the Wisła, or across the park, with streetlights glimmering through leafy boughs, or a number 3 tram rattling along in the fog or drizzle.

Old may be found in city museums as well, the City Museum, the ecclesiastical treasure houses, the library of the Jagellonian University, open 12:00 to 2:00 most afternoons, more than a library, a series of academic rooms and historical treasures dating to the late middle ages. Old may be found in the city wall barbican, in what remains of Jewish Kazimierz, contiguous with Old City. Old is to be found in ulica Kanoniczna down by the southern end of old Kraów, a winding road of ecclesiastical edifices, cardinal's hats and bishop's miters carved above each doorway, still quite deteriorated and eerily untrafficked. Walking this street is like walking into a post-war movie set: nothing except the rats in the rubble.

Old is the University auditorium, where in 1939 Nazi officials invited the entire Jagellonian faculty to a scholarly convocation, then packed them off to Auschwitz—Jews and gentiles, Poles and foreigners.

Old is the statues on building corners—no replicas or restorations these.

Old is a random glance down some Krakówian back alley at an upper story balcony in half-timbered brick.

Old in this city is a cobblestone in the street, a brick in a wall.

Old is the trumpeter's call played live each noon from one tower of St. Mary's (broadcast from Kraków on Polish radio throughout the country), repeated four times from each side of the tower and broken always in mid-call, in memory of the trumpeter who took an arrow in the throat while sounding the alarm at one of the Tartar invasions.

The most important Krakówian Old is Wawel, a hill overlooking the Wisła, a complex of buildings surrounded by a walled fortification including Wawel Cathedral, the royal palace—*the* Polish royal palace, accept no pretenders—and the foundations of several other buildings, which trace in gray limestone rubble the outlines of what is no more. The royal palace is an opulent display of Polish royal wealth hidden or reclaimed from foreign invaders, including enormous tapestries containing hundreds of pounds of gold and silver thread, and recently mended cuts where Poland's conquerors cut away chunks of tapestry to accommodate windows and doorways of Russian or German castles.

The Italian influence is obvious at Wawel, both inside and out: King Zygmunt had the palace redone between 1506 and 1531 by Florentines Francesco Fiorentino and Bartolomeo Berecci. Berecci's next commission was a mausoleum for the King, a magnificent Renaissance structure attached to the right nave aisle of the Cathedral, covered with a dome of golden scales, which clever Poles painted green during the occupation, and less-than-clever Germans mistook for the copper-covered domes of the rest of the Cathedral. One of the more interesting features of the castle is an unfaced section of stone wall near the museum entrance, said to be a surface outlet for some great source of subterranean power—magmatic, electromagnetic, psychic, or just plain superstitious—into which tourists can plug by backing their bodies against the wall for a cosmic recharge.

Wawel Cathedral is a sensory overload of Gothic and Renaissance abundance, touristed enough to necessitate "Direction of Visit" signs during the high season, but a true architectural monument to the Glory That Was Poland: marble, stone, brick, silver, gold over gold, oriental carpets and inlaid floors, Flemish tapestries on the walls, wrought iron gates of incredible delicacy, columns with golden capitals and marble bases, sculptured saints and bishops in flowing robes, silver and crystal reliquaries, angels and cherubs, lambs and skulls, relics and national treasures. The church building itself was consecrated in 1364, the third building to stand on this site. It is Gothic in shape and design, piers of solid stone, gray unpainted stone roof supported by a simple system of arches, some brick work in the nave walls. Fifty years after completion, it was surrounded by other Gothic chapels, all subsequently replaced or razed. Most of the interior is now baroque, including the shrine-mausoleum of St. Stanislas, a marble altar and a silver coffin, made in Gdańsk by Piotr von der Rennen. This tomb was designed by Giovanni Trevano; the tomb of King Ladislas Jagiełło, ornate marble carved a hundred years after his death, was designed by Giovanni Cinci of Siena. Around the outside aisles of the nave, a series of Renaissance and baroque chapels filled with carved marble of every imaginable color, none matching the richness of the Sigismund Chapel, but some coming very close, since most were built, like many other chapels all over Poland, in imitation of the Sigismund Chapel. Some—like Bishop Tomicki's chapel in Wawel Cathedral—were designed by Tuscan architects who worked on the Sigismund Chapel. In all this wealth, the tombs of Casimir the Great and the crucifix of Queen Jadwiga are nearly lost. And the glass cabinet containing her orb and scepter, an opulence of genuine Old.

My favorite Old in Kraków, and possibly my favorite Old in Poland, is the Collegium Maius of the Jagellonian University, an ancient quadrangle of buildings at the corner of St. Ann's and Jagellonian Streets, just a block off the Great Market Square. One of Europe's oldest universities, the Jagellonean was founded by Casimir the Great in 1364. The buildings of Collegium Maius date to the 1490s, when a number of independent structures were conjoined around a courtyard containing a central well, with an ambulatory around the circumference of the square, atop which a second ambulatory—access provided by ancient stone steps—opens to rooms on the first, and main floor of the quadrangle buildings. Atop that, two stories up, a wooden roof, painted on the underside in a series of medallions with gold floral designs. Pillars supporting the lower ambulatory are, of course, hewn stone, decorated in a pattern of raised, interwoven lines. The ambulatory roof—floor of the second-level ambulatory—is gracefully arched vaults. The walls are brick, of course, but brick of slightly irregular shape and masonry, with a particularly hand-made and pleasing effect. Door and window casements are stone, and because the quadrangle buildings antedated the idea of the University, no two walls, no two doors, are exactly alike, although all are definitely mediaeval: short, square, heavy doors, and small, barred windows. Design on the iron grills protecting each window varies, as do the doors themselves, which tend to be iron-faced: a lattice of iron strips held in place with decorative nails, and behind those iron bands diamond-shaped sections of more iron, designs pounded into them with a nail or punch or hammer. The ambulatory, the eaves, the copper gutter and the dragon-shaped downspouts give off an Italian flavor, especially the second-story entrance to the college library.

Some of the facing on the brick wall along the second-story ambulatory is carved stone, and fragments of ancient artifacts have been strategically

positioned around the courtyard perimeter: a bit of column here, an old cannon there, a heap of limestone facing stones somewhere else. In summer, the stone flowerpots are full of geraniums and petunias, and they are augmented by wood flower pots full of leafy foliage. Along the inside wall of the lower ambulatory, hand-painted watercolors, a mediaeval simplicity to them but probably the work of a more recent artist, depict the town and the University at sundry points in their histories: 1369, 1575, 1582, 1775 (an impressive panorama of a procession along St. Anne's Street to the basilica of St. Anne), 1582. The paintings are in plain wooden frames and show watermarks. They just feel Old.

The well, of course, is dry, but in the wall below the library entrance, the stone head of a satyr spits drinking water into a seashell basin. In one corner of the fountain you will find a brown ceramic coffee cup. The Latin inscription on the fountain reminds visitors that hospitality is a cup of water given to a thirsty guest.

Even in mid-summer, when the Collegium Maius is part of most tours of Kraków, it radiates a serenity you can't find in Notre Dame de Paris, Cologne Cathedral, Westminster or even Chartres. And here is a much more organic harmony: Collegium Maius is just Old Poland being old. The courtyard is still a functioning part of a functioning University. The phone rings occasionally in the porter's office behind one stone-encased, grill-covered window at the corner of the lower ambulatory. University personnel pass under the colonnade on University errands.

The courtyard's atmosphere is artificially enhanced by the Gregorian chant emanating from the gift shop, but the shop is tasteful, part of the mediaeval charm: low plastered vaulting ceiling painted in a woodland scene, with semi-clothed women in a garden setting below, a canopy of tree branches and leaves above, something out of Chaucer or Boccaccio. The shop will sell you tapes of Gregorian Chant, plaster busts of Casimir the Great, chess sets, book plates and books to put them in, slides of the Jagellonean treasures, some wall hangings, posters, nice art, and Jagellonean University T-shirts and sweatshirts, university motto in Latin. Who's to complain about canned music in this 100% class act? Besides, this place is most attractive when the gift shop is closed and the music is silent and the tourists gone home. When, on a slightly chilly afternoon in late autumn, you have time to sit with the bricks and stones that have seen nearly half a millennium of priests, potentates, rectors and professors come and go . . . to meditate on things past and passing . . . to plug yourself into that great power source up there in the library: parchments and codices and missals and atlases and encyclopediae, Copernicus' own works revised in Copernicus' own hand, treatises and histories and polemics and diatribes . . . to imagine yourself one in that long line of students and scholars, and, thus, part of the grand continuum of Man Thinking.

Bread

It is best to go just at opening time, shortly after the bread has been delivered, when the store is heavy with the rich, yeasty smell of raised dough. Show up at seven, take your loaf of *angielka* directly home, cut a thick slab, and watch the butter melt from residual heat. On a winter morning, the warmth of the bread, wrapped in a plastic shopping bag and carried close to your body, is as delicious as the taste of the bread itself. On a spring morning, the scent hangs with you all the way home.

The bread shop is the plainest facade on Nowotki: a blue doorway and window in the white cement wall, blocked most of the day by a queue of taxis. Yellow letters on the glass say simply *Piekarnia*. In the window a white lace curtain, a white lace tablecloth, a basket full of rolls. Sometimes there is also a plaster of Paris baker, Smurfish, hand-painted in primary colors, a larger version of the plaster figurines you painted back in 1958 at Camp Hiawatha, a present for mom (dad got a billfold, sewn through pre-punched holes with plastic gimp) to show that your two weeks at camp were more than just a holiday for you and them. Or maybe this baker is a smaller cousin of those cement lawn statues with which Italians decorate their gardens.

The shop interior is also simplicity itself. Two large rooms, one for sales, one for storage, with a sales counter in front of the wall to the left of the entrance. Two walls of the front room and all walls of the storage room are floor-to-ceiling bread racks built of heavily painted two-by-fours, or—for rolls and smaller loaves of bread—standard heavy duty pine shelving. The racks that hold the round three-pound loaves of *chleb* are a cross between bookshelves and wine racks. The loaves are large, maybe fourteen inches in diameter, five or six inches thick, dusty with flour, which is used liberally in the baking process. A dozen loaves set on their sides fill a shelf. There is something primeval about this early morning floor-to-ceiling bread, a vault of bread, a library of bread, bread behind, bread out front, bread and flour everywhere, and a long, curling, seemingly endless queue out the front door, the great army of Polish workers waiting patiently for their daily sustenance. "Jobs and bread," the workers had demanded; "give us jobs and bread."

47

The shop's interior is not entirely undecorated. On beige paneled walls not covered with bread racks, and on top of some of the bread shelves, rest half a dozen hand-painted plates of the type sold by Lutheran Church Women at annual fund-raiser bazaars. The design is Polish flowers, and the colors are the usual yellow, brown and green. The porcelain-faced clock is also decorated with a floral motif. There are dried flowers in vases, and a flower calendar. A pot of ivy hangs on one wall. Despite—or perhaps because of the flour—this place has the appearance of a clean, well run establishment.

Like early McDonald's restaurants, its menu is limited:

chleb pszenny	1.5 kg.	4000zł
chleb pszenny	,7 kg.	2200zł
angielka	,5 kg.	1850zł
bułka zwykła	,2 kg.	800zł
bułka zwykła	,1 kg.	400zł
rogalik	,1 kg.	500zł
chałeczka	,5 kg.	1850zł

The *chleb*, "bread," is round, dark, heavy, not quite rye but made of unrefined flour, with trace elements of sawdust and plywood. *Angielka* is oblong, white, and crusty. The rolls are doughy, chewy; the larger are butterfly rolls, the smaller simple, round shapes. *Rogalik* are oblong rolls; *chałeczka* is braided bread dough, sweet and almost cakey.

On the counter, right, sits a hand-cranked circular-blade bread saw for halving loaves: many customers request "*pół chleba*" and even "*pół angielki,*" half a loaf of *angielka*. I have seen pensioners purchase a quarter of a loaf.

The line in this store moves quickly. People buy what they have been buying for the past decade, modified to accommodate holiday needs and the presence of visitors. The clerk probably knows what customers will request even before they open their mouths. A new face—mine when first I came here—is recognized immediately. Old timers, I am sure, are missed when they leave town. The community of the bread store, the fellowship of bread.

Like the old McDonald's, this shop sells from directly behind the counter, everything that can be ordered within arm's reach of the clerk. Large loaves of *chleb* are stored on the rear and upper right shelves. Small loaves of *chleb*, rear and upper left. Large rolls rear and lower right, small rolls rear and lower left. One shelf of *angielka* rear and left, with a few plastic baskets of *angielka* and *chałeczka* stacked on the floor to the clerk's right. Bread cutter, counter right. Cash drawer, counter left, with a stack of 50, 100, and 500 złotych notes atop the counter for quick change.

Like a ticking clock, the line moves along. "*Proszę?*" "Six small rolls, one *chleb*, one *angielka*." "6,450 złotych, please." "Thank you." "You are welcome. Please?" "One *chleb*." "2,400 złotych. Do you have four hundred złotych?" *"Dziękuję."* "You are welcome. Please?" "Two *angielka . . . ."*

Unlike the old McDonald's, this is a one-person operation. The shelves behind the counter must be refilled periodically from side racks or storage room by the clerk herself. She shuffles between serving customers and restocking shelves, her motions a dance rehearsed day after day, month after month, year after year. She knows when the shelf of large *chleb* behind her needs restocking, first from the storage room, and as the day wears on from other shelves in the sales room. She sweeps a row of eight large *chleba* from the shelves, holding them at either end, compressed like a huge flour accordion. She empties *angielka* from the plastic delivery baskets to the shelves two at a time, one in each hand, holding them always by the end, stacking the shelves three loaves high, with a single row of loaves across the front, a brick-layer setting rows of doughy bricks into a wall of bread. "Please?" She selects her loaves carefully, for they vary considerably in shape and even weight. There is no E.G. norm to these loaves. Customers may reject a bad loaf, like Sandy Koufax or Nolan Ryan asking the umpire for a different baseball. She never allows her stock at hand to drop so low that she has no choice of what to sell, and I have seen her rummage through the few loaves on her shelf, reject them all as unworthy a particular customer, and bustle off to the back room for another armload of candidates. She operates with the practiced efficiency of a worker worthy her hire.

I respect, admire her practiced economy of energy, the repertoire of rehearsed gestures, the practiced minimalism of the assemblyline worker, the baseball pitcher, the ballet dancer. Nothing is wasted in this ballet of bread. The beauty of economy, the only way to go the distance, pitch the full nine, dance the complete performance for the entire run of the show.

Customers also play a role in this clockwork of bread, queuing always to the right of the counter, winding clockwise around the room, then coiling inward like the spring of a watch, waiting outside if necessary. Those outside wait patiently to enter the small shop: two Poles out, baskets full of *chleb*, two Poles in, baskets empty. Customers have money ready, pocket change quickly, bag their own bread at the side of the counter so the next person can be quickly served. There is not much chatter, and not too much complaining about this loaf or that. Everyone does her job.

This is a well rehearsed system, and it is one system in Poland that works well. In other stores I've seen customers impose their presence on clerks and other customers by being, I thought, a little too deliberate, by taking just a few extra seconds longer to examine and finger and inspect. I understand this impulse to assert one's presence in a society that does not generally afford many opportunities for the individual to have his say in the collective culture, the governed to assert his will against the machinery of government. But this store is only bread, and everybody here seems to understand that fact. Here the system of production and distribution functions, with the consent of the governed, very well indeed.

Jan Filipski, Painter

Understand from the beginning that Łódź is not exactly the Star of Africa in the royal sceptre of Poland. Arthur Fromer's *Eastern Europe on $25 a Day* claims that Łódź "is considered Poland's ugliest city, even by the Poles," and mentions it only for the sake of readers traveling between Warsaw and Wrocław who need a place to stay. Or perhaps, the guidebook concedes, someone keen on architectural history might want to see what an ugly industrial city of the late nineteenth century looked like, with ugly workers' apartments, and ugly textile factories, and ugly palaces of newly rich robber-barons. Such a person might come to Łódź to look at nineteenth-century ugly. Otherwise, forget it! No classy restaurants, no elegant hotels, no Baltic beaches or wood-covered mountains, no restored marketplaces, not much shopping for anything that would interest most tourists. Nothing by way of high culture or art, no old cathedrals, no nothing.

Well, no . . . there is good opera and excellent ballet: the Łódź ballet production of *Zorba the Greek* (an inspired selection for spring, 1990, with its conflict between individual and collective wills, between local and international sensibilities) toured Europe, winding up in Athens, summer of 1991. Those restored owners' mansions are pretty snazzy, and old Piotrkowska Street has a neglected glory all its own. Moniuszki, once a private thoroughfare and not yet entirely gone, has appeared in nearly every Polish film set in the 1900-1930 period, many of them filmed at the internationally famous Łódź Film School ("HollyŁódź" read the graffiti). The Łódź branch of the National Art Museum houses the Polish modern collection, which is well worth seeing.

Still, Fromer gives an honest description of Łódź, 1989. This place is never going to compete with Kraków and Gdańsk, and its citizens admit the obvious. "It's lovely here in the spring," they tell you by way of excuses, as if every place, every person were not lovely in the spring. Unless compelled to stop for business or sleep or dinner, most people just keep on driving through Łódź, toward Warsaw, Częstochowa, Kraków or Gdańsk.

On the other hand, except for the obvious differences between city and country, Łódź is a lot like the land I left in western Minnesota: a nondescript

51

landscape through which one passes on the road between the lovely lake cities of Minneapolis and St. Paul and the scenic beauty of the Black Hills.

Łódź is not too different from most places on this planet: some theaters and movie houses, and some hidden surprises awaiting those who go looking, but not much shaking, really. Just a scene through the car window on the drive of life.

So I was surprised in finding a painting I very much liked at the Światowit Hotel gallery to discover that the subject was a Łódź street scene and the painter a Łódź artist. The scene was one of those old nineteenth-century textile mills—"The White Factory," as it is called, once part of the Geyer works on southern Piotrkowska—reflected romantically in the waters of its own mill pond, across from what was once the private park of its owner. The painter had caught the factory in deep shades of blue and gray, at the end of one of those overcast winter afternoons, with the low, polluted sky so characteristic of this city. It was a scene with which I could identify after only a month in town, something warm and comfortable despite, or perhaps because of, the somber sky and dark colors. The painting was priced at 180,000 złotych, and I almost bought it immediately. For $17, how could I go wrong? Only problems of transportation to the U.S. and wall space back home kept my hand in my pocket.

Something, however, compelled me to seek out the artist, to see other work, to be sure all of my $17 (the average Pole's monthly income in fall, 1989) went directly to the artist. I looked up the name Jan Filipski in the Łódź phone directory, and sure enough, there it was. A Polish intermediary arranged a meeting when we could look at pictures and talk art.

Filipski, I discovered, is 82 years old. Like many of the Old Ones of Łódź, he grew up in Warsaw, came to this city shortly after World War II when Warsaw lay rubblized and Łódź—protected during the war because of its historically German affiliation, and nearly emptied after the war of both Jewish and German populations—had surplus housing. He has lived in Łódź ever since, first in old Bałuty, more recently in one of the tall, anonymous, gray apartment buildings on the city periphery. His flat is comfortable but not remarkable, decorated with a few of his own watercolors and assorted other unmemorable artifacts and reproductions.

Filipski's studio is a small room in the basement of a building around the corner, one room in the depths of an underground labyrinth vaguely resembling the cellar of the barracks at Auschwitz. He, Michelle, I, and our Polish colleague feel our way along brick walls toward a light switch, and then Pan Filipski opens the padlock on his studio door. A single bulb illuminates the windowless cell, filled to overflowing with the artist's bicycle, a very few painting supplies, and many carefully wrapped packages of his work. On shelves to the left of the door are stacked a dozen oil paintings similar to the one in the gallery: old Łódź factories and residences, street scenes from Bałuty, some

fall, some dead of winter, all with those heavy Łódź skies, all the buildings in the same state of semi-disrepair, all with the same peculiar warmth.

The chilly room, more a hermit's cell than a painter's studio barely contains all four of us, and we must shuffle to rearrange ourselves as Filipski moves from package to pile to heap. This room, it occurs to me—this small, dank, subterranean cell—contains what remains of his life's work: sixty years of drawings, paintings, sketchbooks, pictures.

"I have painted many things in many styles in my life," the artist tells us. Untying the brown string on a package wrapped in cheap East Block paper, he shows us cubist work in the style of Picasso. He shows us etchings in the manner of Braque. There are wood block prints and steel engravings, a lovely series of silhouettes of Polish workers which I think I saw exhibited at another gallery in Łódź. He shows us series of rural landscapes, woods and parks, colors electric as those of Kandinski, ephemeral scenes along the lines of Turner. He shows us a slide of one painting, saying, "I cannot believe now that I could once paint this well." Nothing he shows me resembles even remotely the heavy Stalinist sculptures and reliefs I see elsewhere in this city, the socialist realism I associate with East Bloc. No wonder Filipski never made it as a major artist. It's a wonder he survived at all.

I ask about the factories and street scenes.

"This exhibit I put together in 1980," he says, "although I had painted such scenes earlier and I continued to paint them after 1980. For the exhibit, I wrote this explanation, which I then painted on canvas." Our intermediary translates:

53

To preserve in our memories the Bałuty that is now vanishing—this was the desire behind my decision to immortalize in my oil paintings and graphics these doomed buildings. There will come a day when we will look upon such houses as relics of the past, dear to our hearts, dear to the hearts of the people who spent their youth, and sometimes their whole lives in them: their first steps under motherly eyes; first loves; first hopes and disappointments; the morning and evening call of the factory siren rousing them from their slumber. The proletarian neighborhood of Łódź, soon to be gone forever, must be saved from oblivion! These are not the opulent secession-era mansions of Piotrkowska street, but single-story buildings with low hanging eaves, wooden fences darkened with age that enclose tiny gardens and yards teeming with all manner of birds, pigeons circling in the changing sky. This may be why my paintings are gray, melancholy and full of sorrow, sometimes brightened by a sprinkling of white or pale snow.

Jan Filipski 1980

The paintings are scraped and battered: Filipski handles them with a carelessness an artist himself could allow only himself. Paint has flaked off one street scene, although generally the scratches and scrapes only enhance his

54

subject, add more warmth to the art. "A bit of East Bloc realism," I think to myself, "heavily flavored with Polish Romanticism." In almost every scene a 1950s high-rise looms ominously behind the peasant homes, or factories, or older wood dwellings in the foreground. Some scenes I have already seen in pencil drawings and etchings, done either as studies for or revisions of the oil painting. In at least once scene, a high-rise visible in the drawing has disappeared from the painting. When I mention the fact, Filipski responds yes, for sure, it is gone. The new building was "not lovely," not an attractive addition to the scene. Looking carefully at the painting, I see it has been painted out. "Not an attractive building at all," he reassures us.

Is this an artistic statement or a political statement, or both at the same time? One must admire an artist who could accomplish so much within the confines of geography and politics which have circumscribed most of Jan Filipski's years. How to work with some censor looking always over one's shoulder? How to sustain one's self with such small recognition? How to work in this damp, subterranean cell, the only light a naked bulb dangling from an electrical cord in the middle of the room? How many other artists, in Łódź, in Poland, have spent similarly hidden lives?

Thinking about it, I realize that similar confines circumscribe all of us, writers and painters, poets and peasants. All of us live in some Łódź or another . . . but only in falling into what Robert Bly once called "our crummy little place" do we discover at last our own true materials, no matter what we set out to accomplish. Filipski has done for Łódź what poet Dave Etter did for Illinois, Larry McMurtry for Texas, Garrison Keillor for Minnesota, Ken Kesey for the Pacific Northwest, Carolyn Chute for Maine. What all artists worth their salt must do for a community, what any community should demand of its artists: "Give us our place." The artist's first duty is to his own place. Wrote Etter, "The lifeblood of any nation's literature has always come from writers who write primarily about one region, one state, one slice of familiar real estate, and I hope and trust that this will always be true." The same can be said of painters.

Part of me believes that these paintings are a treasure which should never be allowed to leave Łódź: unlike words, oil paintings cannot be endlessly duplicated and reduplicated. But another part of me wants desperately to take home a little piece of this place, even though I will spend only a couple of years among these buildings. So we settle on a price for one of Michelle's favorites, $60 in hard currency. The artist is reluctant to part with his five-year-old child, but he wraps it carefully in brown paper and coarse string, forming a handle with which I can carry it. Then he turns out the light in his tiny studio-bicycle shed and sees us all to the tram. I promise him that I will write something, and I promise myself that I will hustle right over to the Swiatowit gallery and buy that other painting as well.

Which I do. But when I get there the next morning, its price has inflated overnight. To just around $60.

55

This story has a number of postscripts, including the reaction of Gabriele mentioned earlier. The first came a week after my visit, when I was recounting the story at the English Institute by way of commenting on inflation in Poland. "From 180,000 to 650,000 złotych, overnight," I said, shaking my head in disbelief.

My students look at each other and one of them laughs. "You yourself caused the price to increase," Agnieszka Tynecka points out. "A week ago this painter was nobody; today he is an internationally famous artist. Some American is interested in his work. Bought two and going to write an article about him. And in Łódź, of all places! Think of that!"

"So," I think to myself: "by being true to his own place, the artist reaches out to people and places all over the world. That is the way it is supposed to work."

A second postscript came in spring, 1990, after the Marshall *Independent* had published my essay on Filipski, largely as it appears here. The paper sent me a tearsheet, of course, which I photocopied and mailed to the artist, as a redemption of my pledge to write a piece. I heard nothing from Filipski, but when I finally gathered money and courage to buy one *more* Filipski painting (all right, I bought *two* more, the only two remaining Filipski paintings for sale in the city), the sales clerk at the gallery asked me in perfect English, "Do you know this painter?"

"Yes, I do," I said. "I mean, I have bought some of his other work, and I visited him once. He lives in Łódź. He is quite old."

"You wrote an article about him," she tells me. "Your name is David Pichaske. . . ."

The final postscript, I suppose, came in November of 1991, on my return visit to a Łódź half way on its way to the West. "The City Museum in Poznański's old palace has just opened a new section," Agnieszka Salska told me and my Fulbright successor, Kate Begnal. "Would you be interested in having a look?"

So look we did (at a dramatically inflated entrance fee), upstairs at the Rubinstein rooms and downstairs at other exhibits, and what do you think we should find on exhibit in the Łódź City Museum? A whole room full of Filipski oil paintings just like the six on my wall in Minnesota, including several the painter showed me that first visit, and the painted inscription done for the 1980 exhibit.

The Mills

It is not written that dark, Satanic mills must be constructed of red brick, but brick is absolutely correct, embodying as other surfaces do not the the mindless and mind-deadening replication of product units by endless lines of workers manning endless lines of machines running endless hours and days and weeks. Brick in Dubuque. Brick in New England. Brick in Liverpool, brick in Manchester.

Brick in Łódź.

Łódź is a city of factories (most of them now idle most of the time) and a city of workers. It is the paths of the workers that crisscross Łódź, cut a little deeper, as Meridel Le Sueur once put it, by people who carry on their backs the endless weight of that which does not concern them.

And brick is the working stuff of Łódź, although as often as not the brick has been cemented over to form long walls of unseamed beige or khaki. Sometimes the cement—in a superhuman effort that defies all logic but seems typically Polish—has been painted brick red, and then checked with a web of thin gray lines, and thus the walls are returned again to a representation of their actual construction. The characteristic exterior surface of Łódź is gray cement weathered in several spots to reveal red brick and white mortar.

Widzew, to the west of Piotrkowska Street, is the old industrial section of the city. Some factories are long dead. They hunker over the downtown skyline, windows vacant, mute reminders of generations that trod, trod, trod, and of just what the Communist Manifesto was about. Some factories have been converted to museums, or, in the New Poland, used car lots and wholesale grocery outlets. Some, although antiquated and inefficient, still produce cloth. Łódź is still textile town; these dinosaurs play a role in its present economy.

Deceased, active, and renovated factory complexes litter this city; one learns quickly to recognize the nineteenth-century pattern: mill on one corner, mansion on the other (often also an office, and a storehouse, and a place to entertain and impress visiting buyers), park across the street, a few blocks of workers' apartments down the road, leased to those who had proven themselves competent and faithful, the section heads and straw bosses. Thus owners' and workers' families shared the noise and the pollution, although under very different circumstances. Workers were often paid in script, with which they paid the rent, and bought supplies from a company store. They were thus "thrice fleeced," as the Polish saying goes.

In Widzew, or around Ogrodowa Street by Poznański's works one sees complex after complex of mansion, factory, flats. By 1910 Łódź contained over 700 industrial complexes, some of them great ganglia of roads and railroad tracks, warehouses and weaving buildings, dying buildings and drying areas, shipping docks. Of half a million citizens in Łódź, a hundred thousand worked in these factories. Each factory had it own siren or whistle, familiar to employees as the sound of their own name, to rouse them early in the morning and pull them back to work after the dinner hour. Each factory was a cacophony of noise, a cloud of noxious vapor, a sewer of pollution. Each factory devoured people whole, laborers and managers both. Between the middle of the nineteenth century and the beginning of the twentieth, the water table of Łódź dropped 35 feet, drying up whole rivers to provide steam for these factories. Each factory contributed its ruble or złoty to the wealth of Łódź, a city which rivaled anything American or British for rapacious capitalist growth, and gaudy ostentation of the newly rich.

The factories now bear names like Poltex and Textilimpex. The whistles are silent, weeds grow tall across acres of warehouse space and loading docks, and it's not exactly a stream of workers that pours from the gates each

58

afternoon around 3:00 p.m. Still, the very heft of their history oppresses: every brick the spent life of a worker.

Workers today have largely forgotten the founders: when a descendant of the former owner of the Steinert works, questing after family roots, asked the factory gatekeeper if the house across the street might be the old owner's palace, his brusque response was, "I don't know and I don't really care." The lot of those still employed is infinitely better than the lot of their great-grandparents: one worker at the Fako lace and curtain factory tends four modern machines—made in West Germany, and nearly self-operated—with plenty of time for chatter and tea and wandering off. Workers put in 42-hour weeks, get 26 days of holiday per year after ten years' employment. They retire after 60 years for the women, 65 years for the men. Wooden floors help deaden noise and cushion the surface on which they stand all day. On top of their regular salary they are paid a quality-adjusted piecework bonus. Two unions—the old national workers' union and the three-times-more-popular Solidarity—compete to resolve their grievances. Fako at least is clean and well lighted, and computers to aid design and production are on the way.

But what of the thousands of workers no longer employed at Łódź factories? And who knows if Fako, or Poltex or Uniontex will survive the year, much less until a worker's retirement age? Rumor at the 1991 Łódź Textile Fair had Uniontex bankrupt come August, Solidarity or no Solidarity. Old suppliers and markets in the former Soviet Union are in chaos: nobody takes responsibility for shipping or receiving anything, and while all parties want payment in hard currency, neither is willing to offer payment except in rubles or złotych. Western markets account for only a small percentage of sales: goods are still too shoddy, production is still too unreliable, redesigning to Western tastes takes too long (in the Far East they are quicker and cheaper both) and the business arrangements in Poland are still too murky. Where will the workers go if and when the factories close?

It is the workers' apartments which are most striking, sometimes renovated with new windows and new cement exteriors, sometimes just the old nineteenth-century brick walls. They are three- or two-story brick rectangles, and they come, usually, in blocks of several buildings. On ulica Przędzalniana is a wonderful square of old workers' flats erected in 1875 by Karol Scheibler: six large two-story brick buildings surround a central green, now shaded by mature chestnut trees. Cobblestone roads flank both sides of the green, in the middle of which stands a large public water pump of the type still found all over this city. Behind each building, on the side away from the center park, are out-buildings for storage and small private gardens and back alleys. In the nineteenth century, the complex contained a school, a hospital, and a social club for the workers. Through each apartment building runs a central corridor, dark and dirty, off which flats open to either side, stark and simple and replicated almost endlessly, like the barracks at Auschwitz.

59

Externally, I can't imagine these apartments have changed much in the past century. White lace curtains fill the windows, and invariably some potted plant is framed by the white high-gloss enamel inner window frame (exterior frames are always either Forest Service brown or Kelly green). Outside, geraniums and hollyhocks and red roses. In a more prosperous Łódź, these flats would have the renovated trendiness of the mews section of, say, Earl's Court, London.

The kids who play near these flats today are thin-legged in the manner I imagine workers' children of a century ago. A small boy, exploring the neighborhood with his puppy, kicks his way through a puddle. A slightly older boy bounces a nearly black soccer ball off one brick wall with his feet, his chest, his head. A couple of girls play a jumping game with some enormous rubber band they have stretched between the two support poles on a rug-beating frame: skip over, hop on the band, skip to one side, hop back, on with one foot, on with the other foot, straddle, skip over. Stop, raise the band a few inches, repeat.

Stop, raise, repeat. Repeat. Repeat.

The old White Factory at Piotrkowska 282 houses the City Textile Museum, ten cents admission. Although the windows are usually dark, this museum is usually open, usually empty. The city is conserving electricity. Attendants will light rooms ahead of you, and darken them as you leave, one floor at a time.

The Textile Museum celebrates the history of the Łódź textile industry. Its interior preserves the oppressive gloom of the nineteenth-century factory: low ceilings of heavy plank floors, supported by massive one-foot-square timber pillars. Along the center of the ceiling runs a pipe with a sprinkler system, and a few undisguised electrical cables. A visitor's first impression of the museum is dejection: this is exactly how it must have felt to come to work very early on a gray Łódź Monday morning, looking down the tunnel at another long work week. Only the dust is missing, and the noise. First floor is devoted to displays of every imaginable spinning and weaving device, either there on the floor or in scale model: spinning machines, weaving machines, carders, dyers, rollers, dryers, dates like 1767, 1769, 1808, 1880, 1928, 1964, 1973, all combinations of wood, brass, machined and forged steel, wires, wheels, pulleys, spindles, shuttles, belts, chains. Equipment from England, Germany, Poland. At the back of the first floor, backlit by fluorescent lights which have bleached them almost unrecognizable, large color photographs of the really big machines still used in the really big Łódź factories.

It is the second floor which most impresses a visitor who has spent even a couple of days in Łódź: the nuts and bolts of the city's commerce, told in enlarged photographs of one mill after another, in artifacts like swatch books and accounting records, in the reproduced office of a factory owner—elaborately carved, glass-front bookcase behind a high Victorian desk, facing the Victorian visitor's chair backed by a huge tapestry of a boar hunt—and the austere simplicity of a factory worker's apartment at the turn of the century. Much of the signage in the photos, much of the print in the advertisements and swatchbooks, is in Russian, reflecting the market orientation of Łódź. There are huge depictions, which probably hung once in the offices of their respective owners, of the Scheibler works, the Poznański works, the Grohman factory, the Geyer works as they appeared in their heyday: little cities of warehouses, production buildings, warehouses, sales rooms, owners' mansions, parks, ponds, workers' quarters, walls, gates, train tracks, horse-drawn trucks, loading, unloading, trucking bales of cotton here, heaps of fabric there. There are maps of Łódź, and photographs of Piotrkowska Street, chronicling the transformation of village and street from rural mud puddle four streets wide and a hundred lots long into the Manchester of the East. There are photographs of buildings now gone and of complexes outside Łódź city limits. There is a Singer sewing machine, and a silver platter celebrating 100 years of the Geyer works in 1929.

One display recreates the typical worker's flat in turn-of-the-century

Łódź: unpainted pine table, two ladderback chairs, a corner cupboard. A bed. A mirror. A coal-fired heater. A cookstove. A small wall decoration. A life not much different from the lives of turn-of-the-century workers in the United States or Great Britain or industrial Germany.

And there are photographs of the workers, posed photographs before the factory gates or at the edge of a loading dock, and unposed photographs of workers' protests and rebellions, including the Rebellion of 1905, the first shots of which were fired at barricades in Łódź. Grainy faces stare at a visitor, the grimy faces of multitudes long dead, not as they went to their graves, but as they looked when still young, strong, full of dreams and anxieties: the men with their brave moustaches, heads of dark hair, and work suits with suspenders; the young spinning girls with broad faces and strong shoulders in their high collars and long skirts. The unending numbers of workers, not yet dead in the eyes, but dirty to the bone, and weary in every fiber of their being. The people are nameless now, but not faceless. And these people are not strangers to anyone who has been long in Łódź. The faces staring out of those old photographs are the faces one meets every day walking down Piotrkowska, in the Cathedral praying, in the markets buying and selling, by the old mill pond fishing and drinking. These are the workers who built Łódź in the nineteenth century, who claimed it as their own in the early twentieth century, who—let us be candid—allowed it to collapse upon itself in the past decades.

These are the workers who, if anyone can, will build the new Łódź, and the new Poland. They are the soul of Poland, and whatever it is to become.

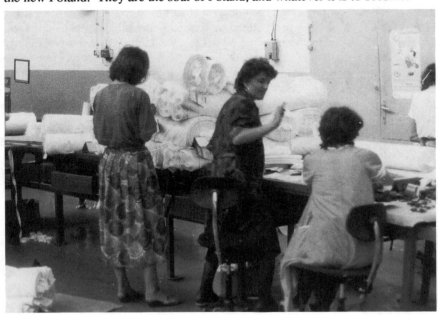

On the Road, Part I:
The Night Train to Berlin

It seems like a good idea this October of 1989 to two Americans as yet unacclimated to East Bloc gray: use a long weekend to visit old friends in West Berlin. Take an overnight train from Warsaw on a Thursday, return Monday (also on an overnight train) in plenty of time to meet the first class of the week. Tickets will be cheap if we disembark in East Berlin and cross on foot to the West, and the visit will mean good food, good friends, and the chance to buy sugar, coffee, drinking glasses and a low wattage 220/110 transformers.

Tickets are indeed cheap: $2.50 for two round-trip, second-class seats for the ten-hour ride from Warsaw to Berlin. They are also surprisingly easy to purchase: I walk naively up to the foreign travel window at Łódź Fabryczna station, whence no trains depart for foreign cities, write on a sheet of paper "Warsaw —> Berlin X. 19. 22:05 Berlin —> Warsaw X. 23. 19:00 2 Klasse" and hand the paper to the clerk, smiling my most ingratiating American smile. She studies the sheet of paper, asks something of her colleague (I catch only the word *Amerykanin*), and agrees to sell the Americans two tickets for the train in question. I hand her two American passports, and she writes out two train tickets (by hand, as international tickets are produced in Poland), and by golly, we have our tickets to Berlin.

"They sold you those tickets at Fabryczna?" asks Krzysztof Andrzejczak incredulously. "Are they valid?"

I show him the tickets and, by golly, they are just fine. "Nothing to it," I boast, unaware that never again will I be able to purchase an international train ticket in the city of Łódź.

"But you also need reservations. Did she give you reservation cards?"

There is the rub. At this late date, reservations can be had only in Warsaw. So Warszawa Centralna it is, two hours up, two hours back, four hours waiting at foreign reservations windows 17 to 21 (only two windows open at any given time, sometimes only one, what with clerks taking half-hour tea breaks and lunch breaks and break breaks), each reservation requiring at least fifteen minutes as the clerk behind the window telephones some central office, in

63

which sits another clerk with a telephone in one hand and a car-by-car, compartment-by-compartment, train-by-train chart of everything leaving Poland during the next thirty days, and your clerk talks to the other clerk, who looks through the charts of the train you have requested for an empty box among the second-class seats, and if she finds one she tells your clerk "yes, we have a seat," and writes your name and ticket number into that formerly empty box while your clerk writes a corresponding name, car and seat number on a 1" by 2" piece of cardboard, which she hands to you to keep with your tickets, and of course with clerks all over Poland dialing into this same office, it takes ten minutes just to get connected, and welcome to the East Bloc, although it serves you Amerykanskis right for refusing Poland the computers that might make this nonsense a memory of the buried past.

By the time I reach window 17, I've have had plenty of time to write on another small scrap of paper the symbol for sleeping car and a question mark. The woman in window 17 places a telephone call, waits several moments for an answer, says something I do not understand into the receiver, and then, to me, something I do understand: *"Nie Ma."*

No sleeping car berths.

"How about just a reservation?" I ask.

"Tak, tak," she answers. Of course, of course. She writes out two cardboard reservation cards (1,000 złotych each), bearing date, time, car and seat number. "Thank you very much." "You're welcome very much, sir." Make return reservations in Berlin, sir. Thanks for eight hours of your time, sir. Next?

A second full day in Warsaw produces two round-trip transit visas through the Deutsche Demokratische Republik at a price, payable in hard currency only, slightly more than double the price of the train tickets. I phone Gabriele in Berlin to announce our arrival, another major accomplishment, since international lines to Berlin are scarce as 20-groszy coins, and everyone wants to use them. "Dialing for Deutschers" this game is called, and you can play it for hours.

"I hope they let you through," Gabriele says, after I've finally gotten lucky. "Americans should have no problem, but the East Germans are angry now with Poles. Poles come to East Berlin and buy up all the food, then sell it in West Berlin, where Easterners cannot go, at a big profit. Making a big mess on the way. Besides, so many East Germans have escaped to the West through Poland and Czechoslovakia and Hungary. Last week Gorbachev was here, and he was not very reassuring. People have trouble . . . ." The line goes dead, and I'm too tired to invest another couple of hours in dialing.

"What harm can come of trying?" I ask Michelle, turn out the light, and fall into a fitful sleep.

"The overnight to Berlin?" asks a friend, hearing of my adventure. "People call that the Peddlers' Express. Poles need no visa for West Berlin, you

64

know. They buy crystal, chocolate, vodka in shops here or in East Berlin, and sell it in West Berlin, cheap by German standards, but for a big profit. Then they bring back electronic equipment. I once saw a man get off the train from West Berlin with five VCR's. It's quite a business these days. Hope you have reservations."

Thursday evening, 10:05 p.m. finds Michelle and me on platform 2 at Warsaw Central lost in a herd of Polish peddlers, each with several vinyl suitcases stuffed to bursting with chocolate, vodka and crystal. The train's arrival precipitates a mad rush for seats, although nobody is supposed to board this train without a reservation. One trader leaps through the door of the still-moving train to claim two empty seats, then collects boxes and suitcases passed through a window by his accomplice. As we board, a gang of particularly low-life types crowds into the aisle from either end of the car, separating me from Michelle, and diverting my attention momentarily. Two stout men block the aisle, engaging in idiotic conversation, as she disappears into the distance. They wave cigarettes and push bellies at each other, and I have my suitcase and they don't understand my English "Pardon" and "excuse me." People press in behind, crushing against me. Michelle, nearly to the end of the car and intent on finding our compartment and seats, does not hear me calling. I'm losing my cool, anxious about losing Michelle. Then a light clicks on in my brain, and I'm prepared when a hand not my own reaches inside my jacket toward my shirt pocket and my passport. Grabbing it, I confront its owner, telling him in my ugliest American English to get his fucking hand out of my fucking pocket before I rearrange his fucking face. This he understands well enough: the bigbellies disappear, and Michelle and I struggle toward seats 35 and 36 in car number 17.

When we find them, they are occupied . . . by people holding reservation cards identical to ours: same train, same date, same car, same seats. Consulting his reservation chart—the same chart kept prior to departure by the clerk in that mysterious office and delivered to him half an hour before departure—the conductor informs us that these seats have apparently been double booked. "Your reservations are shit," he says in German.

An experienced traveler would have slipped the man $5, and he would have found a completely empty compartment in the first class, with all manner of apologies, but I am not at this point an experienced East Bloc traveler. "Shit yourself," I answer. "My reservation are ten hours in Warsaw Central."

Grumbling, he consults his chart again, then leads us to another car, another compartment, in which are two empty seats. "Take those seats," he indicates, writing something on our tickets and in his book.

But alas, these seats also have been double-booked, we learn when more travelers board the the train in Kutno, claiming our seats.

Possibly they have been triple-booked we realize when, in Poznań at 1:30 a.m. great tides of humanity flood onto the train, including two more claimants to our seats. We hold our own, supported by others in the compartment . . . none of whom, it later proves, have reservations themselves. "The conductor put these people here. Look at their tickets. These are their seats. They are Americans." "Americans"—the word echoes and re-echoes like a totem. The newcomers grumble, looking at the crowded aisle, people taking up every square foot of space, some sitting atop their suitcases and boxes, half a dozen in the entrance at either end of the car, more on the platform trying to push their way aboard. Inside the compartment we squeeze together, folding back the arms between our seats so that five can sit on benches designed to hold four uncomfortably. Children sit on parents' laps. Passengers stand in the middle of the compartment (they will stand all night, and we are still seven hours from Berlin). Suitcases and boxes piled two and three high rock precariously on the racks above our heads. Cigarette smoke, the smell of vodka and snatches of old Polish folksongs drift into the compartment from the aisle outside as the train stutters its way west out of Poznań. Giddy girlish talk, the nervous laughter of students embarked on an adventure, the steady earnest drone of traders passing information, the angry quarrels over territory, the soft *"przepraszam"* of individuals tunneling down the aisle to or from the toilets. The clink of glass as vodka is mixed with mineral water or muddy East Bloc Pepsi Cola. The unwrapping of paper from around sandwiches. The opening of tins of Mazowiecki paté. And then an attempt at sleep, which comes only in short snatches as the train rattles toward East Germany a hundred miles away.

Two hours later we reach the Oder River, the Polish-German border.

And wait.

After ninety minutes, Polish border guards enter, stamp passports, pocket the papers—with photographs—we had used to apply for Polish visas. "These papers are very important," we had been told at the U.S. Embassy when first we arrived in Poland. "Do not lose these papers. Always keep them with your passports." We object when the guard takes them, of course, but he insists: "You will receive new papers when you return," he promises.

"How about the photos?" Each visa requires a passport photo, and we have brought no additional photos.

"Not necessary," he claims; "new procedures."

Next comes a customs agent, clambering through the crowd, inspecting bags and suitcases and demanding the currency declarations we filled out upon entering Poland. "These declarations are very important," we had been told. "Keep them with your passports. Do not lose your currency declarations." The agent pockets our declarations, announcing new procedures, promising new forms when we return.

An East German agent arrives, removes one page of our East German transit visa, stamps our passports, and turns in obvious hostility on the Poles. Carefully, he searches one of the suitcases, finds nothing forbidden, realizes he made a bad choice, grumbles something about only eight persons per compartment, stumbles backwards in exiting the compartment over a leg or a suitcase in the aisle, swears, disappears. ("In Rumania," a student has told me, "they go through your things and keep whatever they like—it's your customs payment.") Another East German enters to check beneath the seat cushion for concealed goods or concealed people. He finds nothing, none. The night grows longer. The train sits in the station at Frankfurt am Oder, not 100 kilometers from Berlin, ten of us sitting, two standing in this compartment designed for eight, more standing in the aisle, untold masses huddled inside and surly guards outside and in . . . and we wait. East German guards inspect everything: the train's roof, its underside, and—with dogs and flashlights—every possible hiding place. Finally in the breaking dawn, we lurch forward two hundred meters.

And halt.

And lurch backwards, slowly backwards, gradually backwards down a siding, backwards toward Poland and a pile of coal or cobblestones in the distance.

The train stops. In the dawn, the sound of windows opening. The train moves forward past a switch or two. Then backwards. Heads crane from windows to see what's going on. Another stop. More noise. Forward past some switches. Stop. Back. Shouts of yard workers, the clanking of two cars conjoining. Motion. Looking out the window, I see travelers boiling from both ends of a single discarded car stranded on a now-distant siding, wrestling their luggage across several sets of tracks toward our train. A Pole says something in German to a worker, who barks angrily, "faulty brakes. This train goes through Berlin to the West. Your Polish brakes are not up to Western standards."

A woman complains in a Berlin accent, "You might have warned the people inside. Look, the old ones. . . ."

The worker shrugs and walks away.

"Saxon swine," she shouts.

He does not respond.

Our train somehow absorbs these refugees, lurches forward and out of Frankfurt. The East Germans have committed a perfect crime: in the interest of safety, they have delayed us nearly four hours—us and everyone else down the line. They have asserted the superiority of German standards over Polish. The PKP, not the DDR, will be blamed for the delay. And somewhere in West Berlin, people holding reservations in that now missing car on this long-delayed train will be pissed out of their precise German skulls when their seats are nowhere to be found.

I curl myself around Michelle, trying for another hour or two of sleep.

Finally, four hours behind schedule, we arrive in East-shabby Berlin Hauptbahnhof, explode onto the U-bahn, which takes us to Friederichstrasse and the throng at Checkpoint Charlie: another interminable line stretching 300 yards outside the building. Nobody knows that in less than a month this place will be swept down the river of history by the forces we have just experienced. All we

67

can do is hope for a friendly guard and wait, wait, wait another hour and a half, inching ourselves and suitcases along the sidewalk toward the low frame shed, down the packed corridors, toward the several gates, the freedom of the West looming easy and spacious beyond. More inspection of papers, more stamping of passports by DDR guards. I am too tired to notice that their questions are routine, their inspections perfunctory. All my attention is focused on that long, low corridor beyond the gates, that long gray corridor to freedom, empty, because no inspectors impede refugees on the West German side. That long, low corridor to open space. These sweaty, desperate masses in the East.

And then we are through.

Tired, hungry, irritable, we have arrived, Michelle and I, in the West. The end of the road—or the beginning: a festival of food, friends, freedom: good wurst, good beer, live jazz at the Eierschalle. We buy our transformers, and sugar and drinking glasses. We meet Gabriele's new boyfriend and her old friends, architects Wolfgang and Brigitte Bleick. With her son Timm we take in a real American football game at the American high school: the Berlin Bears versus some team from an army base in West Germany. Homecoming, no less, with a real American homecoming queen, real American cheerleaders, real American hamburgers and real Pepsi. We hit Brandenburger Tor. We hit the museums. We hit the Ku-damm.

We do not hit the Polish market where 10,000 Poles have come this weekend by car, train, and bus to make their illegal fortunes.

All 10,000 have apparently left before Monday. Our return to Warsaw is as quiet as anyone could wish. Yes, we receive new papers; no, we don't need photographs. Yes, we fill out new currency forms. Re-entering Poland takes all of about fifteen minutes. The only unpleasantry comes when a Polish custom

agent hassles a student from Gdańsk about the VCR he is bringing home, demanding 360,000 złotych in customs. "Polish law forbids me from taking more than 10,000 złotych out of the country," he objects. "Where would I get 360,000?"

Both know the student is carrying probably $100 in hard or soft currency. Neither really cares.

"That's your problem," she answers, writing up an invoice both know he will never pay. He smiles as he pockets the assessment.

My heart lifts just a little as I re-enter Poland. Gone is the anxiety of our first landing behind the Iron Curtain, that first view out of the window at the gray East, The Great Unknown, The Evil Empire. I feel instead an emotion which will grow every subsequent re-entry, a sense of coming home, a sense of lifting, a sense of joy.

"You can tell we're in Poland now," Michelle observes discreetly, pointing to other passengers in our compartment. She is right: west of Oder all was correct silence and decorum; east of Oder, it's more kinetic: quick open the food, pop a drink, and chat, chat, chat. The change from gloom to sunlight is almost instantaneous, a reflex relaxing of abdominal muscles.

Wednesday Michelle and I recount our adventure at the Institute of English Philology. "You were lucky," says a student whose friends traveled by bus this past week to Berlin. "His group waited nine hours at the border. Customs agents went through everything, taking or destroying whatever they considered illegal or over the limit. Then the bus went on to Berlin, where East Berlin guards stopped it. They told people they could either turn around and go home, or go into Berlin without their luggage, which would be burned."

Sławik Wiesławski drove to Berlin. "We waited eight hours at the East German border, another seven hours at Berlin. It was the same coming back. Guards went through everything in the car and charged duty on everything. I ran out of gas 100 meters past the border, in my own country."

Listening to their stories, remembering our emotions upon leaving and re-entering Poland, I nod in sympathy. Genetics and training incline me toward the Germans: Father always said his family was from Berlin. Through high school and college, I studied German, not Polish. My sister, father, and brother also speak German. Ann teaches high school German in Pennsylvania Dutch country. All of have all spent months, years in Germany. I worked, lived in West Germany; I have friends all over the Bundesrepublik. Despite two world wars, my instinctive reaction—which I share with many Americans—is to see things German.

But I am beginning to see history in a new light, and on this one at least I think I'll go with the Poles.

The Mazowiecki Fund

Saturday, February 24, 1990. Temperature near 60, skies clear and bright, buds swelling on the trees and crocuses blossoming on the ground. Last October was a cold, ugly month, full of menace and growl. All of us shivered, physically and spiritually. But December and January moderated, and now February as well, and it looks as if the fledgling Solidarity-led government will survive the first winter of this Polish spring. An oft-voiced anxiety had been that a cold winter would increase demand for coal, which, like everything else in Poland, has quadrupled in price these past four or five months, and people would be unable to afford coal, and thus heat, and heat might have to be shut off as well in government-owned flats and businesses, and the new government might be brought down even before it took off. "Faced with repression," a Czech once told me, "Hungarians eat, Czechs sleep, Poles rebel." Poles are quick to blame whatever ails them on the government. . . . even a Solidarity government.

But things look to be turning out all right, this spring of 1990. Trucks fill the Central Department Store and Magda Supersam parking lots, selling everything from ladies' undergarments to, yes there it is, right on top of the uncovered and unrefrigerated wooden tables, cuts of prime pork and beef, producer-to-consumer, at prices below what's being charged at the meat counter inside.

A warm and well fed people are a contented people, I've always said.

But today is not for shopping: today the English, German, French and Russian faculties of Uniwersytet Łódzki are doing a fund-raiser.

For the government.

"Of course you know about the Prime Minister's Fund," someone says. When I say that of course I do not, I am informed: "People began sending him money almost as soon as he became our new prime minister. He is a man of integrity and intelligence, so they thought that he would know what best to do with it. Then he mentioned in one of his speeches that if every Pole contributed something like 200,000 złotych, the debt would be eliminated. Money really started flowing in. Musicians held benefit performances. Artists donated work to be sold at auction. All sorts of things like that. People brought their wedding rings and jewelry to the banks to contribute."

71

"No, that's a different fund," somebody objects.

Whatever. The fact remains, there is a fund, or funds, to which the Polish people contribute their savings, their gold, their jewelry in the belief that they are helping Poland. It's hard to know whether to laugh at this innocence or weep in sympathy with this faith.

"How can they be sure the gold and silver gets to a worthy cause?" I want to know.

"That's the funny thing. There was a similar fund back in 1938, when it became obvious the Germans were up to something and we had better be prepared to fight. Many people contributed a great deal of wealth, most of which never got the chance to be used. It was hidden in Canada or some other safe place across the Atlantic during the war. Afterwards, it was returned to Poland. The silver is still here, but the gold has disappeared. The new government is investigating where the gold went. So there is more suspicion today than in 1938, but people bring in their valuables. And their money."

"It's mostly the old ones."

"Yes, but they bring their rings. Every week or so you see a letter in the newspaper from somebody complaining that the bank is too slow in processing receipts: 'If people are going to contribute their wealth to the nation, our banks could be quicker in recognizing their generosity, and provide something better than a slip of paper that reads only, "received from Pani Kowalska, one band of yellow metal."' Of course the banks are suspicious that the yellow metal isn't really gold, but. . . ."

The receipts puzzle me, since donations are not a tax write-off in any American sense, there being no taxes to take write-offs from. Still, receipts are given for donations, and the Institute has prepared receipts for today's donations in denominations of 5,000 złotych.

"Translation services in Łódź charge rather handsomely for their work," Agnieszka Salska tells me. "You can see one of them just down the street from our Institute, on Kosciuszko. Some of our students work for them, as you probably know. We ourselves are frequently asked for help by people who need things translated: letters from abroad, old family documents in German or Russian, business letters. Even movie scripts and song lyrics. Today we are offering to translate anything in French, Russian, German or English into Polish—or vice versa—with our fees going to the Mazowieczki Fund. If nobody comes, we will just have coffeecake and tea with each other."

The coffeecake has been baked, as you would suspect, by Dr. Salska herself, Institute Director, mother, wife, scholar, role model, a woman with a hundred things to do other than baking coffeecake for this translation party. But well fed workers are contented workers. . . .

There is also some fuzziness on just where money from the Mazowiecki Fund will go. Some say social welfare programs: children, the poor, the elderly, programs to help Poland's new class of unemployed. Others think it's mostly initiative programs, on the old Carnegie God-helps-those-who-help-themselves model. Others are frankly uncertain. But everyone is here, ready to do her or his part for the New Poland.

Mentally I flash back to December, that tentative December just past, lived in the dark fear of Soviet intervention, of collapsed reform, of reinstituted martial law, when the Institute staff had a proper Christmas celebration, in the office: no tree of course, and no exchange of presents, but some boughs of fir and some red ribbons and candles. A special Christmas host—blessed by the Polish Pope himself—was broken and shared among all present, according to the Polish custom of the season. Bottles of Bulgarian red were opened. Krzysztof Andrzejczak had brought carp in aspic, the Americans had bought Oreo cookies purchased at the Embassy commissary, and the British contingent had prepared a figgy pudding. There was poppy seed cake, of course, and very delicious coffee cake baked by the director herself.

An odd lot it was: Professor Witold Ostrowski, 78, not yet retired, who lectured from notes yellow with age and used a metal coat rack as a cane while ambulating around the Institute. Our secretary Iwona, 28, lovely, gracious, full of love looking for someplace to attach itself. Professor Janicka-Swiderska, who, legend had it, used her sweater as a cover while wriggling into—or out of—her blouse while lecturing in front of a class of 60. Former members of the defunct Party raised a glass of Christmas cheer with colleagues who had just received personalized Christmas greeting from Solidarity headquarters in Gdańsk.

British Council appointment Stephen Romer, the picture of a disheveled Poet in Exile, and American Fulbright Dave Pichaske the picture of a North Country lumberjack. Various other natives and foreigners, all with their own small schemes for holiday vacations and their own even more dubious visions of Life, dreams they were scarcely confident enough to utter, let alone realize. We were all living in "interesting times," just on the edge of daring to hope. It was a modest but particularly cheery gathering, something out of Dickens, a small moment full of good will among people whose lives had been petty politics and small aspirations. It was, I imagined, the brightest, most hopeful Christmas these people had had in a decade, and the closest I have ever been to the true spirit of Christmas.

And now, here were these same people, doing a benefit for the new Polish government, the same kind of tentative good cheer.

During the high sixties, we had a joke: "Wouldn't it be something if schools had all the money they needed, and the Air Force had to hold baked goods sales to raise money for another new bomber." But today Poles are doing the equivalent of a baked goods sale for their new government.

How very remarkable!

Once in my life, and only once, I heard an American—Michael Boedigheimer, a Minnesota professor of accounting, no less—say aloud over lunch in the Southwest State student center, "The national debt in this country amounts to about $5,000 apiece. If I really thought everyone else would do the same, I'd kick in my five grand."

"What a fine state this Minnesota is," I thought to myself, and told him that never in a million years would he be called on his offer.

Yet here are private Polish citizens doing their part to reduce the national debt.

"A man of integrity and intelligence"—the phrase rings in my ears. Can I imagine a George Bush Fund? A Dan Quayle Fund? Even a Ted Kennedy or a Dan Rostenkowski Fund? How many Americans, old or young, would donate their wedding bands, or even their talents "for the good of the Republic"?

Yet here are the Poles this fine February day, doing just that.

What a fine city this Łódź is, and what a fine country is this Poland.

The Fog Machine

Night driving in Poland is dangerous. East European headlights are about as bright as a forty-watt bulb. Polish country roads, especially in the south, snake around in woods and ravines, and Poles above the age of fifteen dress in dark colors: blue denim and black leather for the teens and twenties, gray and dark blue cotton or polyester on the oldies. It often rains, and sometimes there is fog. In cities people step without warning into zebra-striped crosswalks from which the paint has virtually disappeared; in the country they drive bicycles without headlights, tractors without reflecting triangles. In both city and country drunken men stumble along the road at all hours. Trabants, Ladas, Syrenas and old Polski Fiats, many without tail or brake lights, putter along at thirty kilometers per hour. I will be pressing ahead through a driving rain, straining to see through the oily grime of diesel fumes and sandy road grit deposited on my windshield by trucks lacking mudflaps, and out of nowhere a dark figure on a battered bicycle will loom up twenty feet ahead, a gray apparition on one of those heavy Soviet one-speeds, weaving toward the highway, then back to the shoulder, then onto the road, oblivious to my lights or horn, and I will swerve quickly left and back again, and almost before I notice it, the figure will have receded forever into the Polish dark.

Or I will come with equally short warning on a tractor hauling a wooden wagon, a cow or pig riding along or a load of turnips, or maybe a horse-drawn cart filled with potatoes or black coal, taking its own sweet time and the whole width of my lane, and then a sudden braking, and down-shifting, a quick check for passing room, and the apparition is gone again into the dusk. Sometimes the specter is a hitch-hiking soldier (always I am long past before I have decided to pick him up; always I feel regret and guilt), sometimes a pair of workers on their way to the job (Poles are very early risers) or young girls dressed to the nines on their way home from a party (Poles party late). To drive at night in Poland is to transverse a foggy landscape out of which rise and into which vanish a series of figures from the void, archetypes from the great Collective Subconscious.

Night driving is a good metaphor for life in Poland in general, for even in the New Poland the fog machine is usually on.

If you have read Ken Kesey's *One Flew Over the Cuckoo's Nest*, you will remember the Fog Machine:

> Right now they have the fog machine switched on, and it is rolling in so fast I can't see a thing but her face, rolling in thicker and thicker, and I feel as hopeless and dead as I felt happy a minute ago. . . . And the more I think about how nothing can be helped, the faster the fog rolls in.
>
> And I'm glad when it gets thick enough you're lost in it, and can let go, and be safe again.

"She" was Nurse Ratched, and the hospital ward jelled to slow-mo was Chief Bromden's image for what The Combine had done to modern America, one of the novel's central metaphors and one lamentably lost in *Cuckoo's Nest*—The Movie. At the I.F.A. I frequently use the fog machine as a metaphor for life in Old Poland. Colleagues and students familiar with Kesey seem to appreciate what I am trying to say.

The fog machine is on in New Poland as well, even after the demise of the secret police, party observers, and all the market shortages that might at one time have legitimatized obfuscation. People are never really sure what's happening, what's supposed to happen, or—by extension—what really did happen. The psychological landscape is nearly as melted as the physical landscape. Or perhaps they know, but they are not telling. Who's giving the American literature exam? What requirements govern a master's thesis? When and where do classes meet? Is attendance required? Are both May 1 and May 3 (Polish Constitution Day) official holidays? What about Wednesday, May 2? What about Monday, April 30, and Friday, May 4?

Yes.

No.

Maybe.

We don't know.

Now that he's elected, just how long will Poland's new president serve? Well, the term has yet to be decided. When might general elections be held? The date is not set. What rules control foreign investment in Poland? They are subject to change. How will privatization work? The process has yet to be worked out. When you do get an answer, it is as likely to be wrong as right—like talking to three different people at I.R.S. Pick the response that pleases you. (My predecessor in Łódź inquired three different times, of three different clerks, on the price of an airplane ticket to Egypt, each time receiving a different answer. The first price was attractive enough to make him book the flight; when he returned with his money, the price had doubled or tripled. He walked out of the office, returned a day later at a different time, and bought his seat for less than he had been quoted the first day.)

Usually people avoid giving precise dates, exact translations, direct answers to even the simplest question.

"What does the sign up there say?"

"Something about an award."

Frequently people simply don't know: when Piotr Salski was elected alderman in one of the small towns near Łódź, I congratulated his son Łukasz and asked, "What does a town alderman do in Poland?"

His response was, "We are not sure. I suppose his first job will be to discover what his job is."

An especially foggy matter was my 1989-90 visa, on the surface a perfectly good 180-day, multiple-entry visa but, as events revealed, another one of those Polish deals. Just before leaving the country for a mid-term vacation, I noticed that, depending on the meaning of certain dates written on the passports themselves, our 180-day visa could expire with Michelle and me out of the country. I asked a colleague what to me seemed a simple question: "Does this visa expire 180 days after being issued, or 180 days after I entered the country?"

Examining the passport, she noticed the date 09. 08. 1989 written in pen on the visa. "What's this all about?"

"That's one thing I hoped you could tell me," I answered. "It might be September 8, the day Michelle and I entered Poland. That date is stamped on this other page, a stamp we got when we arrived in Warsaw. Or it could be August 9, which could well be the date the visa was issued back in Washington. Do Poles write the month or the day first?"

"Well I'm not sure. It was one way, and then it changed. I can't tell what date this is."

"If the date there is August 9, this visa will expire while I am in Germany. If the date is September 8, when I entered the country, we're okay. "

"Tak, tak. I see."

"Does the visa expire 180 days after being issued, or 180 days after I enter Poland?"

"Well this is hard to say. I will ask Iwona, our departmental secretary. She knows about such things."

We asked Iwona, and Iwona agreed: "It must be 180 days from when you enter the country. Some Poles receive 30-day visas to other countries and do not even leave until 30 days after the visa is issued. I am sure that is what it would be."

"What does the document itself say?"

"It says simply 'for a period of 180 days.' It is ambiguous."

We phoned the central bureau in Łódź. The secretary there was also unsure how to interpret the date 09. 08. 1989, but she agreed with Iwona that my visa would expire 180 days after I first entered Poland.

Finally my director drew me to one side. "David, this is Poland. Do not worry about this thing. If you cannot get back before the term begins, that is our problem, not yours."

I shrugged my shoulders: another one of those "Polish deals."

The rest of the story you can easily guess: on the Berlin-Warsaw train, at the Polish border, at approximately 1:30 a.m. on February 22, 1990, classes to begin in three days, Michelle and I handed our passports, fresh currency declarations, and new application for visa, copies B and C to the immigration officer. He stared at them for a couple of moments, frowned, and looked at us sternly. "Problem," he said.

More outraged than enraged, I exploded. "This visa runs through March 8, 180 days after September 8. Look at the stamp over here. Officials in Łódź said everything is fine. Here are more papers, my health insurance, my university appointment, my monthly bus pass, my *Legitymacja* . . . ."

A small crowd gathered in the corridor, and the word *Amerykanin* echoed up and down the length of the train car. The officer left, with passports, to collect his colleague officers. Together they studied the matter over.

Well, our papers were impressive, but these visas had definitely expired, but apparently Łódź needed us, and since we did have some dollars handy, as a special favor, just this once, the immigration officer in charge was going to issue two-day, single-entry visas that would get us to Łódź, where we could apply for proper 180-day, multiple-entry visas. This was being very kind, he gave us to understand, since no entry visas to Poland are ever, under any circumstances, issued at the border. Then he took our $10 and filled a whole

page of each passport with his two-day, early morning special. The crowd dissipated, and the train, behind schedule as always, ground eastward.

"Anybody who comes to Poland expecting to do business as usual is in for some surprises," an official of the Marriott Inn once warned in print. Results of the periodic government-sponsored International Business Forums suggest that Western businessmen understand his warning: always there is tremendous Western interest in Polish opportunities, and always equally tremendous Polish interest in joint ventures. For three days the Marriott is a beehive of activity. But very few finalized or even pending agreements come out of these forums. Westerners are too wary of the fog.

In some ways the Polish fog surprised me: one Polish sterotype I grew up on was the super engineer, the mathematical genius, the guy who got 100+ on his physics exam, resolved quadratic equations without paper or sliderule, was certainly headed for megabucks as a systems analyst. Copernicus was a Pole. Scan the masthead of any computer magazine and tally up the Polish names. But the Poles I met seemed so completely and contentedly muddled: how to resolve this contradiction? Now friends in computers and physics tell me that mathematics is not all black-and-white, that there's room for slip and slide, the computer is as mysterious as a Blake poem. Maybe I had it wrong. Maybe the Polish ability to navigate foggy landscapes is entirely compatible with the national genius in science and math. I don't know. I was just surprised.

"No never means no," we were told when we arrived in Poland, the Old Poland, or at least a Poland in transition. By extension, yes never means yes. Job descriptions, election dates, the price of an airplane ticket, who is in and out of jail and for what reasons, who is being detained and watched or questioned—these matters had been negotiable so long as to make obscurity a norm. Westerners face a double difficulty in Poland. The first is not insurmountable: adjusting to a world in which in which everything is ambiguous, nothing fixed, enshrouded in real or pretended ignorance. That adjustment can be made, although each detour in the fog provokes new rage. Gradually one learns the first lesson of Poland: *"Spoko, spoko.* Easy, easy." You get there when you get there. If you get there.

Having made that adjustment, however, the Westerner perceives that he too is being bargained with, that perhaps he is only being bargained with, that friendship, smiles, invitations to dinner and drink are only counters in negotiations he does not fully understand. Having perceived the infinitely fluid nature of Polish society, the Westerner begins to hear a tiny voice in the back of his head each time he meets a native: "What does this person want? Visa? Connections? The status of having American friends? An invitation to visit the United States?" Is this possibly a Pole in search of a Passport? This voice can poison relationships almost from the beginning. And if the Pole, for whatever reason, disappears abruptly into the fog from which he or she emerged, the Westerner wonders just what he failed to provide.

79

From an historical perspective, I suspect, a deliberate obscurantism helped during what amounts to two centuries of occupation, first by Germans, Austrians and Russians, then by German Nazis, most recently by Soviets. Confusion could at times protect, might even save. "I'm glad when it gets thick enough you're lost in it, and can let go and be safe again," Chief Bromden admitted in *Cuckoo's Nest.* When nothing is certain, all things become possible. Members of Solidarity, for example, jailed during the martial law years for arbitrary and obscure reasons, could hope for freedom for reasons equally arbitrary and obscure. For so very long, hope was all Poland had to live on.

Other foreigners spoke to me of the Polish fog during their visits in Poland: "I'm not really sure why I'm here," one after another confided. They were not talking about the dull whir of mental gears that comes from hearing one's self, a specialist in Victorian novels, introduced to a class as "Professor Jones, here from England, who will speak to you about Irish drama." They were not referring to the buzzing of a brain and tongue confronted with clusters of five and six consonants, or to a landscape of whole blocks of nineteenth-century buildings now scaled, weathered, blistered, crumbled to a dreamlike parody of Reims Cathedral. They were talking about a genuine loss of purpose. "I'm not exactly sure myself what I am doing here."

Even Poles returning from abroad seem disoriented at first. "Can you imagine, after just three months in London, I couldn't make myself do anything?!" Complaints of health problems, especially headaches, are common, and about weather: "This high pressure always confuses me." "I've been feeling lethargic lately: I think it's this low pressure." "Winter always slows people down." "Spring makes me so sleepy!" At first I honest to god thought it was air pollution, chemical residue in the building, or something in the water, like the saltpeter additives in refectory milk during the fifties and sixties. Gradually I realized it was neither the weather nor chemicals: it's the Polish fog. Gradually I understood I would never understand . . . and I wondered just who does.

Describing the Old Poland, Czesław Miłosz once wrote, "One always had the feeling that life is not completely real; hence the constant yen to drink vodka in the hope that an inaccessible normality will be restored." The Westerner finds the Polish unreality a little like a drunken walk home through a landscape that is only half familiar, a landscape with which he is never quite permitted to make full contact, a landscape sealed off by some glass wall. Or to shift metaphors, an extended stay in Poland gives one the feeling of walking literally on the flotsam and jetsam of a once-fine civilization, as it floats down the sluggish and polluted Wisła toward deposit on the doorsteps of the West. Frequently he feels the shoulderings and heavings of whatever runs beneath, and on rare occasions his footing will slip, and a water-stained boot will be jerked hastily from below. A real dive might propel a body terribly, thrillingly waist-deep into the soup. But never is a Westerner permitted to dip fully below the surface. Not for an instant, and certainly not permanently.

Cityscape: Gdańsk

The three steel crosses that comprise the Gdańsk Shipyard Monument rise through brick pavement deliberately fractured, as if to suggest three towering steel flowers thrusting irresistibly skyward from some great organic bulbs buried deep in the Polish soil. Rough at their bases as dried, husky stalks of corn, they smooth as they rise to streamlined shafts as graceful as the prows of oceanliners. At the crossbeams, a hundred feet in the air, three steel anchors hang like three crucified Christs, underscoring the metaphor of death and resurrection, of life triumphant. On the faces of the various shafts, representations of the Polish spirit, figures a little drawn but neither suffering tragically nor triumphing heroically, just working Poles doing working things like cleaning the yard, welding a ship. Around the perimeter of the monument, memorials to the dead in the 1970 strike for a five-day week, victims of the 1981 imposition of martial law, and other Solidarity martyrs.

The monument is a striking monument to one of those glorious moments in human history which are at once both tragic and magnificent. It was the striking shipyard workers themselves who decided, in the summer of 1980, to build a memorial to the dead of a decade before. They decided on the memorial one day before they formally organized a strike committee to formulate a list of grievances, and a week before the first appearance of the newsletter *Solidarność*. The monument was completed four months later, with steel appropriated from the yards, in temperatures well below freezing. In December 1980 a celebratory mass was said at the partially completed monument. In January 1981, martial law imprisoned workers and sympathizing intellectuals and supportive clergy alike. The Gdańsk shipyard workers had built a monument commemorating themselves.

*   *   *

In the dining room of the Grand Hotel in Sopot, a resort city just north of and contiguous to Gdańsk, broiled salmon with boiled potatoes, salad, cooked asparagus or cauliflower, and a Polish beer costs less than ten dollars in spring, 1991. A flaming ice cream and fruit desert adds another dollar. The food is

83

served on porcelain plates, pink or white napkins at the side, by suited waiters who are professionals. A three-member band, possibly Hungarian, in folk costumes provides live guitar, violin, and accordion music: classical compositions, folk dances, songs from "Fiddler on the Roof" and "The Fantastics." The violinist's eyes glisten like a gypsy's.

From the dining room itself, high-ceilinged, all aqua and white and turquoise, diners look out through broad glass windows at the aqua and turquoise waters of the Baltic Sea, toward ships anchored in the bay, toward the long wooden pier that projects far into the Baltic, toward Hell on the peninsula 25 kilometers in the distance. At night, lights on the distant shore glimmer and are gone: ganglia of lights that are ships headed out to sea move serenely across the waters. During the day, especially in high season, vacationing Poles pack the beaches and the pier, turning Sopot into a kind of Atlantic City of the Baltic. Many camp along the shore; the more adventurous defy posted warnings and swim in the polluted waters. A few join the Marina, where they can swim in indoor pools, or play tennis, or shoot pool, or bowl.

Once, in the old days when university-provided documents allowed us to pay Polish rates instead of prices for "visitors from communist countries" or "visitors from capitalist countries," when hotels were empty anyway because it was very early spring . . . once in the old days, Michelle and I stayed a weekend at the Grand Hotel in Sopot, for $4 a night. It was the most elegant weekend of our lives: a room of enormous space, hardwood floors, fourteen-foot ceilings and tall doors with silver handles opening onto a balcony overlooking the Baltic.

We thought we were in New Haven, Connecticut in 1927. I half expected Jay Gatsby and Daisy Fey to walk into the nearly empty dining room.

*   *   *

Gdańsk took World War II pretty much on the chin, and most of the old town here, like Old Warsaw, is restoration. The main difference is that Warsaw got razed to the ground, while Gdańsk crumbled to eight or ten feet above street level. All the quaint old buildings along Długi Targ—Landeshütte Strasse in the days when Gdańsk was Danzig—are restorations, as are City Hall, the Swedish wharf crane, the Jantar Hotel, and the churches. Photographs in the City Museum show Gdańsk just after the war, and a visit to the interior of any church will suggest just how much of the wall surface, roof, and furnishings is restored or new. Look carefully at the carved parapets on the old homes along Długi Targ, Mariacka, or Chlebnicka, especially from the back side, and you can see they have been pieced together like jigsaw puzzles from fragments left after wartime bombing. Many restored buildings display photographs of ruin and various stages of restoration, including the triumphant moment when an ornate metal dome, all multiple bulbs and filigree spires, was hoisted atop the church tower.

Still, the restored Old Town of Gdańsk has a magic unmatched by Warsawian restoration or even Kraków ian originals. Its spires reach with a Scandinavian lightness not often found in Poland. Especially in the off season, when a visitor has these enchanted streets mostly to himself, when the purveyors of tourist paintings and amber souvenirs have quit the streets and gone home, when the restaurants are closed and the Jantar is empty. In the early morning hours or the gathering twilight of a winter Sunday to walk from the entrance gate at the head of Długi Targ down to the old moat is to walk through a dream landscape. Then Gdańsk is, with Kraków, Budapest, Paris, Berlin and Prague, one of Europe's great old cities.

*   *   *

The old train station, Gdańsk Głowny, tidy, elegant and light. The waterfront, and two yachts sailing Soviet flags. The underground café, in what used to be the crypt of an old cathedral. The indoor market, full of stalls selling meat, clothing, souvenirs, perishables—and vendors outside selling fruits and vegetables, flowers and meat and fish. The small parks nearly downtown, with fountains and benches. The statue of Neptune on Długi Targ. Sections of mediaeval wall, including one fourteenth century tower which now houses a photo processing operation. Street musicians in the summer: violinists, guitarists, somebody playing Bach's "Toccatta and Fugue in D Minor" on a Premier vibraphone. Sidewalk stands and glamorous shops specializing in

85

amber and silver, come in, take a look, very good prices, $40 buys you an art nouveau brooch, $150 a string of rounded and graded amber beads, $2 an amber heart for your girl friend. Wear amber to mitigate arthritis pain. Wear Amber to ward off sickness. Distill amber in alcohol, take three drops daily on a spoon of sugar, and you will stay forever young. . . .

*   *   *

Checking into the Poseidon Hotel, a man with a stack of złotych three inches thick. The top bill is a 500,000 note. A pool game these days costs 15,000 and a small drink of wine 16,000. The loveliest of lovely Polish women drift like barracudas through the lobby, nostrils alert to the smell of foreign currency and passports.

*   *   *

In Old Town, on ulica Minogi, one of the back streets, the church of St. Jana, a building that has not yet been restored. The wooden gate in the fence surrounding the church is open, and the side door to the church as well, an oversight, perhaps, on the part of workers intent on getting home this Friday afternoon. Through the yard choked with weeds, piles of cement bags, and heaps of bricks and blocks I slip inside the building like a ferret.

A thicket of scaffolding above, piles of rubble below. The walls have been rebricked, and the ceiling closed over. The underside of the ceiling in the chancel area and transept has been plastered and painted, and frames for new windows are in place. The rest of this fourteenth-century building, however, is still in post-War ruin: bashed altar, columns stripped to bare brick, facing stones in a heap in the transept. In one aisle, on makeshift wooden shelves, assorted fragments of carved limestone, jigsaw pieces yet to be fitted together, fragments of an altar or tomb or decorative facing from the building itself. On the altar, half an inch of dust and small debris, and pieces of the old altarpiece: the raised arm and hand of Christ, the head of some disciple or onlooker, a bit of drapery or ornament. In the floor, the pulverized grave slab of some long-deceased bishop. Probably his bones have disappeared as well, for the earth has been dug out below the slab as vandals, unable to break through the top, dug around and under. The tomb of one Nathan Schroder is also mostly rubble: one of the stone decorative statues lies, at present, in front of the basalt and marble sarcophagus—or what remains of the basalt and marble sarcophagus. Funny things can happen between burial on 12 July 1638 and May 28, 1991 . . . and this mischief, Herr Schroder, is the work of your own countrymen.

Well—in a few years, St. Jana's will be as restored as St. Mary's on Długi Targ, where tombstones are also reconstructed fragments. Herr Schroder's grave will be quite as lovely as Mary's altar. The bones, and whatever this man

86

took with him to the tomb? Dust in the wind, spoils of war, a lesson on the vanity of all sublunary life.

*   *   *

The huge cranes of the Gdańsk Shipyard—now no longer the Gdańsk Shipyard Lenin—are idle much of the time these days, perhaps to the benefit of greater Poland, since vessels produced for the Soviet Union were not always a net economic credit. "We built them beautiful ships," one of the old timers explains, "filled with expensive electronic equipment, just what they ordered, usually things we had to buy in the West. And the ship would be delivered on time, guaranteed for one year, the ship and everything on her. After 364 days, she would be back in Gdańsk, and you would not recognize her: all the electronic equipment gone, and other machinery too, anything that could be removed. A shell of a vessel. 'So where is all the equipment?' we would ask.

"'Well, it was not working, so of course we had to remove it. It needs to be replaced with equipment that works.'

"'That was the best equipment, we got it from Sweden, from Germany. Of course it works.'

"'No, comrade, it was not working.'

"'So where is the broken equipment. We cannot replace it if we do not have it. Maybe it can be fixed.'

"'I have told you, comrade, the equipment was not working, so we had to remove it from the ship. Now you must replace it.'

"'I will have to call Warsaw about this matter.'

"Then we would call Warsaw, and they would say, *'Tak, tak,* the ship is under warranty. Replace all that expensive equipment for our Soviet comrades.'"

*   *   *

Up the coast from Gdańsk, contiguous with the resort town of Sopot, is Gdynia, Poland's major port city, filled with cranes in docks and repair yards. Many vessels came to the Gdynia yards during the winter of 1990-91 to escape the storm gathering in Suez, some to be refitted for service in the North Sea. Many vessels fly the colors of old East Bloc trading partners of Poland: sailors on a freighter from the People's Republic of China once invited Michelle and me to tour their ship after we had walked, unchecked and unchallenged, directly into the repair yard docks. (Wary of being literally Shanghaied, we settled for exchanging a few Budweiser Beer patches for a People's Republic pennant, and congratulated ourselves on contact with the Far East.) Many vessels fly Western flags: Gdańsk and Gdynia have always been more cosmopolitan than the rest of Poland, and therefore less isolated, and therefore less easily deceived about realities of life in the East as contrasted to life in the West.

87

To the south of the repair docks, on a long pier off Washington Street, a string of museum ships: the three-master Dar Pomorza, built in Hamburg in 1909; a naval ship, the Błyskawica, built in the United Kingdom in 1937; and even a Belgian ship, the Bouesse, built in Tampa, Florida. The Polish Yacht Club headquarters are on the opposite side of the pier from the Dar Pomorza. Ice cream and U.S.A. Popcorn is sold everywhere along the pier. A crazy motor vehicle gussied up to resemble a pirate ship offers free rides. Young couples stroll arm in arm toward the sailors' memorial at the far end of the pier, and on a fine summer Sunday afternoon there are more lovely Polish girls in Gdynia than at the Poseidon Hotel or on the boardwalk in Sopot.

*　　　　　*　　　　　*

One hour southeast of Gdańsk is Marienburg, now Malbork, home of the Teutonic Knights after their eviction from Hungary and a subsequent invitation by the Duke of Mazovia to subjugate the heathen Prussians. That was after 1226, and before a series of wars, starting with Grünwald in 1410 and culminating in the absorption of Order territories into Poland-Lithuania in the middle of the fifteenth century. A huge heap of brick and cement, much of it dating to the high middle ages, Malbork is under almost constant reconstruction and is one of the great mediaeval castles of Europe. As Poland opens increasingly to tourism, Malbork becomes increasingly touristed, and prices have risen accordingly. On my first visit, Michelle, Allen Weltzien, and I found the

88

castle closed, and paid a guard one thin U.S. dollar to let us inside. On our second visit, Michelle and I paid about a dollar apiece admission fee. In spring of 1991, ticket prices have risen to two dollars, tours of the museum section with a tour guide only . . . English-speaking guides, $18 a whack.

Still, Malbork is a bully sight—all one would expect of a complex that at any given moment could host 500 monks, 500 priests, and 500 knights, plus 1,000 servants—and one more reminder of the incredible layered richness of Polish history.

*   *   *

St. Brigid's, Gdańsk, is less impressive than Malbork: a small, rectangular structure with a modest tower, eclipsed in every architectural way by neighboring St. Katherine's. The interior of St. Brigid's lacks the old ornaments of most other Gdańsk churches: a small fragment of decorated plaster wall; an oil painting by Herman Han, 1612, of the assumption of St. Brigid; another oil painting on the arch of the right aisle, God the Father receiving the body of Christ, borne up from the tomb by a pair of angels; a grave slab on the left aisle of the nave; and the carvings of Christ, St. Mary, and St. John, high above the nave. St. Brigid's looks like any one of a hundred, of a thousand smaller churches scattered all over Europe, a church with some small history and some small art, a church battered by the War, a church renovated after the War into simple functionalism.

Increasingly, however, St. Brigid's is ornamented with art of a different nature: pine, iron, steel, brick. St. Brigid's is the Solidarność Church, where shipyard workers met and demonstrated and prayed during the 1980s, where in the 1990s national mass is celebrated on important Polish holidays. Its memorials are to the Polish dead of World War II, to the officers murdered at Katyn, to Solidarność priest Father Jerzy Popiełuszko, to the heroes of the struggle of the 1980s. In such a context, it is somehow appropriate that pews be modern, functional, uncarved working-class pine. That confessionals be clean, simple, unadorned boxes. That light fixtures be basic iron, and walls, like the factory walls of Łódź, be working-class brick. That at least one of the side altars be shipyard steel, and the grillwork around the altar in front of the right side aisle be black wrought iron. That the iron art on the rear balcony resemble figures on the Shipyard Memorial: drawn, gaunt, hard. In such a place, workers can still come to pray and meditate—workers and those who remember the years of struggle now too much forgotten in the New Poland.

If the simplicity of this place causes tourists to pass St. Brigid's lightly by, perhaps so much the better. Keep it quiet, keep it holy.

89

Auschwitz #821

I met him in the fall of my first year in Łódź, before the collapse of the old East Bloc and long before the collapse of the Soviet Union, when 50-50 was considered generous odds on Tadeusz Mazowieczki's Solidarno ść government lasting half a year, when private shops, open borders, and a two-day-old *International Herald Tribune* at the Łódź newsstand were pie-in-the-sky pipe dreams. He introduced himself after a talk I'd given one evening at the Institute as a Polish-American businessman eager for American contacts. His presence surprised me, as the lecture, although public, had hardly been well publicized (my audience was mainly area English teachers less interested in ethnic American writers of the 1980's than in contact with a native speaker). Well, Poles always have been good at finding things out.

"You are an American," he said. "I am Polish, but I have American citizenship and I spent many years in America before retiring to my own country. This is common: many retired Americans live in Poland, especially in the South. I am pleased to make your acquaintance. I invite you for dinner."

I shook his hand, begged off the dinner pleading previous commitments, and wrote down a name and a telephone number in my address book, mostly as a token show of sincerity. I found the idea of another American in Łódź unsettling: a Polish-American, no less, someone with my own feel for the States and an infinitely more intimate with Poland. Łódź seemed less exotic, and my own situation less remarkable. The wall was not so impenetrable. Łódź was no distant planet. Others had been here before me. Others were here with me . . . not only teachers and itinerant businessmen, but working Americans retired to Old World roots, where monthly Social Security checks made them wealthy beyond imagination. This man, possibly, knew more than I. Probably he told a better tale than I. What was he doing in my movie?

But Poles are also insistent. Three weeks after my talk, the phone in our flat rang with a direct personal invitation to dinner, at his home (not a flat, but a real private house) just outside Łódź, meet his second (younger, Polish) wife, meet his little daughter as well, whom he wanted to learn English. "I have some proposals I wish to discuss with you as well," he added. "I will greet you and Michelle at your flat at 5:00. Then we will drive to my house in my gold Mercedes. Thank you very much."

91

Dinner was Polish elegant, especially for the fall of 1989: borscht, roast pork, potatoes, green salad, red beets, coleslaw, home-baked cake for desert, wine, tea, vodka, even American whiskey. The daughter, shy but charming, took an immediate liking to Michelle, who is very good with kids. The wife, who spoke no English at all, was less shy, and charming in the manner of all Polish women: gracious to guests while being absolutely attentive to her husband. The house, in what would pass for suburban Łódź, was large and well furnished. It was built of cement block and painted stucco, located on a rutted dirt road, surrounded by fence, guarded by a pair of watch dogs. A speaker phone was embedded in the gatepost and electronically-operated lock secured the gate. The picture windows and hardwood floor suggested America; the wainscoting and leather-upholstered furniture were European.

On the lower level he had built himself a spacious study, complete with a personal computer, on which to track his various business deals. In a large room beside the garage, he had set his wife up with a printing operation that involved, among other things, a plate-maker, a medium-sized offset press imported from West Germany, and a heavy duty saddle stapler. Word-processing software and a laser printer for the computer were on order. One item on the business agenda was word-processing programs; another was copyright law; a third was my sense of texts useful in Poland's English language classrooms.

We discussed these topics and a dozen entrepreneurial schemes that evening, and in subsequent meetings: a Polish version of the *Reader's Digest* "Improving Your Word Power," to be written by me, typeset and printed on his wife's machine, then distributed to English language classrooms throughout the country; a combination accrediting board and trade association for English language instructors; a similar bureau for independent Polish tourist bureaus; an escort-translator-liaison service for western businessmen exploring joint venture possibilities in Poland; several specific joint venture schemes, the outlines of which remained fuzzy to me, never getting much beyond "business arrangements and possibilities"; and liaison services for American Airlines, a new-comer to Poland, which would put American "miles ahead" of Pan-Am, British Air and Lot in the competition for Old World-New World travel. "Just the name—'American Airlines'—every Pole will love it!" Caught up in the wide-open possibilities of an economy that reshaped itself weekly, I wrote, revised, edited, and mailed a dozen letters to various American corporate offices and officers. What became of them, I never learned. Gradually I wearied of vision, and by the end of 1990 I began to lose faith.

My fault entirely. *Mea culpa.*

These schemes were not entirely hare-brained. After the War, my friend had worked for a variety of large corporations before opening his own tourist agency, organizing excursions into Poland and the Soviet Union for all kinds of organizations, including the Chicago Association of Trash Collecting Agencies, who traveled through Poland to Mother Russia (five cities, three weeks) for the laudable and legitimately tax-deductible purpose of examining East Bloc modes of trash collection and disposal. "Chicago waste disposal is entirely in the hands of the Polish mafia: they were mostly old Slavs going home to visit. Two weeks we spent in the Soviet Union, and we never saw a single garbage dump. Not a single machine. Every day it was, 'The workers are having a special meeting,' or 'Unfortunately the facilities are closed this holiday,' or 'We made arrangements for two brand new, state-of-the-arts People's Republic garbage trucks to be driven right here to the hotel for your inspection, but what do you think? The men who were to drive them both took sick at the last minute, and they cannot be here. Tomorrow, American comrades in trash disposal, we will have a first-hand look at Leningrad dumps. And if, perchance, we miss the dumps of Leningrad, you will surely visit the dumps of Moscow. Meanwhile, we have arranged this special tour of the Winter Palace. . . .'"

Ultimately the Westerners got what they wanted—a cheap holiday in the East—and the Soviets got the hard currency they wanted, and the tour, having failed in its primary goal, was a resounding success. A good Polish-American businessman understands the way the world operates in the States, in Poland, in Russia. I don't know how my friend's life has worked out these past few years (he haunted every Warsaw Marriott joint venture conference, got himself quoted at least once by *The Wall Street Journal*), but he knows his stuff and would make an ideal partner in any business.

Even in explaining his years in America, my friend did not volunteer his status as a concentration camp survivor. I noticed the tattooed numbers on his arm and asked.

His answer was at first simple, direct, and brief: "I was in Auschwitz during the War."

Only after several dinners and many vodkas did he offer any detail, and even then, whole rooms remained sealed. Always he underplayed the significance of what he told me. "You should write a book," I told him once. "That is what should be printed on the machines downstairs."

"What is to tell?" he wanted to know. "It is the familiar story: 'Another town fell to the Germans.' The Germans imprisoned millions. And the Russians. Some of us survived."

Still, 821 is an incredibly low number. He must have been there even as the camps were constructed.

Yes, that is true. Arrested early during the German occupation (for the crime of listening to a radio), he remembers construction of camp buildings by prison gangs. He remembers the early times when Auschwitz was a detention camp, a work factory, more than an extermination facility. He remembers Auschwitz before it became part of "the final solution."

"What saved me, apart from the facts that I was Polish and I was very young, was being assigned first to the tailor shop. I spent my first year there. That put a roof over my head. Nobody was healthy, nobody had enough to eat, but a roof over my head made the difference between life and death.

"My second year, I was reassigned to the kitchen. That gave me not only a roof, but some warmth. It also gave me access to food. Of course if I got caught stealing food, that would have been the end. Still, some things we could do, some things we did. The prisoners, who had been told they were being 'relocated,' arrived with baskets of food, sausages and meat, jars of preserved fruits and vegetables and meat. This was all taken from them as soon as they arrived, and sent to the kitchen. I remember most of all the jars of preserved food brought by new prisoners, the jars of canned peas, each pea in the jar lined up carefully, so exquisite and precise, like a piece of embroidery.

"Most of it went to the Germans, but sometimes we could hide a jar of beans, a half a loaf of bread. I would bury something in the cabbage scraps. The garbage detail would bury it in a corner of the compost pile, or deposit it, when the Germans were not looking, in a hiding place on their way to the compost heap. At night it would be reclaimed. All of this was very secret.

"One of my jobs was going to the butcher for our meat allotment. I collected the ration coupons and off I went. On my way back, I would hide maybe a sausage in my pants, tied by a string. One day an SS officer caught me stealing meat. The penalty was immediate execution, but somebody saw this, and informed my superior. He came running. 'What is the problem here?'

"'This boy is stealing meat. He will be shot.'

"'Look, I know. I am his boss. I have a package of cigarettes. . . .'

"I was ransomed that day for a package of cigarettes. That was what a human life was worth: a package of cigarettes.

"I was stealing meat for my boss. This was late in the war, and things were not going well in Germany. He sent the meat home to his family . . . meat, chocolate, coffee, other supplies. He was good to his family. He could have been shot as well, although they never shot their own.

"Of course I was stealing food for myself too, and for others."

Number 821. The whole history of Auschwitz in this man's brain.

"After a while, we all knew what was going on. You could not conceal the smell, the disappearing people. All you could do was hope to survive.

"The Russians closed in on Auschwitz in January. They loaded those of us who could still work into box cars and moved us west, toward the German heartland. I'm not sure where we were sent—Dachau?—but there was some delay. For two days we sat in the boxcar, on a railroad siding somewhere. When we finally reached our destination, we were not permitted to enter the camp because of a quarantine. We stayed in our box cars for several days more. Someone said it was typhoid, that everyone in that camp died. If we had arrived on schedule, we would have been inside that camp and died as well.

"Then the Russians approached, and we were moved again. This was late in the war, and everything was falling apart. Security was minimal, especially on the train, and a number of us decided we would try to escape. This was a calculated risk: if we stayed, we might be exchanged, liberated, rescued. If we tried to escape, we might be shot. The quarantine convinced me."

How did you escape the box car?

"That was the easiest part of all. There were air vents, and I was very thin. Besides, the car itself was battered and rotting; everything was falling apart. What kept you from jumping out was the thought of being shot. So we waited until night, when the train slowed for an underpass or a tunnel, and then we climbed out and dropped into the brush. No shots were fired. I doubt the guards saw us. Maybe they had no guns. Maybe they had no bullets. Maybe there were no guards by then.

"As that train passed, we all ran in opposite directions. There were four of us. We never saw each other again. I just ran and ran. It was after midnight when we escaped, and I did not stop running until two or three hours. You can run when your legs are full of fear. I ran through fields and down dirt roads. This was farming territory. There were no police and not even many dogs. I just ran.

"Finally I was exhausted, and a long distance from the train tracks. It was cold. I came to a farm which was quiet, and there was a tool shed there, and I climbed into the tool shed and fell asleep. I had no idea what time it was, no idea what day it was. I was very tired.

"Well, it was Easter. It just happened to be Easter, and the farmer was doing no work that day. Any other day, he would probably have come to the

95

tool shed, and there I would have been. But it was Easter. I will never, in all my life, forget the feeling of sunrise and freedom on Easter, 1945. I just slept and slept. The next morning, I moved out of my tool shed.

"I was caught the next week, but again I was lucky. Everyone knew it was only a matter of time, and the German official was afraid, I suppose, of one more death on his hands. I was sentenced to help the farmer, to live with him and do farm work. That lasted a few days. Then he told me, 'You better get away from here. We don't need you around here any more, we have problems of our own.'

"I didn't really want to go anywhere. Where could I go? I surrendered to the first troops to come by, and they were the Russians. Then I was in prison camp again, not much better that Oswięcim [Auschwitz], very little food, and a very precarious position.

"The Russians also used prisoners for work detail, and they were no better than the Germans. Russians have no use for Poles, and they had even less food then than the Germans. But then I was offered a deal: they wanted to send me up north, where they needed help opening liberated harbor cities. I realized that if I got to the west side of the Rhine, I might be able to escape again, and be recaptured by the Americans or the British, which I thought was much better than being captured by Russians. Everybody preferred the British and the Americans, but I especially, being Polish, wanted to escape the Russians. So I took their offer, and was put on another train, and again I escaped from the train, and again I surrendered. I never fought in World War II, but I surrendered twice."

The second surrender took him to Belgium, one of very few Poles among a United Nations of prisoners, and thence to the United Kingdom. It brought him one semester study at a Belgian university, which he prolonged into a second year with the help of a teacher-priest.

Finally it brought him to New York, where he took a job as custodian for an apartment complex, working his way through jobs and course work, to Pan Am, to the travel agency, and finally, the great circuit completed, to Poland again, and a wife, and a daughter, and a house, and a big yellow Mercedes diesel.

To me this story is remarkable, enormous, heroic. To him, nothing exceptional. "Another town fell to the Germans." Life pushes ahead. Perhaps because of his American experience, perhaps because of his toughness as a survivor, my friend felt very little self-pity, very little victimization. He was not inclined to look back, even at his age. There was only his new business, "Renitex, a Foreign Company in Poland." Only the future, limitless as the Easter Sunday sky.

In his vision, he is a perfect model for the New Poland and for me.

In retrospect, I realize the real source of my uneasiness around him: his vision shames my retro-gazing Romanticism. We met each other in crossing, he moving forward, I moving back.

I doubt he would even bother to read this book.

Klinika M. Kopernika, Łódź

"I can almost guarantee you it's benign," says the doctor at the British Embassy. "It's in the wrong place, and it doesn't feel like cancer . . . although one cannot say with absolute certainty, and a lump is a lump and ought to be removed. My advice would be to have it taken care of as soon as possible."

This is both what I want to hear and what I do not want to hear. "In Poland?" I ask. "Or in Berlin, or Austria? Or in the States?"

"Certainly not in Poland. You might go to Berlin, of course, where you will find excellent hospitals and very competent surgeons. But who will care about you in Berlin? Berlin will be expensive, as will Vienna. I would go home to the States, have this done among your own people."

"Right now, in the middle of the fall term? Could it wait until Christmas break, or perhaps until the term ends in early February?"

"No one will want to see you at Christmas, believe me. As for February—I would act as quickly as possible. Make yourself a bit of a holiday, a fortnight in the States on your insurance company.

"But this is only my advice. You do as you wish. I am merely saying what I would do. If you need a letter, for your insurance company or your university, I would be happy to write one. Just come back here and let me know."

I thank the man, pay his nurse $30 in hard currency—cash, no checks, please—and walk out onto Fryderyka Chopina Street, heading vaguely toward the American Embassy where, for another $25 and half an hour spent filling out forms, I could get a second opinion. Or I might drive to Berlin, visit Gabriele for a few days, enjoy myself as best I can, and get a second opinion there. I could indeed fly to the U.S., although if I am going to take a vacation home, I'd really like to wait until February. Or I could wait and watch, measuring the size and the pain.

Or I could consult a doctor in Łódź, just for the advice.

"My uncle is a surgeon," says Tom Bednarowicz upon hearing my story. "I can telephone him tonight and get you an appointment to see him tomorrow. He is very good, people have told me."

99

Well now I've done it. I can insult Tom, his uncle, and the entire Polish medical establishment by declining his offer. I can visit Tom's uncle, but I know the escalation of favors and gratitude in matters such as this: if his diagnosis confirms that of the British doctor and I then skip out to the States or Berlin, Tom has spent a favor for nothing, and I have seriously insulted his uncle and the entire Polish medical establishment. The bottom line is that if I agree to visit this man, I am virtually committed to surgery here in Łódź. Meanwhile, the phrase "certainly not in Poland" ricochets off the cushions of my skull.

The following morning, during a break between classes, I see Tom's uncle, who most certainly concurs with his British colleague in Warsaw: this matter should be attended to immediately. He phones his colleague, Doc. Dr. Professor Jeromin, urologist at the Klinika M. Kopernika, who will see me immediately. Dr. Jeromin takes one look at the lump and schedules me for admission on Monday morning, surgery on Tuesday. "I can almost guarantee you this is benign," he assures me in perfect English, "but a lump is a lump, and it will only cause you more discomfort if it is not removed immediately."

Neither Michelle nor I sleeps much on Sunday night, but by Monday morning I've convinced myself this will be a quick snip-and-stitch operation, something like a vasectomy, of which Dr. Jeromin is certainly more than capable. Probably this will be out-patient surgery—nothing to get anxious about. My major concerns are two: anesthesia and infection. I have an old fear of being put to sleep only to wake up dead. It's never happened, but who knows about Polish anesthetists, how much training, experience, and equipment they have? Rafał Pniewski's medical school education has been absolutely general: six weeks of bones, half a year of nerves, a course in blood diseases, two years later another course in viral infections. What if my anesthetist's curriculum in anesthesia amounts to two months' study and an exam passed back in 1985?

Maybe I can get by with a local.

As for infection, I have heard repeated tales of nurses wiping hypodermic needles on their slightly soiled aprons between injections. Not much to do here except to insist upon new needles.

At 8:00, accompanied by Michelle and Ewa Bednarowicz, I present myself at Klinika M. Kopernika, the second most modern hospital in Łódź, behind only the new maternity hospital, "the State's monument to Polish Motherhood," where none of our Institute women ever seem to have their babies. We are directed to a basement "Depository," where I exchange civilian clothes for a pair of hospital-issue blue striped pajamas and a fork and a spoon. In the pajamas and my Nike airs—slippers are not hospital issue—I take the elevator to the fifth floor, where a nurse separates me from my support team and escorts me to a bed in room 538. I last see Michelle headed for the elevator, fighting tears: she has never been in a hospital herself, never known anyone to come to a hospital except to die, can think only of cancer and death. I stifle a cry: there's nothing for it anyway.

100

Room 538 is small and semi-private: three beds, while other rooms in the ward contain eight or twelve. The widow commands a broad view of the tram stop below, where I think I see Ewa and Michelle waiting for a number 2 or 11. In the distance, apartment complexes and the three huge smokestacks which dominate the Łódź skyline. My bed is narrow and iron, painted white. Steel springs. No crank, hand or electric, although the head end can be raised by means of a bar-and-notch mechanism similar to that on an aluminum lawn furniture. The spring sags, of course, and the mattress is not particularly thick, but the sheets are freshly laundered, as is the cover of the featherbed. The single wool blanket, though worn, is clean. I settle in with a copy of Annie Dillard's *Pilgrim at Tinker Creek* to kill the Monday before surgery. Tuesday I'll be groggy from anesthesia, but Wednesday I'll recover, be out of here Thursday. A piece of poppyseed cake.

But Monday is not for rest. Dr. Jeromin has ordered a battery of pre-operation examinations, including a sonogram (American machine) and blood tests (with sterile needles). By Monday evening I am reassured about Polish medicine, at least insofar as it treats foreign patients. Tuesday when I am wheeled into the immaculate, if slightly old fashioned, operating room, I feel pretty confident. Aqua and white tile walls, fixtures I saw last in Mercy Crest Hospital, Springfield, Ohio, in the mid-1960s. For staff, Professor Dr. Jeromin, his assistant Prof. Dr. Marek Rozniecki (who specializes, I later discover, in sex-

change operations), not one but two anesthetists, a veritable bevy of young Polish nurses, one lovelier than the other. "Let's hear it for Polish hospitals" I am thinking to myself as I drop off to sleep. "Especially the brunette."

Polish hospitals are not much for ice when it comes to post-op recovery, I discover later Tuesday afternoon, lying alone in my bed back in 538. It sticks in my head that after my hernia operation (Springfield, Ohio, mid-1960s) there was plenty of ice, and ice helped reduce swelling and pain. No ice here. No water either for the cotton mouth. No ice, no water. No nothing, just me, my bed, a couple of roommates. No Michelle, and I could really use Michelle. No Michelle. Where Michelle? Ice. Water. Michelle.

Later that afternoon Michelle phones to describe her long, anxious vigil outside the operating room, waiting and waiting, catching finally just a glimpse of me on the way out, I still unconscious, a cloth sheet up around my chin, looking dead as a Thanksgiving turkey. It is a tearful conversation, and she is over pronto, with flowers. I grateful for her voice, although still too groggy for coherent conversation, or to notice much about the room, the hallway, my roommates. Hell, at least I woke up alive.

Wednesday brings a new me: hungry, alert, prowling the halls, restless, impatient with Annie Dillard, ready to get back to my flat, to my life, to my wife. The walls of the hallway are white on top of dirty yellow, the same thick cream color of my Skoda, the dominant color (with battleship gray and barf brown) of hallways at Bradley Polytechnical Institute when I taught there in the 1970s. At one end is a locked balcony overlooking scenic Łódź; at the other, the secretary's office and the office of Dr. Jeromin. Nailed to the walls are faded color photographs of Wawel Castle, Gdańsk Shipyards, some Polish fortress I do not recognize, a marsh somewhere in eastern Poland, and the bastion of old town wall in Warsaw. Also two posters campaigning against the evils of alcohol, another illustrating varieties of edible and inedible mushrooms.

Half of the rooms along the hallway contain patients and beds. There are two sets of toilets, one filthier than the other, neither containing a shred of toilet paper, both littered with cigarette butts. Several lounges for nurses and staff, one meeting room where each morning at 7:00, below a four-color chart illustrating every possible dysfunction of the urinary system, the staff of Klinika Kopernika meets to review patients' progress and the day's schedule. Although meals come from some central kitchen in a lower level of the hospital, this hall contains a small kitchen with shelves, sink and stove. Always there is a pot of hot water here, from which patients can draw water for tea at any hour of the day or night. There is a small laundry room, where each morning sheets and surgical gowns are ironed by hand. And of course the nurses' station, with a chart of room assignments and open shelves stocked with gauze pads, jars of this and that, glucose and, yes, copious supplies of sterile hypodermic needles.

Hygiene in this second finest of Łódź hospitals is not good, but not, except for the toilets, as bad as I had feared. Each morning a maid with a broom and bucket and mop cleans the floor with a combination of soap and alcohol. Most of the trash she removes, but some inevitably gets pressed into the cracks between linoleum tiles. Between clean-ups, a good deal of medical litter—blood-soaked gauze and bandages, cotton swabs, spilled urine samples—lies strewn on the floor: nurses giving blood tests or injections make a habit of leaving alcohol-soaked cotton swabs in the hands of patients as they hurry on to further duties. Most patients hold the cotton in place for a second or two, then drop it absentmindedly on the floor as they return to watching television or munching the goodies—chocolate, cakes, cookies, fruit—brought by visitors. There the cotton lies, or the gauze, until the cleaning lady maybe sweeps it up. I know why I am shot full of antibiotics four times a day.

My roommates are contrasting types. One is a young lad in his late teens, the New Poland incarnate. He has survived enough operations to tattoo a topographical map on his chest. On his portable television set he watches only Western programs: *Dallas, Santa Barbara, Sesame Street, CNN News, MTV,* a couple of spaghetti westerns. His English vocabulary amounts to "good morning" and "good evening," but his wardrobe, which he changes daily, is all in English, including a sweatshirt which reads "STADIUM Major League Baseball ALL AROUND THE WORLD Baseball Team good game fine play."

My other roommate is old enough to be my father, whom he in many respects resembles. His bed chart suggests he has been in this room a long while, with no results beyond a significant stabilization of body temperature. He is in considerable discomfort, although the first thing he did on my arrival was to assure me that the doctors in this people's hospital are absolutely first rate and I have not a thing to worry about. Each evening he is visited by his two grandchildren, eight and twelve, with whom he speaks in the most leisurely and gentle manner. As soon as they leave, he evidences great pain, usually calling the nurse immediately for an injection. Each morning he throws up most of his breakfast. The rest of the time he grimaces from the bed, or pads up and down the hall with others in their striped or plaid cotton bathrobes.

Meals are the high point of most patients' days, and a remnant of the Old Poland. A large cart is wheeled up to our end of the hall, and, beginning with room 538, dinner or supper or breakfast is ladled from 5- and 10-gallon buckets onto white plates and passed out to queueing patients. Rolls come in huge plastic laundry baskets, tea in a bucket. Butter is slab butter. Apples or tomatoes come in a basket. Patients receive their portions like bums at a soup kitchen, then retreat to their rooms to eat. After supper they wash their hospital-issue utensils in the sink, set their plates, with whatever food remains, on tables in the hallway to be collected sometime in the night by staff. Sometimes food remains there all night long, attracting small squadrons of large and lazy gnats.

The brightest element of the hospital is the staff: intelligent, articulate surgeons, both of whom interned in the States. And the nurses, Polish women, vivacious as ever, demure brunettes and fiery redheads, one tough sparkplug of a head nurse with flaming eyes and a full figure . . . and the uniforms, not so severe as in the States, low cut and loose enough to show a generous flash of breast each time a nurse bends low to extract blood or give an injection. And the patients, characters out of Polish literature, one with a cousin in Trenton, New Jersey, several with brothers in Chicago. One with a can of Noxema medicated cream sent by a relative in America, *"Bardzo dobry, bardzo dobry,"* he assures me.

And the nurse when I check out: "How many days shall we say you were here? How long would you like to be away from your work? Would two weeks be enough?"

*   *   *

A week after being discharged, I return for results of the biopsy: benign as expected. I bring a thank-you card with some cash for Dr. Jeromin, another for Dr. Rozniecki, a big bunch of flowers for the nurses. Bottles of cognac for the anesthetists and Tom's uncle, who recommended me to Dr. Jeromin. Much discussion has gone into these gifts: none of us are too sure just what gratuities are in order, and we want the staff to think well of Americans, should somebody else one day need hospital services. By my standards, it is cheap enough, practically 1950s prices: $200 for five days in the hospital (Fulbright insurance, to my surprise, honors my claim, although I don't charge them for the cognac or the flowers) with major surgery and a retinue of attendants and nurses and surgeons. When my daughter had a lump cut off her right wrist, out-patient surgery no less, the pirates in Peoria charged well over three times $200, of which the bandits at Blue Cross paid but a fifth. And when Jack Hickerson nicked his finger with a power saw, the bill ran to $4,000.

One week after surgery I am home again, and Michelle is happy, and I am entirely reassured, and ready to tell the story of an American patient, probably the only American patient in the past half century, at Klinika M. Kopernika in Łódź, Poland.

Souvenir of Poland

When it comes to souvenirs, I am more eccentric than most Americans: I go directly for the workaday, the off-beat, and, usually, the cheap. No cuckoo clocks from Bavaria, no overpriced Hummel figurines, no coffee table picture books on *The Royal Wedding*. From a two-week stay in Great Britain a couple of years ago, I brought home only a wooden fish crate, used by Scottish fishermen to ship the day's catch from Tarbert, Scotland to Liverpool, Manchester, and London. "James MacFarland and Sons, Ltd." is stenciled in black letters across each end. I fished the thing from debris in the Tarbert harbor below the bed-and-breakfast place in which I was staying, and you should have seen the people at Pan Am when I checked it as a piece of luggage headed for Minneapolis-St. Paul airport. From Rome I once brought a small red brick, a bit of the old Roman Forum; from Paris a piece of Notre Dame (a weathered ornament that had been removed from the cathedral for replication and replacement; I did not chip it off the building proper, although I did liberate it, using a long stick, from behind a protective fence); from the coastlines of Europe and America I have collected an assortment of rocks and shells and even, from Greece, a bit of wood from an old Greek fishing boat, weathered and painted that lovely Grecian blue.

So what will return with me this summer, 1991, from Mother Poland?

Contrary to what you might imagine, souvenirs of Poland are not hard to come by, even in Łódź, by no stretch of the imagination a tourist city. The country—and this city—is full of tourist claptrap, although at this writing I have yet to find the one typically tourist thing I really want, namely, a T-shirt or sweatshirt with some Polish writing on it. Some tourist junk is junkier than other, but visitors have options: amber and silver jewelry, most of it from the Baltic coast; hand-knit sweaters in gray and red designs from the mountains in the south; crystal Polish and Czech, clear and colored, some carefully etched with hunting or fishing scenes which no two pieces duplicate exactly; little dolls in the peasant costumes, which nobody in Poland wears any more, except in Łowicz on All Saints Day. Cepelia stores sell hand-embroidered peasant costumes for living dolls small or large, and tablecloths, and woven wall hangings (quite popular with Poles, although they have risen in price so much that I don't know anyone who can afford them). Cepelia stores also stock carved wood mugs and boxes, cards and paper cuttings, and wood carvings, including Polish peasants, Jewish fiddlers, and chess sets great and small, painted and unpainted. I appreciate Polish wood carving for its peasant vitality, something that long ago disappeared from the more professional—and more mechanical—productions of southern Bavaria.

In major tourist cities like Gdańsk, Torun, Kraków, Warsaw and Poznań, artists hawk watercolors, etchings, and even original oil paintings of local scenic attractions—exactly what my father brought home from his trip to Germany in 1952, exactly what my Aunt Esther brought back from her trips to Rome and Florence and Milan in the 1960s—at prices, comparable to what they paid then in those now-affluent countries. In local market squares you can also buy postcards and photographs from an army of pre-teen merchants who buzz like flies around all suspected Westerners. They all use the same hustle: one ten-year-old boy will sidle up beside you and ask, *"Proszę, która godzina?"* ("What time is it?") If you tell him the time, in proper Polish, he is off in an instant with a simple *thank you.* Sometimes he'll leave you alone if you show him your watch. But if you look puzzled, or answer in your clearest English, "I'm sorry, I don't understand, kid, I'm from Minnesota," he will call in the troops: *"Marek! Krzysztof! Piotr! Chodzi tu!"* Each kid has a deck of postcards, a map of the city or a booklet about the cathedral . . . each costing one dollar.

Religious shops sell wood-and-pewter reproductions of the Black Madonna of Częstochowa, wood carvings of the scorned and scourged Christ, and

all manner of Pope paraphernalia: cards, calendars, pennants even aluminum foil helium-filled balloons. In the bookstores, several options: Polish translations of English classics like *Dr. No* and Cooper's *The Prairie*; selected volumes of the 18-volume piano scores of Chopin, edited by Paderewski, the less popular volumes at maybe 500 złotych, the more popular (and more recently restocked) volumes at 25,000 złotych, or, shock of shocks, the *études*, back in stock only this month, at 80,000 złotych, or nearly eight bucks. There are lovely coffee table art books, gorgeous four-color printing on thick coated stock, weighing several pounds each, printed in Warsaw or Leningrad (often in Russian—although English and Polish texts can also be found) and therefore usually full of paintings from the Hermitage Museum, at ridiculously low prices: a few dollars for 250 pages of "French Impressionist Paintings," 450 pages of "Soviet Folk Art," or 350 pages of Pablo Picasso. In bookstores you will also find horse calendars, art calendars, and those Polish girlie calendars that hang in offices all over this Catholic country, including offices staffed only by women, including the office of the Institute of English Philology, whose director, assistant, and entire secretarial staff is female.

You may also find comic books—Kaczor Donald and Myszka Mickey are popular—a few nicely illustrated children's books, and more postcards and maps. And cute little stickers, probably Disney characters or Smurfs or television-promoted junk. There is even, in the philately shops, a series of Disney character stamps.

Finally there are photographs: everything you are permitted to shoot and many things you are not permitted to shoot (everyone, it seems, takes at least one photo of the NO PHOTOGRAPHS ALLOWED signs that mark railroad stations, military instalations, and even utilities). Use East German Orwo film, and your photos are nearly free. Like everything else in the East, it's a little grainy, not Kodak Gold Ultra 400 by a long shot, but why not make your photograph of Poland a true presentation of the landscape itself?

But we can be more imaginative than this. How about a book: *Satysfakcja: Historia Zespołu The Rolling Stones*? How about *Ronald Reagan w Białym Domu,* a gift for comrade Bill Holm, who so admires the ex-president? How about half a dozen Solidariność pins, T-shirts and even daybooks bought in Gdańsk at a table in St. Bridgid's?

I have four wind-up Soviet bears in peasant costume, one yellow and female, the other three males playing balalaikas . . . Goldskilocks and the Three Bearskis. I have a set of children's blocks in Polish, and a set of toy print shop letters, also with Polish alphabet characters. I have a Polish "monopoly" set. Michelle has bought a couple of HO scale model railroad cars, green and grey, PKP (*Polskie Koleje Panstwowe*) painted on the side. I bought one elegantly carved and painted chess set in Poznań for $50, and one workaday set for a buck from a Russian in the street market. (If you want to play like Kasparov, you have to learn on a set like the one he learned on.)

Actually, I have collected quite a pile of Russian paraphernalia: a dozen or so matrioszka dolls, three or four silver and red enamel stars with the caption "Workers of the World Unite," a medal or two that read "CCCP," one of those heavy winter fur caps with flaps that fold down over the ears, several watches ("perestroika" designer watches for Michelle, who has a collection of over a dozen different designs, and for me either the gold-plated watches with date and time functions, or the heavy pseudo-Rolex models with the red star and CCCP logo). I have several children's toys, including a socko battery-powered tractor with two speeds forward and reverse, and lights that flash red and yellow as the engine cylinders pump up and down.

I have a tin Żywiec beer tray bought from the proprietor of a mountain hostel last November for $1 ("That's *a lot* of money," Pawel Krakowian objected in astonishment at the time), and a "herbata" tea tin bought on the street for another dollar. I have one of those twig brooms used by Polish street workers. For Ron Koperski I saved the Christmas host, blessed by the Pope himself, and distributed at the beginning of Advent to each household in Łódź by a team of priests. I have Łódź boy scout patches bought at the camping store on Piotrkowska, and some hand-painted, hand-thrown dinner plates shipped to Poland from Vietnam, sold here in stores for 39 cents each. I have one place setting of Uniwersytet Łódzki silverware. (I bought six place settings of silverware for the apartment—fair trade, I'd say.)

I have, of course, the iron balance scales, and an aluminum cream can, and a cobblestone from the street on which I live. And I have six Jan Filipski oil paintings of old Bałuty, if I can get an export license and find a way to get them onto an airplane.

There are a dozen records of Polish folk music and jazz, and four Paul McCartney Live in Moscow albums, bought for $1 apiece in the music store on Piotrkowska, bringing, I'm told, $25 in New York.

If I can figure a way to get them onto an airplane, I have also one genuine wood, cloth, and leather rocking horse, two and a half feet high and three feet across at the rockers, its wooden head hand-painted and metal stirrups and real horse hair mane . . . and a child's peddle car, Russian-made, three feet long by foot and a half wide, headlights that light, horn that goes "beep beep," a heavy sheet metal toy which some kamikaze kid of five would have a ball pumping all over the house, and half a dozen Polish kamikaze kids eyed ruefully as I brought it home on the tram for Michelle's Christmas present.

I have the case of an old cuckoo clock I bought at the weekend Superbazaar by Kaliska football stadium, its wood all eaten by worms, its face replaced with a scene, reverse painted on the glass, of some World War One soldiers riding to attack—or defend—one country or another on brown motorcycles.

I have a Coke bottle in Hungarian, a Pepsi bottle in Russian, and another Pepsi bottle in Polish.

108

There are several posters advertising various plays, concerts, elections, and art exhibits, including the "HollyŁódź" poster and the "Łódźstock" poster, which nobody back home is gonna get, because Americans don't understand that in Polish "Łódź" is pronounced not "Lodz," but "Woodge."

But the best souvenir to date, the most curious, the most preposterous, is the set of "Stainless Steel Tool for Miniature Trees and Rockery" made in the People's Republic of China. The set contains seven tools, each with a steel head and wooden handle: rake, clippers, saws, spades. It resembles stainless steel about as much as the Metro-Goldwyn-Mayr lion resembles Goldilock's ailing aunt, to borrow a phrase from Thurber, but the manufacturer was thoughtful enough to include a whetstone on which to sharpen cutting tools, and an explanation in Chinglish: "Our factory is the special manufacturer of the tourist's gardening tools, which are the most ideal ones for daily gardening, and picking miniature trees and rockery when traveling. This product is made of stainless steel, cleverly designed, small and exquisite nice-looking and easy to be taken. Painted with scenery of famous spots on handle, it also has the unighe local traditional style."

This set of tools, with English explanation, was carefully packaged in hand-made wooden carrying case, with plastic leather handle, then shrink-packed in plastic and shipped from somewhere in the People's Republic of China to Łódź, a textile-manufacturing city of 900,000 blue-collar workers in the very center of Poland, where it was bought for $1.45 by a visiting American professor without a miniature tree or rockery to his name.

Now isn't that the funniest thing ever?

On the Road, Part II: A Tale of Two Crossings
(in which are exhibited certain national character traits
of Poles, Germans, Greeks, Americans, Brits, and Czechs)

We arrive at the Yugoslav border just after eleven a.m., coast to a stop behind a short line of Volkswagens, BMWs and Mercedes, and turn the ignition off. We're a little short tempered after several times losing our way in Thessalonica, where no roads are marked, and outside of Thessalonica, where blacktop disintegrates at frequent and unannounced points into pre-Roman paving stones. And we are not happy with our host of one otherwise exceeding pleasant week on the beaches for announcing, at the point of settling accounts, that breakfast was not included in the price of the room. And we are still pissed about the bank strike, which made cashing American Express traveler's checks almost impossible . . . and at this morning's electrical strike, which shut off all the traffic lights in Thessalonica during morning rush hour, adding to the confusion of unmarked roads.

So okay, we are in a really lousy humor, and the hell with this goddam country, let's get back to Mother Poland. We cut the engine and roll down the windows of the Skoda for a bit of cool morning air, and wait patiently, relieved finally to be out of the city and on the road home.

And we wait.

And we wait some more.

Since nothing seems to be moving, and I've sat in this car for six hours already, I volunteer to go see what's happening.

"Not much," says the couple in the VW Rabbit with the Austrian decal, lounging beside their car parked at the head of the line. A police vehicle blocks half the bus lane, and twenty or thirty trucks stand parked in the right hand lane. A few border guards drift in and out of the customs shed. "We've been here since about 10:00," the husband says. "The electricity is off because of the strike, and they can't raise the gate." I mutter something about Greek hospitality, then turn to go back to Michelle.

That's when I notice the sign on the window of the customs shed: "On: 20 and 21 September 1990 The Customs are in Strike."

Today is September 20. I ask the Austrians about the sign, but they hadn't seen it. "It can't mean much," the wife says; "Several cars went through around 10:00, just in front of us."

I retreat to the Skoda, grumbling to Michelle that there is a strike here too, but not to worry, the front car has been here only an hour and several others crossed just this morning: this will probably be one of those off-again, on-again, off-again deals. Remember the electrical strikes? Power out for fifteen minutes during rush hour or the evening television news, and then back on? This will be over in no time. Michelle slips a pair of jeans over her swimsuit and we return to the crossing gate.

"So hier ist ein Strik?" I ask one of the guards in German.

He understands. "Ja."

"Wie lange dauert dieses Strik?"

Taking a slow drag on his cigarette and striking a pose, he announces, "Perhaps a couple of hours, perhaps a couple of days."

"If this is a strike, then you are doing no work."

"Ja."

"Then the border is not guarded and the crossing is free today."

He smiles and turns his back.

More people arrive, mill around inside and outside of the customs house. Questions are raised in Greek, German, Croatian. Cars and buses pile up behind ours: Yugoslavia, Poland, Hungary, Great Britain, Greece, but mostly Germany and Austria, big fast cars ready to blow our doors off on the Yugoslavian autobahn, big, fast cars which, like ours, have pissed and piddled around the back streets of Thessalonica this morning, inching their way through gridlock at intersections they did not even want to cross.

A couple from Great Britain pulls up to the front on a motorcycle. He is a football player—American football, mind you, halfback, quite popular these days in the U.K. They have been on a London-to-Istanbul race to raise money for muscular dystrophy, documents and visas all in place, notes of explanation in several languages about what they're up to. They have returned from Istanbul through Athens, and now north to home, and "god, do not ever go through Bulgaria, only two petrol stations on the whole country, lines longer than this one at both places, and I had to work some black market deal just to get gasoline for me bike. And the restaurant, if you want to call it that, two sides, one just filthy and the other side filthier, foreigners eating on one side and natives watching them form the other, and they have nothing there, absolutely nothing, don't ever go to Bulgaria, ever. . . ."

The crowd grows. Nearly noon, and the line stretches far behind my Skoda, around a bend to who knows where. Exchanges between travelers and guards grow more heated. Greeks especially are unhappy, and the Germans, whose juices have marinated two or three weeks in Greek incompetence, who have a long and winding trail before they reach even the Yugoslav autobahn (longer still before the good roads in Austria and Germany), leapfrogging up the

111

mountains over assorted trucks, ox carts, donkey wagons, bicyclists, tractor-drawn wagons, horse-drawn carts . . . and then tolls on top of tolls in Yugoslavia, and those long backroads of Slovenia with their endless villages, one backed up against the other, 60 kilometer limits throughout, and more bicyclists and tractors and donkey carts . . . and beyond that, on the psychological horizon, the traumas and uncertainties of reunification.

"Is this strike against us or against your regime?"

"Are we hostages here? Is this Iraq?"

"We demand to talk to an official."

A Mercedes at the front of the bus lane explodes suddenly to life, and in a scene out of *The Blues Brothers,* swerves around the crossing gate, which does not entirely block its path, and disappears in a cloud of Macadonean dust up the road toward Yugoslavia. The crowd erupts in cheers, looks expectantly to the next vehicle in line, a Polski Fiat loaded to the roof and not likely to roar anywhere in a cloud of Macedonean dust. Embarrassed guards rush to block their escape with a car, and a police vehicle moves to fill the side lane of the bus and truck line. Then guards return to their smoking and tea, to their doing nothing.

"If you want to have a real strike, you should let everybody pass without inspection," I tell one of them.

He smiles and raises his tea cup.

Michelle fiddles with the crossing gate. "Look," she announces; "it's not locked. It goes up and down by hand." She demonstrates by raising the striped beam in front of her. "No, no," shouts a guard suddenly no longer on strike, hustling her away from the gate and warning of dire consequences if she doesn't behave.

"Go back to your tea," she tells him in English. "You're on strike."

Recognizing, as they say, a photo opportunity, I fetch the camera from the car, shoot three quick ones before the guards are on me. "No photographs," says the one with the cigarettes.

"Where does it say no photographs?" somebody else wants to know. "I see no signs. Are we in Russia here?"

"I do see a no smoking sign," I tell him, pointing to the sign over his head.

"You want to take pictures here? This is such a beautiful place?"

"This is news," I respond. "Tomorrow you will be in the newspapers."

"You follow me," he orders.

"Your pictures are okay here," a Greek woman tells me.

A German van threads its way to the front of the line. A heavy set man with thick gray eyebrows gets out of the driver's seat, pleading with the guards. "I have children back home and they are sick. I have been called back to Germany this past morning. I must get through for my children."

The posing guard with the cigarette and three chevrons quits striking long enough to demand his passport.

112

"You will just take it from me and not give it back," the German protests. "Take a picture of this guard taking my passport," he asks me.

"Passport. Passport. Give me your passport." I click off a few shots.

"You will not give it back," the German cries.

"Don't give it to him," the crowd chants.

"Passport. Passport," the guard insists.

"Come with me," the guard demands, and the two disappear into the customs house, not to be seen again. Some of the crowd wanders into the Duty Free shop, others argue with various officials, most just churn about.

"Do you speak English," one of the guards asks Michelle.

"Yes," she answers.

"Then please return to your car."

"Because I speak English?"

"No, I just told you in English so that you would understand. You must return to your car."

"We return to our cars when we are allowed to cross this border," she tells him.

"We're going back to Athens," the Brits on the motorcycle announce. They wrestle their bike around, rev it up, and blast off on the 600-kilometer ride back to Athens.

Imagining a newspaper piece—"Hostage situation at the Greek border"—I scribble notes conspicuously. The tea-drinking, cigarette-smoking guards are not threatened by this American pseudo-reporter.

The crowd gathers, the crowd disperses, alternately docile and angry. The Poles sit in Polish resignation in their Fiat. "Isn't this stupid?" a Greek woman asks rhetorically. "Stupid of the Greeks. These people are not our problem." All I can think is, "My problem is not having gotten here one hour earlier. My problem is the traffic, the signage, and the lights in Thessalonica. My problem is Greece, that's my damned problem."

It is nearly 2:00 p.m. This is not, apparently, an off-again, on-again strike. It will not be a two-hour strike. It just may be a two-day strike. "Border Guards Sip Coffee While Travelers Burn" runs the headline across my brain.

A kid with large dark eyes stands patiently by the curb in his red baseball cap.

Brits in a camper break out the awning and card table for high tea.

I drape a blanket across the rear window of the Skoda to shade the insides, and take a swig off the Pepsi we bought for this journey to nowhere.

We wait for whatever will or will not transpire.

The sun arcs slowly toward the west.

A thin breeze blow.

But the Germans have had enough of this shit. From somewhere far back in the line of waiting vehicles comes a wiry, animated man of about fifty, gathering followers as he heads to us and the gates. People turn, watch.

"Everybody who speaks German, come with us. Sprichst du Deutsch? Come with us."

We join the brigade of angry Germans, marching toward the front.

Faced with this ugly crowd, the guards glance uneasily at each other. They are not quite as self-assured as they let on, Michelle observes, especially the young ones—not DDR killer-guards by any stretch of the imagination, just a group of macho Greeks in uniforms with chevrons and caps and cigarettes.

"We want an end to this strike," the German leader demands of no one in particular. He is answered by a Greek out of uniform, a man who seems to be coordinating activities here. There will be no end to the strike until the strikers' demands are met. But the strike is not against travelers, it is against the Greek government which is not inconvenienced even the slightest by their strike. Old arguments are repeated with new intensity. Still, there will be no end to the strike. "We are hostages," somebody begins shouting. "Hostages, hostages, hostages." Another begins a chant: "Wir wollen raus! Wir wollen raus!" The crowd surges toward the guards, closing around them. The pounding on windows continues.

The Austrians in the Rabbit start their engine, and somebody—not Michelle— raises the black and yellow pole. The crowd melts in front of it as the Rabbit moves forward. A striking customs agent positions himself directly in front of the Rabbit, inviting the driver to run him over. "Come, hit me," he shouts. The Austrian disengages his clutch, but the crowd is in no mood for compromises. A dozen people, including my Michelle, push the Rabbit forward into the guard's chest, once, twice, three times as he stumbles backwards. "Wir wollen raus!" the chanting continues. Crowds press against the windows and doors of the shed, threatening to break glass and plywood.

"Eine Stunde," announces the head of the strikers in German. "The strike will end in one hour."

"Now. We want to leave now."

"People backed into a corner must find at least some small escape hole," I tell Michelle. "Otherwise they get vicious. We better settle for an hour."

"Halbe Stunde. The strike is over in half an hour."

The crowd talks this over.

"Okay, half an hour," the fifty-year-old German agrees. For all to hear he announces in German, "The strike is over in half an hour. Go back to your cars. If the line is not moving in half an hour, come back here and we will talk again to these men."

Within minutes the yellow and black gate has been officially raised and cars are passing up the backroads of Yugo, toward the toll road, toward Austria and Germany far in the north.

*   *   *

114

We have been driving through Greece, Yugoslavia, and Czechoslovakia now for two days, 27 hours of road and border work, sleeping overnight in the Skoda in some parking area on some backroad of northern Yugo, exhausted, twisted, smelly, sweaty, moss growing on our teeth, broke, bleary-eyed, nerves on edge from driving across the Czech mountains in rain I haven't seen since last year's mid-summer thundershowers in eastern Iowa. But we are now just one thin border and three hours of pretty good Polish roads from dear, dirty Łódź and home. We will be in our own beds by midnight, teeth brushed and warm-showered. This is gonna be okay.

Now the narrow road threads its way downhill, toward the Czech border town of Cesky Tesin, a small village crossing through which we passed with no hassles whatsoever ten days ago on our way south, a lot less tan and a lot less poor. Traffic is light, and the rain seems to have let up. A hand-written sign on a tree indicates border traffic to the right, center city to the left. We turn right.

At another sign we turn left.

Then we turn right.

Then we turn left again, alone on this road, threading our way, it feels, "out back by the river."

Another left, then a right across railroad tracks where international trains pause for customs, around another bend in the road . . .

And right into a long line of cars, the Mother of All Border-Crossing Queues, their engines stopped, their headlights dead, their owners leaning beside the doors and talking to each other in low, hushed tones, mostly in Polish. A sign pointing left indicates "border 2 km," but the queue extends far to my right, and I am too familiar with Polish etiquette of the queue to think I can get away with cutting ahead.

"This could be a bad one," Michelle says as she turns right, finds the end of the queue—well down the narrow road—negotiates a tricky U-turn and pulls in behind a Polski Fiat 126p. The night is very dark.

"You think I should leave the lights on so as not to get rear-ended?" she asks.

"Until somebody pulls in behind you."

In the darkened vehicle, my stomach sours at the thought of yet another night sleeping in the Skoda, awakening every ten minutes or so to push our car ahead (we will push it by hand, Polish style, to save gasoline) then falling back into sleep, then pushing. . . .

"Maybe I could walk on down and see how long this line is."

"You want your passport?"

"No, I'll just see how things are going."

"I'll wait here."

I mentally mark the Skoda's location and strike off in the direction of the crossing, walking past Ladas and Fiats and a very occasional Mercedes with Polish plates. The queue of automobiles extends nearly three kilometers, past

115

stands where enterprising peddlers sell food and drink, past a knot of Poles talking in low and patient voices, past the railroad tracks and the train station, around a couple of bends. The cars are loaded with Czech goodies headed for market tomorrow in towns like Łódź and Warsaw—if they arrive in time for market tomorrow, which seems unlikely enough at this owl-blinking hour. This is not the same crowd I saw at the Greek-Yugoslavian border, full of piss and vinegar, in no mood to take nothing from nobody. No, this is a different crowd indeed. I curse aloud: this is going to be one long motherfucker of a night, all right. Friday night—I should have remembered!

The rain begins again.

Past the railroad tracks, a small plywood shed with a coat of yellow paint, no windows, and a red light. A sign in German and Polish: "No cars beyond this point without permission from the border patrol." None of the vehicles are moving.

Around the door of the shed, people converse in Czech and Polish. One woman pleads another case of sick children. The guard—no uniform at all—just smiles and tells her no. Others ask questions about time delays. No definite answers, but plenty of resigned shrugs of shoulders. These Poles have been there before. "Spoko, spoko," goes the old Polish saying. "Easy, easy."

I am immediately recognized as an American, which, I blush to admit, was my purpose from the beginning, the reason I wore my denim jacket with the WYOMING patch on the breast pocket and the baseball cap with ROCHFORD, SOUTH DAKOTA across the front.

"You are American?" the guard asks in English.

"Yes, American. Is here a strike? Is border here closed?"

"Here is big problems. Too much work. You far back in line, big distance?"

"Thirty minutes to walk. Two or three kilometers, I think."

"You bring passport, come back here in one hour. I take care of you."

"Passport, this place, one hour?"

"Yes, here. You American."

The Poles hanging around the shed shrug their shoulders. They know what's going on, and they would just as soon, for themselves, wait things through. Easy, easy.

Sixty minutes later I am back at the wooden shed with my passport. The guard motions me inside, closes the door, examines the passport, asks a few questions which lead nowhere. Then a couple of minutes of embarrassed silence. "You have money?" he wants to know. "I am very sorry to have to ask, but tonight is very busy. You far away in line?"

Oh, for stupid, I think to myself; for very, very stupid. "Of course. I have $10 in the car. I bring the car and the money here."

The guard smiles. "Bring car, park 100 meters down road, come back here with passport. American."

116

I am smiling as I walk out, again, from the yellow plywood station with the the red light, past the long lines of cars, to Michelle and the Skoda.

"For a change," I tell her, "the USA sticker on this car is going to work *for* us. That sticker and $10. Remember Meridel Le Sueur's line, 'Money will get you into and out of anything'?"

We drive slowly past the line of silent Fiats, past the yellow shed with the red light. We stop about a football field down the line. I slip a $10 bill in my passport, return to the guard, who is now handing out white passes to the front fifteen cars in line, and wait respectfully. He motions me to the shed and closes the door. I offer my passport with the money. He pockets the ten bucks, asks my license number, writes it on one of those pieces of white paper. I thank him, he thanks me. Michelle and I and the Skoda are off to the border. In fifteen minutes we are out of Czechoslovakia.

At the other side of the crossing, a Polish official handles currency declarations: we list $1500 in cash and $6,000 in traveler's checks, all of it back in Łódź, although we don't tell him that, and he doesn't ask to see our money. Another agent, yellow band around the fourth finger of his right hand, peruses our passports.

"Where is your visa application?"

"Visa application?"

"Copy C of your visa application. Where is it?"

"We do not have them," Michelle answers. "You took them from us when we left Poland ten days ago."

"You must have application form C," he replies. His English is very good.

"They were taken. Here, at this very crossing."

"I do not have them," he tells us.

"Neither do we," responds my Michelle.

Silence.

He walks away from us, returns in a moment with two applications for visa, copy A. "Pull over to the right side of the road, fill these out, and when you are done, bring them to me in the station."

We do as the man directs.

Five minutes later, applications for visa all filled out, I join him at the desk of the border station, this one clean, well lighted, substantial. There is no smoking of cigarettes, no drinking tea. Although they do not have to check the cars of Polish peddlers, these guys are serious and up to their ass in work.

My guard looks at me. "You teach at the University in Łódź?"

"Yes, at the English Institute. Here is my *Legitymacia.*"

"Do you have a flat?"

"Yes, I have a flat. Żrodłowa 29, apartment 2. In Łódź."

"I have no flat," he smiles. "I am 24, I am married, and I have no flat."

I would like to tell him that at his age I lived in a college dorm eating mostly rice and chicken wings. Alternately I'd like to say, "Look, I am forty-six years old. I have a Ph. D. I have published twelve books. When you have done that, you too will have a flat."

Instead, I shuck and jive. "It's the University's flat actually. They just assigned it to me for the year."

I can't decide whether he's waiting for $10, or is just young, or happens to be in a pissy mood. He fingers my application for visa, copy A, consults my passport, stares long at my 180-day, multiple entry visa.

"That's last year's visa," I point out. "This year's visa is toward the back of the passport."

He finds it, copies the number onto my application, crosses out the A and writes in a C. He stamps my passport and the form A or C, puts the form in a box at his right, and picks up Michelle's passport.

"You keep form C?" I ask.

"Yes, I keep it here."

"Then I will not have a form C when next I leave Poland. The visa is a multiple-entry visa."

Smiling, he turns to a thick pad of application forms. "How many do you want?" he asks.

"One for me, one for Michelle," I tell him.

He tears off two complete application sets, copies A, B and C.

"I hope you get your flat soon," I tell him as I leave.

Five minutes later, Michelle and I are off in the Skoda, headed into the twisting and unmarked backroads of southern Poland, feeling our way toward the A-1 interstate, toward Łódź, and, finally, toward home.

118

The Łódź Cathedral

No old leaded glass and no oil paintings in heavy gold frames. No shining mosaics, except one over the front entrance, quite plain and quite dirty. No elaborate bronze doors, like those on the cathedral in Poznań; no eighteenth-century memorials on floor or walls, like those which grace churches in Gdańsk; no mediaeval or Renaissance tombs, like those in Kraków's Wawel Cathedral. None of the magnificent contemporary stained glass that dazzles you in Wrocław. None of the elaborate baroque elegance of the Łowicz church, forty kilometers away, nor even the rich history of village church at Rzgow (ten kilometers outside of Łódź), which dates to the late middle ages. No tour buses. No heat. No gimmicks. The Łódź Cathedral is simply, strictly business.

In fact, the Łódź Cathedral is shamed by the nicely restored and repainted building across the street, formerly part of the Scheibler-Grohman complex and more recently the gilded headquarters of the Party youth organization. At a moment when ecclesiastical buildings all over Poland are heavily into (expensive) repair, the Łódź Cathedral supports no scaffolding inside or out, despite serious structural cracks. It hasn't been cleaned, or even tuck pointed, in years. The young trees in the surrounding park are neither sheltering nor elegant; the benches badly need paint. Plain cement steps lead to all entrances, absolutely without ornamentation. The statue of Christ carrying his cross with one arm and pointing with the other onward and upward, set on a raised pedestal to the south of the front entrance, lifts the spirits, especially when dusted lightly with snow. And the memorial to the unknown soldier, north of the front entrance, is noteworthy, especially on All Saints' Day, when it's littered with flowers and ablaze with votive candles. But for the most part, the Cathedral sits huge and solitary on the south end of Piotrkowska, open always for prayer and meditation and confession, in no sense alluring.

The Łódź Cathedral is yellow brick, erected between 1901 and 1912, with yellow brick buttresses and a single spire atop the front portal. The Cathedral is plain Gothic, a pleasing architecture, but a clean texture. If it does not lure, it pleases in its simplicity . . . especially when dusted by an early winter snowfall.

119

The interior is also pleasing in its simplicity. Relatively new, it has not been elaborated—or violated—with memorials in foreign styles, as have older Norman and Gothic churches around Europe, around Poland. Simple cross vaulting in the aisles and heavy stone (cement disguised as stone) piers in the nave support brick ribbed vaults above. On either side of the nave, not the tangle of privately endowed chapels common to older cathedrals, but a row of businesslike confessionals, with stations of the cross set between. The high altar is fine Polish neo-Gothic (1912) as are altars at either end of the transept: carved wood, polychrome, light gilding. In a small chapel behind the high altar, the obligatory reproduction of the Black Madonna of Częstochowa. A fine carving of St. Joseph on the canopy of the pulpit. Two wooden crucifixes flank the narthex door, the paint on Christ's feet worn away by lips of the faithful. The neo-Gothic clerestory windows of the choir date to the early years of this century; windows along the nave are clearly 1950s, each illustrating a New Testament verse in glass of a pure, ungradiated, bright primary color. A white panel onto which slide images can be projected folds against the wall beside the high altar. The carpet is basic red, and the pews are a basic weathered pine.

Every visitor I have taken to Łódź Cathedral has been moved by its uncluttered architecture. In this regard it approaches better than more celebrated rivals the Gothic idea of space defined by a series of arches, with just a dusting of gold leaf and colored glass.

I spent limited time in the Cathedral myself: Easter, Christmas, a few private visits during the year. Easter was memorable mainly for the bad weather and the cold drafts, me without a cap covering my nearly bald head. What I got from Easter in Łódź was mainly a cold.

Christmas, 1989, was a different story, an insight into Polish Catholicism. Michelle and I arrived half an hour early for midnight mass to find the Cathedral nearly deserted, except for a small group collecting contributions for Rumanian relief. This when Poland could barely feed itself, when the nation's economic and political future was by no means secure. The emptiness of the Cathedral confused me: in the Lutheran tradition I knew as a boy, you get to midnight Christmas Eve service well before it begins, ahead of preliminaries like carol-singing and organ preludes, which extend, owing to the high holiness of the event, to thirty, forty-five minutes. Otherwise, you sit on folding chairs set up in the aisle invariably at the last minute. Or you stand in the doorway.

Here, however, Michelle and I sat in doubting solitude until ten minutes before the hour. Then people began arriving, pouring in, flooding the pews and the aisles of the nave and the transepts and everywhere, half the city of Łódź, chatting, chatting, chatting. Suddenly this Christmas Eve was standing room only. The procession began not with tremendous organ fanfare, but with the ringing of a soprano bell and the clattering of clerical shoes on cold Cathedral pavement. Most parishoners gave it no notice.

Still people streamed in, most of them dressed to the nines, all quite awake including the kids, having a ball, seeing and being seen, almost nobody paying the slightest attention to the mass, perhaps because from where they sat they couldn't see anything. I had a fine view of St. Joseph, but not of the altar, and the bishop delivered his sermon not from the pulpit, but from the transept. Even during his sermon, children and adults tromped up and down the central aisle, and crowds milled around both sides of the nave. Throughout the service a priest heard confessions in one of the rear confessionals, giving off a low murmur which nobody heard. Or minded. When a couple of drunks entered midway through the service and started a bit of a ruckus, the priest suspended his business, left his confessional, and ordered them out of the Cathedral in a voice none too *sotto voce*. Christmas mass proceeded oblivious to the drama.

When time came for communion, some partook and others did not: the whole operation was disorganized and confused. The music was remarkably bad—before, during, and after the mass, for liturgy and for hymns. Polish Christmas hymns are anemic, nineteenth-century sentimental in contrast to the robust eighteenth-century *Adeste Fideles,* sung in heaven by angelic choirs on this feast of Christmas Eve. Many worshipers left before mass ended, as many had arrived after it began, and the whole evening struck me as irreverently Polish loosey-goosey.

I felt the same about the wedding of one of our students, held again at the Cathedral, sandwiched between 4:00 and 5:00 mass, a hurried and apparently ill-rehearsed affair witnessed by friends of the bride, friends of the groom, and doddering, slightly confused parishioners left over from the 4:00 mass, or come early for the 5:00 service. Did anyone here know what was going on? Where I come from, you rehearse weddings, and Christmas eve services, days in advance.

121

The subject of the Łódź Cathedral raises the issue of religion in Poland, how much Polish Catholicism is faith, how much is national consciousness, how much is political struggle. Early in my stay in Łódź, Agnieszka Salska gave me a postcard-sized cartoon of a priest and a bureaucrat standing on opposite sides of the street, staring in apparent nonchalance at each other, hands behind their backs, eyes empty. Behind one, a church topped with a cross; behind the other, an East Bloc bloc flying a red flag. The two figures just stand there, hands in pockets or behind the back, contemplating each other, so much left unsaid, so much said. That cartoon came to mean more to me as I watched the East Bloc crumble, watched the red flag of international communism become the red and white flag of Poland. Today the Catholic Church collects its dues, the price of its support in a bitter and protracted social and political struggle. Religious education is offered in every Polish public school. The Sejm debates a strong anti-abortion bill. During papal visits, condoms disappear from public shops. Even devout Catholics fear the Catholic hierarchy may become in the New Poland, as the Who once put it, "the new boss, same as the old boss. Don't get fooled again." The fact that John Paul II is Polish merely clouds with national pride to an issue of faith . . . or politics.

I can't answer the question I just raised, and I doubt many Poles could separate faith from nationalism from politics from superstition and habit. It's easy to sentimentalize the Łódź Cathedral, or even the various Solidarity churches in this city, and it's easy to intellectualize with analysis. This cathedral, that Christmas Eve mass was not sentimental nor intellectual. It was people doing what they do, a bedrock Given borne of habit or necessity, an action beyond volition, the great yellow brick foundation of the Polish soul.

Cityscape: Warsaw

The joke goes something like this: "What's the best view in the whole city of Warsaw?"

"I don't know; what's the best view in all Warsaw?"

"The view from on top of the Palace of Culture."

"Why's that?"

"Because from there you can't see the Palace of Culture."

Yuck, yuck, yuck.

Joke's on Warsaw. Humbled as it must feel these days, with a yuppie-puppie shopping mall inside and armies of Polish and Soviet capitalist wannabes in the parking lot, peddling their wares out of suitcases and boxes and the trunks of Ladas and Fiats, this mountainous stone memorial to Soviet-Polish communist friendship is probably the least pretentious thing in the city. True it does not fit into the Warszawian architectural style, but also true that the dominant Warszawian architectural style, despite a restored church here, a rebuilt Old Town there, is East Bloc drab. Boring, boring, boring. And pretentious, pretentious, pretentious.

Besides, how are you going to appreciate Old Town when you're always looking over your shoulder toward the car, afraid that somebody is swiping the radio or the tires (not without cause do German auto insurance companies decline coverage on trips east of Oder), and you got one hand in your pocket holding onto your billfold, which you better hang onto because you'll need it to pay for your $150-a-night room at the Marriott or Victoria or Holiday Inn, which is where you better stay while in this town, or you'll wake up morning with the billfold and most of your luggage AWOL. And you are talking out of the side of your mouth trying to fend off the kids selling postcards, and the other hand is heavy with a bag full of Gorby dolls and Polish wood carvings, for which you know you paid three times the street price in Łódź or Zakopane, but these things are hard to find in Łódź and Zakopane, because they bring triple price here, and what the hell is a Gorby doll doing in Poland anyway?

The guidebooks bring you to Warsaw as one of Poland's two or three major attractions: restored Old Town, the capitol buildings, the King Sigismund

Column, the Adam Mickiewicz Monument, the St. John's Cathedral, the opera, museums, gift shops, restaurants, Ghetto Monument, other churches, art Museums, University, Polytechnic, parks, embassies, riverfront . . . not to mention the country's major international airport. But people, can we talk here a minute? Old Warsaw disappeared in 1939, the people, the life, the joy in life. The buildings disappeared in 1944, when Adolf Hitler sent a telegram and the Warsaw skyline was leveled to a pencil line. You can see the film and the photographs on display in the Historical Museum. As for the city rebuilt, let me refer you to the appropriate chapter of Jack Higgins' remarkable anti-tourist book *Season in Hell*.

Warsaw is the New York City of Poland: overpriced, arrogant, dirty, dangerous, noisy, overcrowded, living off its past, basically unlovely for all the parks, memorials and monuments. The odds on your pocket being picked while you photograph the Chopin statue in Łazienkowski Park are probably about one in ten. The odds on your parked car being vandalized are about one in fifteen. The odds on a private home inhabited by a known American being burgled during any given 12-month period are better than fifty-fifty. Fulbright lecturer Tom Samet was robbed in Warzsawa Centralna not just once, not just twice, but three times. The third time his attackers used mace. Killing time one night in Centralna, Michelle and I witnessed, in the space of ninety minutes, one robbery, two muggings, and a drunken brawl in which one man's head was smashed against the glass edge of the snack counter. When a middle-aged man started dragging his protesting wife up the stairs feet first, we decided to leave early for

the airport and hang out there. The cab driver wanted $15 for what should have been a $2 fare; I found a night bus for 40 cents. One published story about cab drivers in this city is that at the very moment they're gouging tourists on fares, they are radioing ahead in Polish, alerting accomplices at the tourist's destination who will further abuse the visitor.

And trust me, the beggars moaning at you from every street corner are not *all* Rumanians. Nor are the panhandlers with their death's-door faces, moth-eaten sweaters, and hand-written signs: "Please help me; I have AIDS."

True, Warsaw has a river front, but this river is the Wisła, Queen of Sewers, its water unfit for use as the city's water supply. True, Warsaw is the capitol of Poland, but it hasn't always been the capitol: the old capitol, the city with all the fine old buildings, is Kraków, 250 kilometers south: same river, a different story entirely.

True, Warsaw offers better shopping than most other Polish cities, but today that difference is almost negligible, except in the area of prices, and for clothing Poles still shop Łódź. Warsaw has a McDonald's, but so does every American town over 10,000 inhabitants. Warsaw has a sushi bar . . . but sushi is for yuppies. True, the Russian market sprawled around the Palace of Culture is the largest in Poland . . . but you get better goods, cheaper, in Białystok, on the eastern border. Warsaw's Bong Sen Restaurant has better food than the Golden Duck in Łódź . . . but not much better, and the Bong Sen will cost you twice as much. Yes, the opera here is bigger and better than the opera in Łódź, but if it's big opera you want, go the whole ten yards, go to Berlin. Besides, the new director of the Warsaw Opera is, you guessed it, the former director of the Łódź Opera. What's happening at the Warsaw Opera today happened in Łódź two years ago. Last time I poked my head into an art museum in this city, the special exhibit was a collection of modern art on loan from, right again, the museum in Łódź. (By the time you read this, all those paintings will be back home again in Łódź.)

And while the Marriott Hotel is one striking edifice, with brass-plated restaurants and chrome-plated shops, it's just a typical American Marriott. What makes it stand out in this city is the contrast it offers to Warsaw drab.

Like New York, Warsaw is full of people who are irritatingly full of themselves, and for no compelling reason. Like New Yorkers, Warszawians go to work late, leave for home early, charge you double for making you wait. Like New Yorkers, Warszawians have been brutalized senseless by their environment, and they take their troubles out on you. In effect, the rest of the country is made to compensate inhabitants of this town for their misfortune in having to live here . . . although part of the compensation is that they get to remind you repeatedly of how swell they are. After a few years, even resident westerners catch the Warsaw Virus, becoming more native than the natives. Worst of the lot seem to be Americans who marry into the city, take jobs peripheral to the American Embassy, set up offices more or less in proximity to the Embassy, which they decorate with proper yuppie furniture in all the proper yuppie colors, install complex security systems and secretarial barriers to keep visitors away, post restricted working hours on their office doors to further discourage people from knocking, and set about flaunting their Polish-American eminence at U.S. government-funded receptions at the Marriott.

Fortunately, most Warsawians—like most New Yorkers—do not often venture into the hinterlands, so they will leave you alone unless you pester them. Unfortunately, there is too much power concentrated in this city for most Poles—and most Americans—to ignore it entirely. Besides, trains from Berlin arrive here, and airplanes from overseas. So probably you're gonna see Warsaw, and you're gonna stay at the Marriott or the Victoria, the Forum or the Grand. And you're gonna get ripped, for at least one night. But the next morning, do yourself a favor: take your morning tea and cake at the Victoria, visit the Stare Miasto shop that sells those exquisite greeting cards decorated with dried wild flowers, visit the Russian market, and check out the open-air railroad museum just south from Warzsawa Centralna, with armored railroad cars and old wooden boxcars and steam engines of all descriptions.

Then return to the Centralna, catch the next train out of town, and see Poland.

A Meditation on Work

I am no economist, and no political scientist either, but I do know
enough to understand that what failed in Poland, and in the rest of the former
East Bloc, was not communism as a recognizable economic or political system,
but an experiment in high idealism: a system which undertook to feed, clothe,
house, educate and employ all of its citizens, all of the time, to the best of their
mental and physical capabilities, to the best of its own resources. I don't know
how others feel, but I would like to see any government so conceived and so
dedicated succeed resoundingly. I am saddened to see such ideals scrapped with
the failure of this particular attempt.

The Swiss dramatist Dürrenmatt, visiting Warsaw in 1989, said that
capitalism isn't a system, it's just human nature. And what has triumphed in
Poland and the rest of the East is not a system of free markets, but old habits
bred in the bone. Apparently, as Andrew Carnegie warned only a century ago,
the utopias dreamt by idealists are indeed "the work of aeons," and people's
republics are not builded in a few decades. Perhaps, as Andrew Carnegie really
believed, workers' paradises are not going to be built ever. I can only speculate
on what went wrong, and my speculations—the semi-informed opinions of an
outsider newly come to the country—change daily.

In the first place, Poland did not afford optimal conditions for a test
case. Where the United States started with vast expanses of rich soil, tall
timber, untapped mineral deposits—the whole bank account built up century
after century by Native Americans and stolen in a few swift raids by immigrant
settlers—Poland began with an old and depleted land battered by two world wars.
When you construct a nation only to have it razed, reconstruct it only to see it
razed again, and then reconstruct it a third time without help from any Marshall
Plan . . . well, you work under a handicap. I doubt that America, capitalist or
socialist, would have succeeded under such circumstances.

World War II and the Nazi occupation didn't help the Polish work ethic
any. In a *Kultura* (1985) essay titled "The Knoll," Bohdan Korzeniewski recalls
the advice of his work detail commander in Auschwitz: "Now mark my words
carefully. You mustn't work, but even more important, you mustn't make it

obvious that you're not working. If you're not careful and make it obvious, you die even faster than the ones who work, understand?" The stereotype of the lazy Pole is, as much as anything, a tribute to the acting ability of these clever and, given the proper incentives, industrious people in the presence of gullible German masters. In another sense, however, what you see is what you get; we are, finally, what we appear to be; dancer cannot be separated from dance. At nonwork disguised as work, Poles are still quick studies.

After the War, Poland remained, for all practical purposes, occupied territory, underwriting the Soviet economy in a dozen ways, large and small. You can't expect an economy to function well when drained this way. When I suggested in 1990 that Poland could trade potatoes and grain to Russia, a colleague laughed in my face. "We've been sending them free potatoes for decades!" he scoffed. You can't expect an economy to rebuild itself and its neighbor to the east . . . to rebuild itself while supporting a large and useless military, and a large and even more useless secret police.

And a hierarchy of directors who are appointed to their directorships not because they know their business, but because they are members of the Club, the only club in town, from whom all directors must be chosen. And the Party clubhouse is built at the people's expense, with public money. And the people lose hope. And the arms of the workers fold once more. People invent lines and stand in them, a little longer each day. There is sabotage. There are excuses: "We cannot meet our quota, comrades, because parts have not arrived from the supplier."

Well, what did you expect?

There is theft, and workers use public facilities and state-owned machines for their own little projects.

Well, what did you expect?

And in a country which guarantees employment to all, people cannot be fired, not really fired, not put out of an income, whether they work, work hard, work a little, work not at all.

And when a government's hold on its populace becomes so tentative that the least spark threatens its legitimacy, that government is likely on the one hand to intimidate and repress, but on the other hand to grant grudging and select concessions, rewarding not increased productivity but raw political clout. So subsidies serve this group or that, and the price of political stability is milk at .3 cents a bottle and bread at a penny a loaf, and rail travel is cheap, and mothers receive endless maternity leave, and potentially troublesome students receive free parties just before their exams, and long summer holidays as well, all subsidized by a government which just prints more worthless money. Over several decades, this all takes a tremendous accumulative toll, not only on the economy of the nation, but on the nerve of the people, who are weakened proportionally to the degree they are pampered.

And then there is the bureaucracy, the endless bureaucracy, which antedated the communists, which Warsaw was no more able to contain than Washington, D.C. The endless, growing, absorbing bureaucracy takes a tremendous toll..

And behind all this lies a century and a half of partitioned Poland, a nation divided into thirds, from the First Partition of 1772 until the Republic of 1921, a country and a people not in charge of their own affairs, without real incentive to greatness. A country that was not a country.

And behind the Partition of 1772, a tradition of the small nobility, the *szlachta*, a warrior class long retired from battle, become small-potatoes politicians "hard on their subjects and people of the lower orders, careless of their speech, used to living beyond their means" (this from a contemporary historian, Długosz), who sold their loyalties to higher and sometimes foreign lords, who frustrated serious constitutional reform until far too late. Who, when impoverished in the nineteenth century beyond their ability even to feed themselves, chose to complete their ruin rather than work as a cook or gardener in the household of some German factory owner. "We are angels. We have titles. Work for us is a mistake."

And behind all that, centuries of the Roman Catholicism, the Papacy a bureaucracy all its own, and countless other bureaucracies besides, and a philosophy of life as well: "Ask not for much on this earth, where moths eat up and rust corrupts. Your reward will be in heaven. It is easier for a camel to pass through the eye of a needle than for a rich man to enter the Kingdom. Nor is it wise for a man to know much beyond his *credo* and his *ave*. Mother Church will take care of her own. Have faith, and do as the priest tells you."

Not without reason are Polish elections held just after Sunday mass.

129

The entire East Bloc system, designed to manufacture jobs and minimize work, found its most characteristic embodiment in the queues which maddened Westerners to the extent that many Americans I knew actually hired natives to wait in line for them. I never noticed much genuine Polish resistance to queuing: waiting in a queue is the ideal non-work: it's necessary, it's apolitical, it beats the hell out of working your ass off on an assembly line or a construction crew. And the Polish system of commerce increases, rather than decreases the number of, and thus the time spent in shopping queues. At the usual Polish shop, for example, there is no fingering merchandise directly, picking out what you want yourself, hustling through a check-out counter where a scanner reads a bar code and automatically computes price, tax, total, cash tendered and change. No sir. You queue at the counter, and when you reach the counter, you ask for what you want.

Maybe it's gloves.

"Do you have gloves?" you ask when, after half an hour in line, your turn comes.

"Why, yes, we have gloves," the clerk answers, and she fetches a pair of gloves from a drawer behind her. You examine them, feeling the leather, checking the stitching. You try them on, decide they are a tad too small and ask about a larger size. She fetches another pair of gloves, and you try them on.

"Do you have brown as well as black?"

She fetches a pair of brown gloves, your size. Others wait. On one occasion—the matter was boots, not gloves—the clerk, who was alone at the counter, herded all his customers outside the shop, locked the front door, and wandered off to a storage shed in search of a pair of size 37 black boots.

Having settled the matter of gloves, you ask about scarves. The clerk fetches you scarves, you study the selection, the rest of the queue waits. When you finish, the clerk totals your bill by hand, writing an invoice (with carbon) describing your purchase and its price. At the grocery store, and in some private shops, you may pay the clerk directly, but usually you walk, invoice in hand, to a cashier's window, where you wait in another queue to pay the cashier. Then you return with the original invoice (now stamped "paid") to the counter at which you purchased your merchandise. A clerk there has meanwhile been wrapping your purchase in cheap brown or gray wrapping paper, folding edges upon themselves in that miraculous manner Polish clerks have of making a tightly bound bundle without using a bit of Scotch tape or string. You wait your turn (queue to the left of the counter—not with people waiting to purchase goods), present your receipt, pick up your package, and off you go.

In a large department store you queue at different counters, often on different floors, for toys, radios and television sets, crystal, cooking utensils. Probably you will make several trips to the cashier's windows, as it's unwise to leave purchases waiting too long.

This is an old system once used in the States. It has nostalgic value, and I've seen variations alive and functioning in, for example, Foyle's Book Shop in London. But anyone with a double-digit I.Q. could devise a more efficient system of shopping.

The cashier's office may even be in a separate building entirely. Foreigners buying green card insurance for automobiles traveling outside of Poland apply for their insurance at the Warta Agency, Piotrkowska 99. After filling out appropriate forms there, they are sent with their invoices, to the Central Bank of Łódź, Piotrkowska 211, a thirty-minute hike or a short tram ride from Warta, to pay in U.S. dollars, queue first at window three, where a computer generates five (5) copies of a deposit slip which are stamped four (4) times each, signed (all copies) by both depositor and clerk, and taken, with the U.S. dollars, to window *six,* where a clerk collects the dollars, the five deposit slips stamped four times and initialed twice, issues a certificate of payment (duplicate), which is stamped twice, signed once, and handed to the owner of the foreign car, who may then return to Piotrkowska 99 and pick up his green certificate of insurance. If he carries only Polish currency, there will be one additional detour, with one additional queue, to buy hard currency.

You can kill an entire day buying Warta insurance . . . or collecting your salary, paying the telephone bill, and buying a train ticket.

I am following a thread here not because I want to plaster blame, but to trace the arc of a nation, to discover why a people so spectacularly industrious and successful in other countries made such a mess of their own.

To see how my students fit into the larger picture.

"They are confused victims of a system that makes no sense—not to them, not to you, not to anyone," said my predecessor in Łódź, Donald Morrill. "Just talk to them, and you will be the only teacher who cares about their lives and their success, and you will be appreciated."

"These students are very clever at inventing excuses and lying their way out of any situation," a Polish colleague at the Institute advised me just after my arrival. "Polish students are the best liars in the world."

After two years, I still don't know what to make of them.

They are bright, even the dullest of them, brighter than most of my students in the States. Their presence at the Institute comes after a long winnowing process, genuinely competitive testing for not too many seats in not too many universities (the process did give sons and daughters of doctors, teachers, and Party members undeniable and probably insurmountable natural advantages). Higher education in Poland comes tuition-free, even providing room and board stipends, and further stipends for need and for good grades. Some of the married ones make more money each month than Michelle, their teacher. Who would not fight for a seat at the University? And with English now so popular in Poland . . . a seat at the Institute of English Philology!

They are indeed clever, especially with excuses.

They are as fogged in as I am. As workers they are underpaid, although here I agree with the State: their work is indeed "non-productive," so they deserve less. Still, like all European students they are subsidized in a number of attractive ways: travel, associations, the discounts attendant on having a *legitymacja*. Some deliberately delay graduation to retain a dorm room or a stipend. In contrast to American students, who work all summer and half-time during the academic year to pay half their tuition, room, and board, while borrowing the other half, so they can graduate $10,000 in debt to take some 30-hour-a-week, no health care, $1-an-hour-over-over-minimum-wage job . . . well, these kids live very comfortably.

They are wonderful sitting in the café drinking tea, chatting. They can survive a lecture just like that, although I get a lot of what Americans consider rude chatter—not only during their teachers' lectures, but also during student presentations.

On paper their week is long—more hours than American counterparts put in. However, they manage to trim two-hour blocks of class to 90 minutes, including a fifteen-minute break for sandwiches and tea, so that two hours distill quickly to one. A three-or four-hour marathon, like the evening classes many American students endure, would be unthinkable in Poland. Absenteeism is very high in all classes, although in this regard Poles are no worse than Germans or Brits. It is not uncommon for an entire class to blow off a lecture, or for individuals to spend a week or two in mid-semester skiing in the mountains. The academic calendar is plump with holidays, rector's days, and other days of officially canceled classes. Medical excuses provide another source of time off, as do children, ailing parents, even conferences at other universities. In the spring of 1991, the entire third year at Wrocław took rector's leave from classes to join two of their younger teachers at a conference in Poznań. Not one showed up at the conference. The net result is that Polish students are not in class any more minutes per week than American students . . . who, studies indicate, come on the average nowhere near a forty-hour work week, not even combining class time, study time, and transit time.

My Polish students are good at watching films, and very good at throwing parties.

Three things about them concern me. First, they are genuine sheep. They think as a group, they act as a group, and on exams they frequently— after consulting each other orally in Polish— answer as a group. What we would consider cheating, they consider group effort. They are surprised when Westerners are offended. Returning from a year at the University of Missouri-St. Louis, Agnieszka Leńko told me in surprise and admiration, "Americans won't cheat! When I offered to help one of my friends with grammar study, he was horrified. In Poland, that's how we get through exams, by helping each other."

Polish students spend most of their education in group, even at the Institute: before their first year they are assigned to, say, IC, a small group of fifteen first-year students which meets together every class, every week for the whole year. IC then becomes IIC, and so on until VC, the same fifteen students, always in classes with each other. Only when they specialize (pedagogy, American literature, British literature, linguistics) do they break from the group. They may not like their group or its collective nature, but they will not actively work to transfer to another group, or to change the character of their own group. Individuals fear for their very careers: to stick out too much is bad form, and dangerous.

Thinking on examinations or papers is timid, formulaic: the same clichés resound in paper after paper. M.A. theses are long on recited criticism, short on fresh insight. If a written examination question asks them to spit back notes from a lecture or book, or repeats questions from last year's exam, they fire right at you; but questions that require even the simplest review, sorting, and synthesis leave them stumped. On an historical grammar exam, most simply could not "discuss the ways English has, from earliest times to the present, formed the negative of verbs" . . . although all could have translated the forms *nadde, hadn't,* and *didn't have.* Such strengths and weaknesses do not bode well for their future—or Poland's. (In their timidity, of course, these students are no worse than most teachers—American or Polish.)

I remember especially one occasion when my students simply refused a written exam in my American culture lecture. The whole group stormed out together. "This is not legally required of us," their representative told me.

"It would be a good experience," I argued, "an experience in American culture. And besides, 1990 is not the appropriate time for Poles to be deciding what they are not required to do."

But out the whole group went.

Then back some of them came, individually, sneaking into the room with furtive looks over the shoulder, each with the same tale: "I would not have minded the exam. I think it might even have been fun. But the group . . . if it had come to a vote, I am sure the group would have voted 60-40 against it." After two hours the figure stood at 50-50; the next day only "the vocal few" had wanted to leave. The point is, they all went out together. Solidarity forever!

My second concern is that most of my students are genuinely lazy, which is to say most of them would prefer to work as little as possible, or even not at all . . . at least on their studies. Most are self-confessed minimalists: a passing grade is fine. When Agnieszka Leńko returned from a St. Louis a smash success—bringing with her scores of books, a perfect American accent, enlarged vocabulary, serious cash, Presence, and her own personal computer—they told me by the dozens, "I could never do that. I'm not Agnieszka!"

"Neither was Agnieszka before she left," I told them, but the message fell on deaf, jealous, suspicious ears. Most English language students "give private lessons" or teach at some private school, but I cannot imagine their teaching depletes their energies any more than their day-to-day classroom work. If there is fire in the western Slavic soul, it breaks forth in dance, song, and

133

affairs of the heart, not in work . . . at least not work in Poland. Students burning with intellectual curiosity? I met only a handful, most in their first or second years. By the time theses are completed, the fire is quite gone out, and they are safe and suitable teachers.

I expected more fire, especially in people in their early twenties, and regarding things American. When I point out the obvious, that for the sake of Poland things must change, all readily admit yes, things must change, but "I think for the older generation it is already too late, even for people as young as we are. We have spent too much time in the old school. . . ."

Their academic apathy is matched only by their lack of political activity, which seems limited to striking for fewer requirements and more electives (the American system of elective courses is widely misunderstood, as are many features of American post-secondary education). "If students ran the Polish railroads" a colleague once joked, "there would be train service only in February and June [exam months]."

Dead Poet's Society was a run-away smash hit film in Poland, especially among students, but for all the wrong reasons. "I wish we had teachers like that, teachers who would have us stand up on our desks," they all sighed.

"Which of you would be first to stand on a desk?" I wanted to know.

They're on the edge, looking out that door, sighing, wishing, dreaming. But they still need what Janis Joplin used to call "that old kick in the ass."

My third concern is related to the second: none of my students seem genuinely interested in, anxious over, or even curious about work after graduation. Few take summer jobs, in Poland at any rate, because their education is tuition-free. They travel, they retreat to family enclaves in the countryside or mountains, some claim to read. If they go to the West, they work like maniacs at jobs they would consider demeaning in Poland: waitressing, babysitting, cleaning houses or stables in Germany, picking berries in Wales, constructing roads in Sweden. They are in it for the hard currency and the short haul. (In this regard they are no different from their parents and friends, who work 16-hour days at two or three jobs during their two-year stays in Chicago, piling up $30,000 or $50,000 to take home to Poland, where the livin' is easy.)

Students who cannot travel complain about not having the money to travel. When asked what plans they have to earn the money for tickets, they seem genuinely puzzled: Poland is not an appropriate theater for earning money. Suggestions for an aggressive poster campaign to drum up business as tour guides or translators for visiting businessmen snooping around Łódź fell flat on their face. When, two weeks later, I produced a poster peeled off a wall in Warsaw advertising precisely such a service at five U.S. dollars per hour, the reaction was disbelief. When I suggested T-shirts in Polish might be a real money-maker, their reaction was, "Who would buy them?"

"I would," I replied; "Michelle and I. Every rich foreigner who visited

Poland these last two years has been looking desperately for a Polish language T-shirt or sweatshirt."

In spring of 1990 Michelle devoted two hours of her composition class to preparing vitas and writing letters of application. When she asked if they had found the lecture worthwhile, students answered, "It was very interesting, but I cannot imagine ever having to write such a letter."

Not many of these kids plan to teach high school, although many study methodology, and Poland is so desperate for English teachers that it imports Peace Corps workers and World Teach volunteers by the dozens, and employs other native speakers as well, has set up a whole system of "teacher training institutes" to generate in three years Polish teachers of English, German and French. A couple of very bright students availed themselves of foreign opportunities for the advanced degrees prerequisite to teaching college, although none intend to teach at a Polish university. A few students have broken away from the Institute to form private companies. A few are energetic in translating into Polish English classics, contemporary fiction, and trash novels. One became a television sports commentator. Most just muddle along, unable to connect their education with a vocation, or even a paying job. While I believe in a liberal education, I also understand that what is consumed must be produced.

The candidacy of Lech Wałęsa for President of Poland crystallized the whole issue dramatically for my students—and for Polish intellectuals in general—who dislike and fear Wałęsa. In conversation, they emphasized his awkward use of the language. (The first Polish-language T-shirt I ever saw was, in fact, a satire: Wałęsa announcing in idiomatic Polish, "I am the President.") More than one self-serving academic assured me that intellectuals "made Wałęsa," whom they picked as a figurehead who would appeal to the masses . . . now here he was, full of delusions of grandeur.

What really troubles Polish intellectuals about Wałęsa, I suspect, is that he represents the worker ascended to the office of President. His success threatens their values, especially since they cannot write it off as Party connections, foreign intervention, or the old corrupt good-old-boys network. His election threatened them even more, because their candidate, the intellectual, did not even make the run-off. Wałęsa is clear proof that even in an emerging democracy speaking good Polish is not required for political success; by extension, speaking good Polish, or good English, may not be required for anything at all. Possibly speaking and thinking may, in and of themselves, lack intrinsic value. People must work, and smart people as well, to paraphrase D. H. Lawrence. Not that Polish intellectuals, underpaid and underappreciated, constitute a new aristocracy, as do German academics, but that is the way they would like to think of themselves. Wałęsa denies what they most assert: "We drink tea. We hold conversations. We are angels. For us clever ones, work is a mistake."

Agnieszka Salska and Old Solidarity Days

"It was so much easier then," she says wistfully, eyes bright with remembrance but just a hint of weariness in her voice. "There was only here or there, and you knew where you had to be."

She is Docent Dr. Agnieszka Salska, Director of the Institute for English Philology at Łódź University, author of several articles and an important book on Emily Dickinson and Walt Whitman, published by the University of Pennsylvania Press. She holds the highest rank a Polish university can offer—and she is a former member (some have used the word "big shot") in Solidarity. Today on a walking tour of Solidarity Łódź she remembers the old days.

"Because of martial law, you could be detained without arrest and without charges. Detainment lasted maybe a year for most Solidarity activists. Since there were no charges, there were in effect no 'political prisoners,' although one of the things we were constantly trying to do was get them to admit the fact of political prisoners. Even those formally charged with breaking the law were booked on normal criminal charges and treated like common criminals: made to work, housed with other criminals, sometimes beaten. Two leaders of Łódź Solidarity—Andrzej Słowik and Jerzy Kropiwnicki—started a hunger strike in prison for the recognition of the rights of political prisoners. Słowik was force-fed. I think it did him some permanent harm, although he is back in office as the head of Łódź Solidarity today. He was released in 1986, in the amnesty, after four and a half years in prison for appearing in the window of the Łódź Solidarity building on the morning of December 18,1981."

In the early days of martial law, travel was restricted. You could not travel from Łódź to Warsaw without official permission (shades of life in Nazi Poland); troops blocked the county borders (students living at home often crossed such borders on their way to school each morning; some moved to town and lived with friends, I have been told). "Two of our men went to the December 12 meeting in Gdańsk. Almost everyone there was arrested as they left the meeting, except Słowik and Kropiwnicki. They made it home somehow, but were arrested the next day."

137

Parish priests communicated news about prisoners to family and friends, administered relief to the prisoners' families, provided a rally point for sympathizers and members of Solidarity. In Łódź the so-called "Solidarity Church" was the Jesuit Church—formerly the Evangelical church—three blocks from the English Institute. Sunday mass provided an opportunity for Solidarity people to congregate legally. The sermon, on an appropriate New Testament text emphasizing human rights, would drift back and forth between theology and politics, always implying more than was stated explicitly. Being a priest in such a church was dangerous, although those who put themselves in danger in the early eighties are much admired today. "Last year our priest, Father Mieczykowski, received the City of Łódź award," Dr. Salska says. "It wasn't too long ago we were signing petitions to keep him here."

In front of the church stands a large wooded cross towering over a marble slab commemorating another priest, Father Jerzy Popiełuszko, a modern Polish martyr, one of the unfortunate ones. The inscription reads "14. IX. 1947—19(?). X. 1984." "He was not a strong man," Dr. Salska remembers, but he had a driver who also functioned as a body guard, ex-special forces in the military, a very agile man. Both men were driving one night to Warsaw when their car was forced to the side of the road. The body guard managed to roll out of the door of the automobile which had picked them up, and to escape. Another vehicle was coming by, and the *milicja* could not turn around and get him again. He got to a church, where he told everyone what happened. He was kept in hiding for quite awhile, the only man who could identify the assailants. There were prayer vigils in churches all over Poland."

"Was Father Popiełuszko ever found?"

"A few days later the body was dragged out of a pond behind a dam. He had been badly beaten. We all knew what had happened and who had done it."

Terror and intimidation were the tools of the *milicja*. "They always went for the young men. They were told to 'get the young ones, get the men.' It was part of the intimidation."

Of course there were forged documents and propaganda as well—Solidarity was the enemy of the people. "I was once shown a list of individuals Solidarity supposedly wanted to get rid of," Dr. Salska recalls, " a list I was supposed to have helped put together. It was all nonsense, designed to confuse you." Usually it backfired: writing in the *Warsaw Voice*, Krzysztof Jasiewicz noted, "In the days of communist propaganda, . . . because the Communists were portraying someone in a bad light, the public knew that that person was probably very decent."

The soldiers, recalls Dr. Salska, herself a mother, were pretty young too, and she admits to having felt just a bit maternal toward them. "They were not from Łódź; the boys from Łódź were sent to other areas. And they were frightened too. Scared little boys with these big guns!"

We walk to Holy Cross Church, oldest in the City of Łódź, to another remembrance, this one of the Gdańsk Uprising in 1970: a small slab commemorating those who died in that action. After martial law, the tablet—set in the outside wall of the Church, eight feet off the ground—became a rallying point for Solidarity members. "We held our small protests here, our public rallies. Men would be up there in those windows taking photographs. We would smile, wave. . . ."

"The tablet was not removed by authorities?" I ask.

"It was attached to the Church, you see, so removing it would have been . . . more difficult."

"And the photographs? They must be tucked away in some files. Where are the files now?"

"Oh, I am sure they around somewhere," she smiles. (I recall having seen pictures taken at the Jesuit Church by a Solidarity photo-journalist in an album I bought at the Gdańsk Shipyard souvenir booth.)

Although I can't imagine the Polish Roman Catholic Church needing strengthening, its position was enhanced by association with Solidarity, even during the early 1980's. "The position of left intellectuals became untenable after martial law. The Catholic position was all that was left. There were many conversions then. I don't mean to be cynical. They had nowhere to go. Many members of the new government are Catholic intellectuals, including of course Prime Minister Mazowiecki, who was one of their best writers and editors."

Explicit Church support for Solidarity came mostly on the parish level. "When the Pope visited Poland, he met with General Jaruzelski [then in charge of martial law, later President of Poland, with Mazowiecki his Prime Minister], not with Wałęsa or other Solidarity people. They talked for an hour or more. I remember being in Warsaw, waiting for the Pope to come out and bless us, and the meeting went on and on. We all joked: 'Jaruzelski is making his confession; he needs plenty of time.'"

The goal of Solidarity during the early eighties was, first and foremost, simply to survive. Second, it sought to make things not work as a protest against the denial of basic human rights. Leaders were identified, detained and—after their release—monitored (making contact with them dangerous to others in the movement). New leaders emerged, people with new ideas, new programs. Then they would be identified and detained . . . and replaced as leaders. "Continuity was difficult. And we always worried about informers.

"I must tell you one story," she says. "On the first anniversary of the suppression of Solidarity, we were having a small rally at the Institute. It was on a break between classes, so the students would not be inconvenienced, and the rector—who was our elected rector and should not have too much to answer for—was present, and naturally the secret police showed up, and right in the middle of things who walked in but a group from the American Embassy, Fulbright representatives and all. Elizabeth Corwin was there; she will remember. I don't know what they wanted, and I'm sure they didn't know what

139

was going on, but the police were furious. 'This is an international conspiracy,' they raged. We kept hearing that one for a year."

"You yourself were permitted to leave the country during the early martial law years," I remind her. This was 1983, when Dr. Salska spent time in Philadelphia working on her Dickinson-Whitman book. "Were they trying to get you out of the way?"

"That is a funny thing," she answers. "I had applied for the scholarship in 1979, and been turned down, so I thought I would reapply for the program. This time I was accepted. When I requested a passport for travel to the West, both for myself and for my son, I was turned down right away. I reapplied, of course, and they asked all sorts of questions. There were telephone calls and more visits. What they wanted me to do was identify some leaders for them, admit I was one myself. When they realized I was not giving them what they wanted, the harassment continued. But by then it was just intimidation.

140

"I remember one time, they said, 'Well, why don't you just admit it: this is only an excuse for you to escape from Poland.' Then I decided—and I remember quite consciously making a decision—to make a big scene. 'I am a serious scholar,' I shouted at them, 'and my work is important work.' On and on."

Then, with no explanation, just a few weeks before the start of fall term, the passport was granted. "I have no explanation," she admits, "except total confusion. Or perhaps I had a friend somewhere I did not know about. Sometimes I feel a bit guilty, as if maybe I did not do enough. I just don't know."

Throughout our conversation, I have been remembering my own student activist days during the high sixties: the demonstrations, the rooftops lined with government photographers, the files, the government agents. I remember demonstrations and sit-ins at Ohio University during my graduate school days. I remember learning that my immediate predecessor at Bradley Polytech had been let go essentially because he was advisor to the SDS. I remember one member of Bradley SDS telling me that he and others returned to Peoria from the Port Huron Convention to discover that in their absence they'd been dismissed from the school, no reason given, no appeal permitted. I too felt guilty for somehow escaping jail, staying in school to the Ph. D., taking Harry's job, ending up finally as a department chair and a full professor. Maybe I too did not do enough.

I have been remembering too the collective mind of other sixties types, and one of Dr. Salska final comments strikes a very familiar chord. "There was something quite romantic about it all in those early days, a kind of game we were playing with the police: keeping secrets, avoiding arrest, rescuing our people when they got caught, supporting each other, spiriting people away in the dark. I remember when one of our people in Warsaw was shot and had to be hospitalized: it became a game of springing him from the hospital. And we did it. It was like, 'Hurrah, that's one more for our side!'

"Things were so much simpler in those days, and I worried a lot less than I do now."

A smile crosses her face, a golden glow of battles fought and remembered victories, and I realize consciously something I have subconsciously suspected for a long while: Docent Dr. Agnieszka Salska, Director of the Institute of English Studies, is just another one of those sixties people who made good.

The Mansions

> "It is no matter. They all build palaces, so I had one
> built. They have grand rooms; so have I. People
> ought to know that Müller has a palace of his own."
>
> —Reymont, *The Promised Land*

They lived well back then, the owners. You can tell that just by
walking past their mansions, many of which still stand, scattered around Łódź.
The façades may be darkened with pollution, cement ornamentation may be
chipped or weathered, the buildings themselves may have been converted to
schools, museums, or municipal administration, but these are unmistakably the
abodes of former owners. "Let me tell you about the very rich," Fitzgerald once
wrote; "they are different from you and me."

Yeah—they have more money and they live better.

Two mansions stand out as models of robber-baron luxury: Poznański's
palace on the corner of Zachodnia and Ogrodowa, across the street from the
relocated Łódź town church, and the palace Scheibler built on Przędzalniana for
his daughter. Both are restored and open to the public; either will give a middle-
class visitor a painfully acute sense of life in a two-class society.

Poznański's huge residence on Ogrodowa is worthy of a nobleman . . .
a rank to which Izrael Kalmanowicz Poznański, "The Cotton King," clearly
aspired. The gray neo-baroque palace, designed in 1888 by Hilary Majewski (the
man responsible for many Łódź collages of neo-This and neo-That) and enlarged
in 1902 by Adolf Selighson, contrasts sharply with the red brick wall around the
adjacent red brick factory—now "Poltex"—a contrast not lost, I am sure, on the
masses who plodded each day to work beneath the red brick gate crowned with
the clock which regulated their lives, who must have thought this mansion,
constructed long after the factory was fully operational, at a time when
Poznański already owned two other very impressive mansions elsewhere in Łódź,
a daily personal affront to their lives. Who must have yearned in every fiber of
their being to burn the place down, and blame the disaster on the "lightning" that
struck so regularly in nineteenth-century Łódź. Who must have rejoiced in secret

143

when Israel's heirs found the place too expensive to live in, and converted at least part of it into office space.

From the roof rise two gray tin mansard roofs, from which rise two flagpoles each. Around the perimeter of the third story, silhouetted against the gray sky, obelisks and statues of men and women in various stages of undress. The elaborate wrought iron gates of the factory entrance could compete in Belgravia, London or in New Orleans. Built originally in the shape of an L, then renovated, elaborated and extended, this building is a veritable icon of vulgar wealth: dining hall with elaborate ceiling and more semi-nudes celebrating the initial P, heavy bronze chandeliers, elaborately carved walnut paneling, art nouveau peacock above the dining hall fireplace (again the initial P), inlaid wood floor, bronze figure of allegorized Industry cast by Mathurin Moreau of France, marble entrance hall, dark wooden staircase, large Rubens-like oil depicting Perseus and Andromeda, ornate exterior staircase leading to formal gardens . . . and various other interior rooms in a hodgepodge of styles, pre-Raphaelite, neoclassical, the ballroom a goofy, gaudy collage of neoclassical and early modern, in turquoise and white and gold. Poznański lived in eclectic elegance, all right.

This palace has had a checkered history. Nazi occupational forces made it their administrative seat; photographs displayed in the City Museum show their renovations, now entirely undone. The palace today is used for concerts and receptions—Michelle and I attended an Italian classical guitarist's Łódź concert in the ballroom, and several Institute students, acting as translators, wheedled invitations to the cocktail parties held in the dining hall during the spring textile

and fashion show. The palace also now houses the Museum of the History of Łódź (Poznański's other residence, a neo-Renaissance magnificence on Więckowskiego, now houses the City Art Museum), including several second-story rooms celebrating the city's most famous native son, pianist Artur Rubinstein. Although the rooms themselves are elegant, Rubinstein steals the show, especially the photographs of the pianist with presidents, celebrities, and world leaders, and a French order that came with medal, uniform, and ceremonial sword. And the hands, Rubinstein's hands, cast in bronze. A fellow can do okay for himself playing the piano. Or running a textile mill.

The City Museum in the basement of the Poznański Palace, is again several rooms, not all of them open all the time. Most interesting to me are the hall containing invoice heads, stationery, and notes from various old Łódź textile factories, the rooms filled with photographs and artifacts from the Nazi occupation and the Łódź ghetto (including the battered sign, yellow paint on sheet metal, that marked the home of the Eldest of the Jews in the Litzmanstadt Ghetto), and a display of paintings of old Bałuty by Jan Filipski. The palace-museum thus embodies that odd fellowship common between robber-baron industrialists—the very rich—and artists, writers, and musicians. Whether the robber-barons are Italian Popes, German-American beer magnates, or Jewish textile manufacturers in Łódź; the two poles of this relationship always seem to find each other. Hard-working rich hire often disreputable and indigent artists to play tunes in their palaces, paint pictures for their walls, and chronicle their histories; even as they accept their patronage, bohemian artists despise these patrons (who never seem to quite understand art and are not always pleased with

145

what their money buys). Yet a grudging mutual respect prevails (the fraternity of excellence?), and the odd fellowship sustains itself. Whatever defilement time and the Nazis worked on Poznański's palaces and graves, he has, in the end, Rubinstein, Reymont (*The Promised Land* is the story of Poznański's Łódź, his friends and enemies, their palaces and businesses), Filipski, and all the artists of the Museum of Art. Not a bad end for an old cloth peddler.

The Herbst Palace, built by Scheibler as a wedding present for his daughter, seems warmer, less ostentatious than the Poznański Palace, but that judgment may reflect my own stylistic preference. A marble staircase leads from the entrance hall, past a richly colored stained glass window, to a series of second-story rooms, including Herbst's office, his wife's dressing room, his mother-in-law's dressing room, a library, a sitting room, a dining room . . . each rich with carved wood desks and cabinets, porcelain figurines, art nouveau fixtures, oil paintings, gilded mirrors, oriental objets d'art. The ballroom is a harmony of dark, carved wood and glass, a bust of Scheibler presiding over all. The grounds are pleasant: enclosed park, functioning greenhouse, stables with horses' heads peering out from the peak of each roof, fountains and pathways, a lovely view of the pond. And of the factory, all five stories of it, which must have created an incessant racket when going full blast. The dominant impression here is Old Money And Plenty Of It, which was Scheibler to a T.

Like Poznański, Scheibler owned several mansions in and around Łódź, one of which now houses the Museum of Cinema. These and other palaces are used by Polish film-makers (many affiliated with the Łódź film school) whenever they need a turn-of-the-century interior set; sit through half a dozen Polish movies, and you'll get a good sense of Łódź owners' mansions. The 1991 map of central Łódź, with all the new street names, is bordered by drawings of some of the finer mansions; it makes a good introduction to the styles and grandeur of the owner's mansion. A very handsome book, *The City of Palatial Residences and of One Street,* contains numerous four-color photographs, interior and exterior of the mansions of Łódź industrialists: Herbst, Poznański, Scheibler, Geyer, Grohman, Heinzl, Biderman, Kinderman. Another small publication, *Lodzkie Witraze, the Stained Glass Windows of Łódź,* reproduces windows from mansions owned by Scheibler, Poznański, Kern, Kinderman, Steiner, and the banker Maximilian Goldfeder. From the color photographs, from the drawings on the map, from a first-hand examination of interiors and exteriors of those buildings still standing, from the photos and the museum displays, from the tombs in the cemeteries, one develops a picture of the life of an owner in turn-of-the-century Łódź.

And from Reymont's novel, which photographed their life as clearly as any camera:

Piles of silken cushions, with crude Chinese hues, lay on the sofa
and on the milk-white carpet, which they seemed to tinge like great

146

blots of spilt colour. The fragrance of burnt amber and of *violettes de Perse,* mingled with the odour of roses, floated about the room. On one of the walls there glittered a collection of most costly Oriental weapons, grouped round a large circular shield of Saracenic steel inlaid with gold, and so brightly burnished that the golden tracery and the edgings of pale amethysts shone and sparkled in the dusky boudoir with a variegated display of light. In one corner a huge fan of peacock's feathers formed the background to a large statue of Buddha, cross-legged and gilt all over. In another there stood a Japanese flower-stand, borne by golden dragons and filled with snow-white azaleas in full bloom.

"Why, this is a millionaire's lumber-room!" Charles said to himself.

A walk down Piotrkowska, beginning at Plac Wolności (Freedom Square; note the memorial, pulled down by the Nazis and restored after the war by Poles, commemorating General Tadeusz Kościuszki, with a bronze relief on its base depicting Kościuszki and George Washington shaking hands) will take you past the façades of other residences, factories, and businesses: number 10 Piotrkowska, Moorish façade, Gothic gargoyle downspouts, Romanesque collonade, peeling pink paint revealing lime green undercoat, the wet dream of some half-drugged, newly rich owner brought garrishly into being by some equally demented architect. Number 43, a gorgeous art nouveau façade, its

147

balconies a filagree of graceful curves reminiscent of the ironwork of some stations of the Paris Metro. 86 Piotrkowska, the house of Jan Petersilge (publisher of the *Lodzer Zeitung*), a cement German hunting lodge five stories high, with genuine marble pillars flanking its Gothic portal on the ground floor, gryphones flanking the central tower at the second story, the statue of some Teutonic knight in a recessed niche on the upper flourth floor, medallions featuring the heads of famous Germans below the windows a of the fourth floor, an assortment of other decorative balconies, shields, gargoyles, and whatnot on the façade and across the roof. Growing from the left turret five stories above street level, a small poplar tree. Ulica Moniuszki, once the private street of industrialist Ludwig Geyer, with gates at either end and porters to bar the riffraff, a quiet enclave in a hectic city, a small avenue of mansions designed by Hilary Majewski largely unchanged from a century ago (although in the New Poland even some of these buildings have begun to sprout advertisements), a street brought easily back to turn-of-the-century life and shot from a dozen angles to give it the appearance of many different streets. It is one of the most filmed streets in Poland, thanks in no small part to the Łódź Film Institute.

Piotrkowska 77, Maximilian Goldfeder's bank, now Student Club 77. Walk up one flight to a typical second-story reception room now a jazz club: hardwood floor, ornate plaster ceiling, high folding doors, elaborate brass door knobs, quarter paneling—you'd think you were in some English pub.

137 Piotrkowska: the old Kinderman palace, now office of the Association of Polish Teachers: enter the side door, usually open, and you will

148

confront a bizarre mosaic of tile and sea shells, mostly green and blue and gold, in a clearly Moorish style. In a recessed niche in the middle of the mosaic, the pedestal for a now-lost statue. Overhead, more mosaics. Sneaking up the marble staircase to more Byzantine splendor on the second floor, you will pass a splendiferous art nouveau glass window, all in pre-Raphaelite blues and greens.

On your way away from this building, cross the street and notice its third-story façade: a glittering mosaic illustrating the production process of cotton fabric.

My own reaction to the homes of the very rich—whether they are castles in Germany or England, Gilded Age mansions of Newport, Rhode Island or Summit Avenue in Saint Paul, Minnesota—is always ambivalent, a combination of anger and desire, a forked wish to buy the place and blow it up, a respect for the taste and elegance of which civilization is built, and sympathy for workers short-changed by those who amassed the fortunes which built these palaces. The contrasting drab of Workers' Paradise Łódź, even the modern high-rise blocs of the "Manhattan" complex on Piotrkowska, is enough to tip my sympathies toward the owners, but a good deal of judgmental jealousy remains. I would probably sleep better believing that all robber barons got, finally, their just deserts, but I don't believe that for a moment. Some went bust and stayed or left. Many escaped clean to the immortality of death, died wealthy, in Łódź, surrounded to the end by family, friends and sycophants. Others escaped, with their wealth, to places far away. It's the usual, on-going story of the very rich.

In Łódź, however, in at least one case, it is a story with a twist. This story was told me in the textile museum by a guide who spoke only imperfect German; since my German is none too good either, it may be flawed in details, correct only in outlines. It is the tale of an owner who stayed, Grohman I believe, Scheibler's partner and one of the Old Ones, one of the Germans. And when the Nazis began their ethnic sort, Grohman qualified as pure Aryan, to be registered in the A-1 German log, while others were registered as German-2, Polish, or Jewish. Even at the beginning of the War, people knew, or thought they knew, what it meant to have one's name in the proper book . . . but when the SS officer approached Grohman to register him among the first-class German citizens of the Reich, with all attendant rights, honors, and privileges, Grohman declined the registration everyone sought, the registration which would save a man's life from the barbarisms to come.

Politely but firmly he declared, "My name is German, but my family has lived here many years. I am no longer German. Now I am Polish."

And the SS officer shot him in the head.

149

On the Road, Part III: Białowieża

A hell of a time we've had getting here. Łódź to Warsaw in the late evening, train packed because of the holiday, ten in a compartment designed for eight, and every one a Polish type: one drunk and ineffectual looking male; one stiff and long-skirted mother who crossed herself at every church we passed; one tall, stout, and homely girl of twenty, headed probably for a convent, who also several times crossed herself; one fat Polish mother with an equally fat male child of eight or ten, who clung to her as if he was three; one gorgeous Polish girl of eighteen, engaged in reading a Polish translation of some American bodice-buster novel; one male Polish peddler, who snored.

Then dead time in Central: grime and crime; smelly waiting rooms, smellier toilets; trash cans full of trash, benches full of drunks. The same unintelligible voice over the same crackling loudspeakers heard in train stations around the world. The odor of urine.

The ride fromWarsaw to Białystok, local all the way and a real trash train: windows black with pollution, upholstery tacky with spilled beer, soda, juice. Ash trays jammed to overflowing with bags, bottles, banana peels and apple cores. Stale cigarette smoke seeping into our non-smoking compartment from the outside aisles. The heat on full blast (in Poland, conductors control heat, and that thermostat in your compartment is irrelevant), and the window latch refused to lock down: after newspaper wedges, curtain rod struts, and two-boot weights all failed, I finally removed my belt and tied the window handle to the ash tray, much to the amusement of several Polish women. I tried unsuccessfully to snooze; then joined Michelle in the aisle conversing with other travelers—she is much better at this than I—using a combination of German, English, Polish, French, even Italian and Latin to share ideas.

It was just as well I did, for I finally witnessed one of those slip-the-conductor-a-five-spot-and-ride-for-cheap payoffs my students are always talking about. As the conductor entered our car somewhere east of Warsaw, one fellow moved out of his compartment to the aisle, slouching against the window and lighting up a cigarette, tucking five thousand złotych in his closed fist for the conductor to snatch as he moved down the car. If I had blinked my eye, I would have missed the exchange, but there it was: instead of a 10% commission on a ticket he would have written himself, the conductor had himself 5,000 złotych; the passenger had himself a half-price ride.

Between Warsaw and Białystok constant acceleration and deceleration, as the train slowed—sometimes to a dead halt—for red signals and amber, for bridges and track junctions, for local stations, for unguarded crossings, for crossings where a guard was supposed to have been lowered but was not, for a crossing where a guard was supposed to have been lowered and was. At one point I think the engineer stopped the train, climbed down out of his engine, walked over the a remote tower, picked up a few papers from the yardmaster, and returned to our train.

Then more dead time in Białystok—no bar, of course, and in the restaurant only tea, soda, crackers, moldy sandwiches, congealed bigos, crusty mashed potatoes, and cold fried patties of ground meat—before the ultimate Polish local, Białystok to Białowieża via Hajnówka, no heat at all on this puppy, but precious few passengers either, and time at last to stretch ourselves full length on a second-class compartment seat (those arm rests fold back, but be careful to remove your shoes, or the conductor can and will fine you). Wrapped in one sweater and two jackets, using a roll of two or three T-shirts as a pillow, I catch a few Zs. Jesus, what a trip!

At 7:30 a.m. the train again shudders to a stop.

I awake and check my watch. About the right time. I pull down the window, poke my head out, and stare stupidly at the depot, a low wooden building elaborate with gingerbread ornamentation, more a hunting lodge than a train station. Ahead, the tracks end in tall grass and a stand of trees. On all sides, forest: beech, spruce, birch, oak. A sign reads "Białowieża Towarowa." Somewhere in the distance a rooster crows.

"I think this must be it," I tell Michelle, who is already pulling her backpack from the overhead rack.

Five minutes later we are stumbling down a gravel road toward the village, a double row of peasant homes—each with barn and long, narrow field—flanked by a stone, vaguely Norman structure at one end, and, at the other, a red brick Victorian edifice out of *Mary Poppins,* all cornice and ornament, its roof a forest of chimneys, a stork's nest on one of them. The long night on the trains from Łódź has muddied our thinking, even in the crisp country air.

The road crosses some railroad tracks and turns left, away from the distant village. We opt for the tracks, which head in the general direction of the Victorian chimneys. "We must have missed the town," I say.

"I was watching. I don't think we missed anything."

The rails rattle. Looking over my shoulder, I see a train—our train, the only train around—coming slowly toward us. We step aside and it rumbles on by. A pair of storks stand motionless in the marsh beside the tracks.

Ten minutes later the train is back, backing up now toward us from the

152

village. The storks say nothin'. "This is goofy," says Michelle.

This is Białowieża, edge of the country of Poland, end of the line for the PKP—no crossing here into Mother Russia to the east—a tiny village of some 2,000 farmers, foresters and border guards set in the midst of the Mazurian-Podlasian Natural Forest Province, adjacent to Białowieża National Park, 5300 hectacres of virgin forest, one of only three such areas in all of Europe now included in the UNESCO register of "reservations of the biosphere." (The other 6,000 hectacres now lie in the Soviet Union, land once part of Poland. The national boundaries of Central and Eastern Europe are written in sand.) Because this area has been under protection for well over sixty years, it offers a nearly unique environment for biological and ecological study, attracting scientists from all over the world. Others come to study, photograph, or hunt the wildlife: European bison, foxes, red deer, wild boar, lynx, eagles, storks.

Others like us come for a weekend in the country, a hike through pristine forests, a walk along country streams—well, drainage ditches mostly—and through a country village. 150,000 visit the Park each year, including 5,000 foreigners. Most stay at the Hotel Iwa, a modern building of cement, wood and glass built in the late 1960's with unusually courteous service in both restaurant and reception area. Foreigners pay $20 a night for room plus

breakfast; Poles pay about $2. The Iwa is set inside a "Palace Park," surrounded by ancient oaks and soaring spruce, overlooking a pair of artificial lakes, and across a very picturesque wooden bridge from the new railroad station Białowieża Pałac, built in the late sixties at the end of a spur line constructed for tourists. It was down this spur that our train had huffed after somehow turning around at Białowieża Towarowa, pausing in Pałac just long enough to pick up passengers and mail before backing down the spur for Towarowa, there to head out to Hajnówka, thence to the World. (Thus, we discover on our departure, this train covers the seventeen kilometers between Białowieża and Hajnówka in slightly more than an hour, the first twenty minutes of that trip spent backing up that long spur. Thus station Pałac, by far the cleanest and comeliest I saw in Poland, serves only three trains daily. And that a bottom-line lesson in East Bloc resource allocation.)

We spend our the morning of first day in Białowieża checking into Hotel Iwa, exploring the Park Pałacowy, photographing the village, discovering that visitors in the National Park must be accompanied by guides licensed by the PTTK, and hiring such a guide for the morrow. Finally, seeking more territory to explore, we strike out for the old railroad station, tending inexorably toward the end of those steel tracks now lost in the high weeds. We have nothing particular in mind, just a couple of Americans alone in an adventure on the eastern edge of Poland this Easter holiday season.

The tracks do not end. They extend through the grass, through a cut in the woods, to the east, toward Russia waiting mysteriously two or three kilometers away.

"You know," says Michelle, "these trains did not always end here. When that land was Poland, the trains continued east, and the tracks continue east right now. If we followed them through that break in the woods, we would find ourselves at the Russian border. . . ."

He is on us in an instant, roaring out of nowhere on a motorcycle, white letters on his khaki helmet (abbreviations I do not recognize), a red star on his uniform. "Paszport, proszę," he demands. We have no passports, we explain; they are with our other papers at the Hotel Iwa. Noticing Michelle's German Army jacket, he speaks in German. "Hier ist Grenze. Verboten. Die Grenze ist verboten." Lazer beams flash from both eyes; there is not a soft muscle in his body. Probably he eats tourists for breakfast. Shaken, we raise our hands as if in surrender. After a minute of further warnings, he disappears to wherever he came from, and we return hastily to the gravel road, north into town, making excuses to each other. At dinner we are still cracking nervous jokes. Even sleep comes fitfully here on the edge of the Evil Empire.

Saturday we meet our guide for the National Forest, a retired ranger with forty years of experience, most of it managing the bison herd, first in Wigry National Park (also in northeastern Poland) and then in Białowieża. His name is Wojtek, and he speaks fluent English, having served, he says, as a

154

fighter pilot in Britain during World War II. I'm not entirely sure he really belongs to the few to whom so many owed so much, but it's a good story, and we are off to a friendly beginning, chatting amiably as we leave Hotel Iwa and head for the park.

"Please to stop here a moment," he directs Michelle and me. "This is new Hotel Iwa you are looking at. There was old hotel, all wood, beautiful building. Nazis burn it in 1944, night before Russians came. Our new government told us not to worry, we build new one. Then they build this. We told them we like old hotel better, old style of building. Cement is not so good as wood. In city, people get headaches, sickness from chemicals in cement. Wood is for health very good. So people come here for health, and what they get? More cement! You know, is crazy!"

I nod in agreement, and we walk further. Wojtek must be seventy—he was 24 in 1944—but having lived a lifetime in this healthy environment, he sets a stiff pace. We pass through Park Pałacowy, toward the gates of the National Park, looking at trees, sites, buildings. With a sweep of his arm, Wojtek indicates another modern concrete lodge, Dom Myśliwski. "This too was lovely old building. Then came one time Khrushchev and Brezhnev and whole bunch of Russians. Secret Police came four, five days ahead of time, before big fish arrived, get building ready for big chiefs. They clear it up some, making plenty of plans, playing the cards and drinking the vodka. Finally came Brezhnev and Khrushchev in these big black cars, and there is more playing the cards and drinking the vodka and who knows what. Well, that night whole place catches fire. People from village, they come quickly, but *milicja* tell them, 'Do

155

not go near there, you will be shot, you crazy.' So whole place just burns down. Next day, Brezhnev and Khrushchev get in their big black cars, go back home to Russia." He laughs. "Germans, Russians, they burn place down. Poles, they build it back up."

Crossing an open field, we approach the wooden gate which marks the park entrance. The fence is supposed to keep unaccompanied strangers out, although its wooden lattice is broken enough in one place to admit Michelle and me walking side by side. It's also supposed to keep animals inside, although the bison herd lives in the grasslands. "They do not like forest grass," Wojtek says; "it is too bitter." The real reason for the fence, and the guides, is to keep people under control, away from the border, away from fragile elements of the biosphere.

And to tell the story of this place. Wojtek is good with stories, some of which concern the Park: statistics on size, fauna, flora, history. "And insects. Such mosquitoes. In two, three weeks come such mosquitoes, you cannot imagine. Last year one of these women comes with such a short skirt, and the high heels, and in half an hour her legs are all bitten. 'Well, what you expect?' I tell her. One year comes this bunch of American professors, one so large as this. He walks half an hour, cannot go on. What am I going to do? So I send him back with a friend, tell him, 'You just walk a little, then you rest a little, then you walk.' I got to go on with tour. Why such people come here for?"

"There is an American author who writes a lot about National Parks," I respond, "named Ed Abbey. He believes motor vehicles should be banned from all national parks. People should hike in and hike out. If people are too feeble to walk, that is just too bad, because they should keep in shape. If you are too sick to walk, that is also too bad: you should exercise more. If you have a physical handicap, that is just too bad period."

Michelle asks about the yellow plastic bands around some of the trees. They indicate the sites of tape-recordings of bird songs. Forest birds are territorial and mark their own turf, which may be only a few hundred square meters. They keep to the confines of their territory, defending it from outsiders. You just leave a tape recorder, monitor what was said all night, and then come back in a month, in a year to repeat the process at the same point, the same place. Then you study what you hear.

"This tree here. I was working in the park when it fell. I was called King Jagiełło Tree, a huge tree, growing since probably 1410. In that year the King came hunting in this forest, rounded up all the animals, a huge hunt, plenty of game. They drove a lot of it off still living. Then came the Battle of Grünwald."

We stop in front of another huge oak, 400 years old, 17.5 cubic meters of timber, an enormous tree. But some of the old ones have fallen, and recently: a wind storm five years ago, a spell of bitter cold and wind more recently that snapped trees off just above the roots. Wojtek talks about his daughter Ewa,

156

degree in biology, teaching at the Białystok branch of the University of Warsaw, now home for the holiday. About acid rain losses in the surrounding commercial forests, about the timber industry in Hajnówka, about a woman who lost her way, alone, in this park and died, apparently of a heart attack induced by fright, "It was two days before we found her. By then wolves had attacked. Police were all over—a tremendous inquiry."

In the old days, Wojtek says, he was visited by the police after every tour given to Westerners. "Well, they might be spies," the police told him.

"Spies in Białowieża? Spying on what?"

"Still, they might be spies."

"If they are spies, they are your problem. They are not my problem. Leave me alone, thank you."

Wojtek indicates a memorial in the forest, a stone marker, a cross, a wooden shrine covered with patches left by school children, each patch bearing the number of a school and a city name. This elicits another somber story: "Here the Germans killed about 200 old people during the war. The story is this: they had taken a bunch of children prisoner. Maybe these children were running contraband for the underground. Maybe these children were being children, you know? So old people came to Nazis and said, 'Look, these are just children. They have their whole lives ahead of them. We are old people, we have lived our lives. We will be your prisoners. You trade these children for us.' Germans said that this was okay. Then they brought old people here and murdered them all. What made is especially awful was that they left their bodies for the animals. When school children visit this pace, they leave school badges as a thank-you."

In the forest, now suddenly quiet, Wojtek turns oddly defensive of the Germans: "But you know, they were sometimes merciful. They kill people very quickly, did not make them suffer. One time long ago Cossacks tied a prisoner to a tree and just took his clothes away. They ask questions, eh? When he did not give them the information they wanted, they did nothing at all. Just stand there, do nothing. Then came these ants from below and started eating. Bite, bite, bite. And then these mosquitoes. In four hours he was crazy. In eight hours he was dead, no blood left in his body.

"It was Göring who saved this forest. This is true. He thought he was hunter, and this would be his special forest. One German pilot, maybe it was an accident, I do not know, he bombed the church in town. Of course people could do nothing. But after a year they got to talking among themselves, and finally they complain to officials. 'Well it would be very difficult to help you with this problem, because this land belongs all to Herr Göring.' So the people wanted to know where is this Herr Göring. 'He is in Berlin.' So some people went to Berlin, they sent a little delegation, and told Göring that a German pilot had dropped a bomb on this church on his land. Göring gave them 150,000 German marks to rebuild their church. That was in 1944."

Not all of Wojtek's stories are so dark. As a forester he was often called upon to search out animals for visiting photographers and movie-makers. A French team once came for one day of camera work, intent on all kinds of action shots. "One day they have. I told them they must be crazy. But we go out looking, and what we see? Two bison bulls fighting in front of a group of cows. You cannot see such a thing in ten years. These Frenchmen take such pictures, make whole lot of money.

"One time I sit in tower one hour with this Dutch fellow, and he photographs the little foxes playing below. Very valuable pictures."

Many visitors, of course, are hunters. They bring big guns, and they bring big bucks. "One man from Texas, he is showing me pictures of his house, of his own museum. This man makes a museum of all things he is shooting. I am noticing these things in the back of one picture, and I ask him. Yes, yes, these are elephant's feet. So I ask how many of the elephants he is shooting. Eighty. Eighty! Can you believe this? Eighty elephants? Two, three, maybe. But eighty . . . !"

He continues. "One German comes here, is very rich fellow, I know him. He wants to hunt the elk. So he gets this male elk, very big one. Huge elk. You know, you pay for these trophies by the gram. One gram increases the price of a big elk. So this is very expensive. $15,000 he pays for this elk! I hear him on the telephone to his wife, 'Stop the remodeling the house,' he tells her, 'I spend all the money on the elk.'

"Hunters want big males, trophy animals. What they leave? Little males. Little males are left. Little males make little babies. Trophy bucks get fewer and smaller all the time."

There have been softer moments in the forester's life: "One day I am coming home in the car, and this line of bison is crossing the road. It is spring, and there are little ones with their mothers. This little one comes with his mother to road, and he is afraid of crossing pavement. His mother has him locked between her front two feet, pushing him across road, and he is looking out so frightened. . . ."

There are moments of humor: "A few years ago is coming this British man. He is staying here a week, at the Hotel Iwa, a friend of a Pole who lives now in England. I know he is here for some reason, but he is saying nothing. Several days he stays here. So this man on Easter telephones my house, wants to see me. My wife says to me, 'Wojtek, what you see him for now? It is Easter. You stay home, talk with this man tomorrow.' But I say I will visit with this man, find out what it is he wants.

"Well I go see this man. We talk. We drink this tea with some honey, and finally he tells me, 'Wojtek, I am here on a mission,' he tells me. I tell him this I know. He tells me he has friend in England, and I tell him this I know also. He tells me that his friend sent him to dig up some gold he left buried on his land from before the War, in this town nearby. I say, 'But this is not Poland. This is now Russia!' He tells me yes, he knows, but he wants to go get it. I tell him, 'Get out of my house, you crazy. I do not want to hear anything about it.' He tells me the owner will keep 70% of the gold, and he will get 30% and I will get half of his 30%. 'Get out of my house, I do not even want to hear this.' This man, I tell you, he must be crazy."

"The gold buried in Eastern Europe would probably pay the Polish and American national debts twice over," I muse, "but it is going to remain buried forever."

So our 50,000-złotych tour spins out until Wojtek must leave to spend Easter with his daughter. "Maybe the police will come calling, now that you've been talking to two American spies," I suggest as he left. He just laughs. We tip him in hard currency—but not gold—as a thanks for the stories, and head toward the hotel, dinner, and an afternoon bus rise to and from Hajnówka. (What else are you going to do on the Saturday before Easter in a sleepy farm village on the Polish-Russian border?)

That night an odd thing happens. At midnight, the village of Białowieza literally explodes. Jolted from my sleep by the first loud explosions, my first thought is that these must be fireworks . . . although I'd seen no fireworks for sale during the day, and friends who warned of Easter pranks—mostly involving water, and mostly on the Monday *after* Easter—said nothing about Easter Eve or fireworks. But the loud explosions sound like fireworks, maybe cherry bombs. I look out of the corner of my eye for streamers of sparkling red and blue and white coruscations. There are none.

I listen for merriment in the street. Nothing at all.

And then an instant of real terror, vague but palpable as it is irrational,

159

a terror Michelle later confesses to having felt as well, as if the hotel, the town, the pair of us as foreigners, are all under attack. A scene from *Empire of the Sun* flashes across my mind, the first shelling of the hotel, the attack which signals the coming revolution. Is Białowieża under attack? Are the Soviets finally clamping down on Poland? Will I find myself a Russian prisoner come morning? Is this the reason the border was so carefully patrolled? I listen for chaos in the halls, some kind of response by the hotel staff. There is nothing.

An hour or more I listen fearfully, then fall back into an uneasy sleep.

Next morning Michelle and I discover fragments of aerosol cans scattered along village streets: the cherry bombs of the night previous. Easter Sunday has arrived after all, with excited children dressed in their very visit-the-old-folks Sunday best, with crowds of faithful headed toward Easter mass, with a church wedding for one young couple which has waited impatiently all through Lent, when weddings and other festival masses are forbidden. But it has not arrived without anxiety, an anxiety derived, I suppose, from the border patrol and the tales of Nazi terror in the dark forest, from subconscious acknowledgment of the Soviet proximity, from the strangeness of this world.

And from my sudden realization on the bus from Hajnówka to Białowieża that Michelle and I are in unfamiliar terrain indeed, and lightyears from home.

160

Encounters with the Archbureaucrat, Part Seven

> "The occupation of a bureaucrat may be very necessary; it was not long, however, before I had made up my mind (later my conclusion were verified) that bureaucrats are parasites."
>
> —Czesław Miłosz, *Native Realm*

"This is a country that has lost control of its bureaucracy," observes our dinner guest, Robert Jones, visiting Poland for the first time from York, England. "And until it regains control, all other reform will be in vain."

He pauses for another bite of Michelle's garlic bread, another sip of Bulgarian red wine. "Reminds me of my experience in Brazil. I spent two years at the university there in a three-member department: myself, another native-speaker, and the chairman. During my first year, the chairman spent most of his time trying to get the department upgraded to an institute. The foreigners did most of the teaching, while he went from one office to another trying to get his institute. We got monthly progress reports, usually over dinner at a small restaurant. I kept wondering how a three-member institute would function, but I was young and this was his country, so I asked no questions.

"Finally, after long and complicated delays, all necessary documents were signed, by the director of the humanities faculty, by the university rector, by the local politicians, even by the president of the country, and we had out Institute of English Studies. My native-speaking friend and I were summoned to a victory celebration, where, after the toasts and the speeches, we offered a modest proposal: 'Now that we are officially an Institute, might the Institute to do something?'

"'Like what?' asked our puzzled director.

"We suggested a small conference for the secondary level English teachers, co-sponsored perhaps by the British Council, to help them with methodologies and materials. The director adopted our idea as his own, took it and us to the university rector for approval. After listening politely for half and hour, and finally agreeing to support the conference 'in principle,' the rector

161

shook his head sadly and asked our director, 'Why do you wish to make things difficult? The Institute of Portuguese Studies has flourished for twenty-five years without doing a thing.'"

Yes, I admit, Poland is often an adventure on the other side of the looking glass. "I used to be put off by Kafka's surrealism," colleague Tom Samet once remarked, paraphrasing, I think, Philip Roth; "but since coming to Poland, I have come to consider him the most pedestrian of realists."

I pass the observation along to Jones, who laughs the nervous laugh of one lost in the Twilight Zone.

Jones is right: if nineteenth-century capitalism taught us that owners are selfish oafs who give not a damn about the safety of their workers or the general public; care not at all about product quality, the environment, or national welfare; are interested exclusively in maximum profits on minimal risk and investment, then twentieth-century socialism teaches us that workers are selfish oafs who give not a damn about their own safety or the public's; care not at all about product quality, customer service, or the environment; and will, given the opportunity, work as little as possible, steal all they can carry in two hands, and complain about being overworked. The Worker's Paradise amounts finally to Poland, 1990: sloth triumphant, and not a country you would care to live in.

The day after our dinner, I am off with Michelle to match wills against the arch-bureaucrat herself. Our missions are not complicated: pick up the month's pay at the rector's office and, while there, pay the telephone bill; then stop by the train station and buy a pair of round-trip tickets to Hungary, where

Steve Horowicz has invited me to talk about Bob Dylan and America during the Sixties, and maybe bring along a few copies of *A Generation in Motion* for his students. But nothing is simple, because bureaucrats, having infiltrated into even the most mundane corners of public and private life, are alive and thriving even in New Poland.

Collecting pay at the Rektorat, for example, Michelle and I wait half an hour in line at the fourth floor cashier's desk, watching people check their names against a computer-generated master list, receive their money—cash, counted out one bill at a time, and in front of everyone in the room—and sign a receipt. When our turn comes, Michelle collects but my name is nowhere on the pay list. Do I really teach at the University? "Yes, I do. I am a docent professor at the Institute of English Philology. Here is my *legitymacja*." "Ah, a *docent professor* . . . your pay would be at the *first* floor cashier's window. So sorry."

We walk downstairs to the first floor cashier's window (I remember this room now; it *was* here, not upstairs, that I last collected my pay), wait again in line, check the computer print-out, and yes, there is my name. The clerk opens a brown envelope, 10,000 and 20,000 notes to a total of 850,000 złotych are counted into my hand, and I sign a receipt. I ask about the phone bill.

"Phone bill would be in the other building, room 104. I will draw you a map," says the helpful bureaucrat.

Out the front door of the main building, around the corner onto a side street, in the back door of a second building, down a hall, to office 104, knock, knock, knock. The opening door reveals six major-league bureaucrats sipping

tea around a pair of desks. One rummages through a stack of envelopes, finds my phone bill: 15,000 złotych for January, 60,000 for February. On a small slip of paper she writes *75,000 złotych, I, II 1990*. "Take this to the cashier's window on the first floor," she tells me, "and when you're done there, bring the receipt back here so we can record your payment."

Returning to the window where thirty minutes earlier I received my 850,000, I wait again in a short line to speak with the cashier . . . only to be told "next door, you must take this next door first."

Slamming the door to the cashier's office on the first floor of the main building of the Rektorat just a little, I walk next door, where I wait my turn at the usual gray counter. After ten minutes, I present my little slip of paper and the bureaucrat fills out a receipt for 75,000 złotych. "Take this receipt to the cashier's window next door, pay the bill, and get it stamped," she directs. I notice a little window conveniently set in the wall between her office and the cashier's office next door: perhaps she could pass the receipt and my 75,000 złotych through that window, because I have already been to the cashier office twice today and I'm getting a little grumpy. But this is not possible.

Slamming the door to this office just a little bit harder, and grumbling aloud about withholding and direct deposit, I return for the third time to the cashier's window, wait once more, pay my money, get my receipt stamped . . . whereupon I return again to the office in the other building, wait again, have one of the bureaucrats not busy drinking tea inspect my receipt and record that Pichaske has paid his phone bill for the months of January and February, 1990.

Then I head downtown for lunch.

(I have lied here: actually, I lost patience somewhere around the second—or was it the third?—trip to the cashier's window. Michelle got the damned phone bill paid. I headed downtown in search of train tickets.)

Tickets to Budapest involve an even more frustrating encounter with Polish bureaucracy. Remembering that golden day in the fall when I just walked in and bought two tickets to Berlin, I make a half-hearted attempt at Fabryczna Station. No such luck this time: "Tickets to Berlin, Prague, and Budapest are sold only at Kaliska Station." I've lost an hour waiting in line, but this is useful information, and off I go on a number 12 tram to Kaliska Station and wait another half hour in line, only to be told, "Tickets to Berlin, Budapest, and Prague are not sold at these windows. There is another building down the street. You will recognize it when you see it."

I do. It's the building where the line snakes clear out the door and onto the street. Very long. Very slow. Very futile. Two hours after arriving, I am told, "You are a foreigner. Go to the Orbis agency on Piotrkowska Street."

"No tickets here for Budapest?"

"Not for you. You go to the Orbis agency."

"On Piotrkowska."

Back to Piotrkowska, to the Orbis agency, and, finally, no ticket.

"We can sell you a ticket to Budapest for thirty days from now."

"I need to go in eighteen days."

"Nie ma."

I search my calender for another open weekend. "How about 32 days?"

"Perhaps."

"Could you pick up that little telephone on your desk and find out?"

"No."

Foregetting the number one axiom of life in Poland ("*No* never means no; *yes* never means for certain yes"), I express my displeasure in a string of English expletives the general thrust of which should be evident enough to even the stupidest, laziest, most incompetent of bureaucrats. I do not slam the door, but I am plenty steamed . . . until another plan occurs to me: plane instead of train. As a state employee, I can buy airplane tickets in Polish currency, at Polish rates . . . and airplane tickets inside the East Bloc are dirt cheap. Allen Weltzien flies Gdańsk to Warsaw for four bucks. It's time to assert my rights.

At the Orbis Air Office, another line, another clerk, but, wonder of wonders, after half an hour of talking, I have reservations for two, round-trip, Warsaw-Budapest-Warsaw, days of my choice, 120,000 złotych ($12) each. "I will purchase the tickets now," I announce.

"That line over there, sir," a clerk tells me.

Another line, another wait, and a computer prints out my tickets . . . at a price approximately ten times the price quoted at the other counter. "This is the incorrect price," I tell the clerk.

"This is the foreigner's price," she tells me.

"I pay Polish prices," I reply, producing a stack of papers. "I have documents."

"No. These documents allow you to pay for your tickets in Polish currency, but you must still pay the foreigners' price, not the Polish price."

"Other foreigners have flown to conferences at Polish prices."

"It's different when the University itself purchases the tickets for the professors," she tells me. "But that takes a document from the Rektorat. . . ."

I tear the tickets in half, unleash another blizzard of expletives, and head for a private bureau specializing in bus tours. Another line, of course, and another run-around. "Book your tour in our office on Piotrkowska Street."

To Piotrkowska Street, again. And again, no tickets for eighteen days hence. "How about later this month?"

Nothing.

"April?"

Nothing.

"May? June?"

"In June nobody travels to Budapest, so there are no tours. Sorry."

Hell, I quit. It's supper time. "What did you do today in Poland, Dave?"

165

"I collected my pay and paid my phone bill."

Of course there are tours, and of course there are tickets, and of course appropriate people in the airline bureaucracy could have read my papers—secured, I need not say, only after long hours waiting in various university and governmental bureaucracies—and sold me airline tickets to Budapest at Polish prices, payable in Polish currency. The receipt for my phone bill could easily have passed through the window designed specifically for that purpose . . . and all disbursements at the University could easily be handled in one central bureau. But the bureaucrats, intent on making more jobs for more people in more places, or less work for themselves in their own bureaus, or waiting for a bribe, or just being ornery, chose not to. Bartleby triumphant, they would prefer not to, and by golly, they do not have to. The most important, omnipresent, critical service industries in Poland choose not to function unless bribed.

Or threatened with bodily harm, a bad idea even for an American.

Well, the train ticket saga continues, although not on this particular day. It is a story of continuing bureaucratic intricacies, and one worth telling.

Soon after this adventure, while killing time in Warzsawa Centralna waiting to catch the Telimena to Łódź, I note the line at International Trains is surprisingly short, and having nothing better to do, I wait for a turn at the window and pull the arm of the old slot machine one more time: does the clerk maybe have a round-trip ticket to Budapest for two weeks hence?

"What train would you like, sir?"

I mention the 5:00 p.m., and yes, this clerk has just such a ticket.

"Do you have two such tickets?"

"I have only one ticket."

"I will take that ticket, thank you very much," I tell the clerk, pay her $4, and damned if I don't have my ticket *and* reservation for Budapest, simple as asking at the right time and place.

Trouble is, I have only one ticket, and after another week searching in both Łódź and Warsaw, I still have only one ticket.

Thursday before departure, I suggest to Michelle, "I will go up early to Warsaw and check all the stations, all the windows. If I can get another ticket, I will phone you, and you can pack your bag and come up. If I can't get another ticket, I will go alone, do my thing, and get back to Łódź as quickly as I can."

Which I do. I leave Łódź at 6:00 a.m., arrive in Centralna two hours later, wait in a very long queue, ask one more time about a ticket to Budapest, hear one more time, "*nie ma*." Since it is not yet ten and I have the day to kill, I ask myself, "Trains stop in Warsaw East; maybe they sell tickets there."

Warszawa Wschodna it is. Ignoring signs posted at the International Trains window which read very clearly "No more tickets for any trains departing today to Berlin, Budapest, or Prague," I wait in a short line and ask the clerk about tickets to Budapest. By way of answer, she merely points to the sign.

Returning to Centralna, I meet another American also headed for

Budapest. We exchange tales, and the reply she received was slightly different from the one I got earlier this very morning at this very station.

She was told, "Perhaps. Come back after 12:00."

By the time we arrive at the head of the line, that deadline has passed, and what do you think? The clerk has tickets to Budapest on tonight's train.

"Do you have seats on the 5:00?" I ask.

"No, only 11:00."

"Do you have two tickets for the 11:00 train?"

She does not.

"Could I trade this ticket and reservation on the 5:00 for one on the 11:00, and then buy one additional ticket for my wife?'

"I have only one seat on the 11:00 train," the clerk says firmly.

"I will take that ticket, thank you very much," I tell her, put down my $4. In three minutes I have my second round-trip ticket, with reservation.

"I have another ticket," I tell Michelle on the phone, "but it's on the 11:00. You come up here immediately, and we'll talk to the conductor about letting me use my ticket for the 11:00 on the 5:00. Maybe we can work things out. If we can't, we'll travel separately and meet in Budapest."

When the 5:00 pulls into Centralna, Michelle rushes to claim her seat and, after what I hope is not a kiss good-bye, I join the small knot of Poles negotiating with the conductor further back of the train. *"Nie ma, nie ma, nie ma,"* he keeps repeating. No room, no room, no room. I flash my American passport with two U.S. greenbacks inside. "Get aboard quickly," he commands. I jump through the door just as the train pulls out.

With both Michelle and me aboard!

Hey, Shellsers, we have pulled this thing off! Michelle, honey, it's me, your Davey, I am here with you! Shell, I'm coming! I start working my way up the train, one car to the next, to break the good news.

But the door between cars is locked. Worse, I encounter another conductor, who of course wants to see my ticket, which I show him, and my reservation, which I also show him, and of course it is for the 11:00.

"Your colleague said I could ride this train."

"Nie, nie. You will have to get off at the next station, then wait a few hours until your train comes through. You get off in Częstochowa."

Well, I am not getting off in Częstochowa, you can bet the mortgage to your house on that. I drop back a few cars on the speeding train, run into the first conductor. He is all smiles. "Come with me," he indicates.

I follow him into an absolutely empty compartment, eight unoccupied second-class seats. I give him two dollars, he writes me a reservation ticket, smiles, wishes me a good journey. Four hours later at the Czech border, I finally make contact with Michelle, leading her back to my empty second-class compartment. By 10:30 we're sprawled across the seats, snoozing peacefully.

By 6:30 the next morning, we are in Hungary. Together.

Street Workers

They are an early-to-bed-early to rise lot, already busily at work when I catch the 7:30 bus to the Institute, and usually finished their work—or nowhere to be seen—by early afternoon. I doubt they are paid much (when my students complain of Polish "workers" being paid more than doctors and intellectuals, they mean shipyard workers and coal miners), and their labor has no social prestige. They seem to be a dwindling number in the New Poland, as local government finds itself squeezed for revenue, confronting escalating prices and increased demands for service. But, welcome to western capitalism, the poorest paid and the least prestigious jobs are among the most useful. Poland is one of the neatest countries you'd care to ever visit. It's not Germany, admittedly, where women still scrub the street in front of their house each morning, but it's not Amsterdam or New York either, full of litter and dog droppings. Or London either, a tidy town two decades ago, gone to garbage lately. Polish buildings may be tan-and-gray drab, chipped and crumbling, but you'll not see much litter in the streets of Łódź. And for that I thank the street workers.

You see them mostly in the morning, as I said, the men in their blue or gray uniforms or sometimes in just street clothes, the women in skirt and sweater and bandana, with shovels and pushcarts and brooms, hard at work keeping Łódź beautiful. On the streets, in the parks, on sidewalks and plazas, at the museums and monuments, trimming, sweeping, hauling, dumping.

Three times during one two-hour wait in front of the Gdańsk train station I watched a worker sweep up cigarette butts, litter, cherry pits, and dirt from around the bench on which I sat. In Malbork I saw a small battalion of women sweeping leaves from the cobblestone courtyard. The road to our flat and the waiting area at the local bus stop are swept every morning of every day of the year by our local street sweeper, who is as conscientious a person as ever I met.

In fact, she's a maniac about sweeping. With her twig broom—the

169

same style of broom used by Paris streetworkers years ago to guide trash into the gutter and down the sewer and off, I suppose, to the Seine, this before the Paris streetworkers got themselves proper modern brooms, plastic bristles molded to resemble the old wooden twigs, no less—with her broom, this woman sweeps dirt from sidewalk and leaves from the street, discarded bus tickets from the curb, grass from the edge of the sidewalk. When the weeping willow weeps, she sweeps wept willow from the walk and from the dirt below the tree. She sweeps around the apartment buildings, ours and the neighboring blok. When she's done sweeping, she tends the rather substantial gardens beside both buildings, trimming, planting, cultivating, weeding, coaxing into blossom a whole spring, summer and fall of color, including pansies and hollyhocks, my personal favorites, and roses, the staple of Polish gardens everywhere. I had intended to bring her some nice Western tool—pruning shears, hedge clippers, a rake—from the States our second year in Poland, but of course I forgot. More than once I have felt the urge to drop say 100,000 złotych in her hand as a reward for a job well done. I think that would be a nice gesture, for people to reward public employees doing an especially conscientious jobs, although it might be misinterpreted in Poland, and it might set a bad precedent. Possibly it would offend her: she takes obvious pride in her labor, the integrity of which payment might impugn. Maybe the best gift is a smile and a thank-you, although maybe I'm letting myself off easy.

This woman is not alone in her nearly Germanic thoroughness. They're all out in the early morning, doing the necessary work. Even around the garbage dumpsters, although trash-picking poor are increasingly common, you won't find a lot of trash on the streets of Łódź. Not around the public buildings, not along the shopping district streets. Public markets are a holy mess each Saturday evening, but come Monday it's all gone somewhere.

Man, can I respect tidiness!

Spring it's fallen blossoms; summer it's twigs; autumn it's leaves. Winter is the major problems in this low-technology country. Snow removal,

for example, is mostly by hand. Light snow is swept away with the twig brooms used on grass clippings and leaves. Heavier snow is shoveled with large squares of plywood nailed to machined wooden handles—they resemble the placards waved at American political conventions or demonstrations, two feet by two feet. They're effective snow shovels, I guess, but lack shape and of course toughness at the edge, which is quickly shredded by the cement walk. Gradually the plywood erodes from two feet to a foot and a half, to a foot, edge irregular, not lifting as much as it once did with each pitch of the shovel, increasingly ineffective at chipping packed and caked snow on heavily trodden walks. Get it early, or the getting gets tough.

Especially snow becomes a problem after a period of thaw and freezing. I've seen streetworkers in Łódź banging away at ice with their plywood shovels and with steel bars similar to the one my father uses to break shale in the hills of western Virginia before planting a bush or a tree: steel rods with no particular ice-chipping end, not the tools you buy at Hardware Hank specifically designed for ice removal. Bit by bit, however, workers clear whole walks, piling ice in heaps, before hauling it off in carts or wheelbarrows. It's cold, tedious, unpleasant work, but gradually the job gets done.

Carts are used by streetworkers for hauling more than litter and chipped ice. I see them frequently in downtown Łódź, pushed down the middle of Piotrkowska or Kościuszki by older men and even women, loaded with paper and cardboard collected at the larger stores and headed for some centralized recycling centers. Whether or not the cardboard recycled justifies that tremendous amount of human energy involved in this particular recycling process, it's good to see natural resources conserved, and it's good to see people at work.

Again the impulse to walk up and hand somebody a 100,000-złotych note, and again the fear of paronizing them. One afternoon I did insist on helping an especially older woman with a very tall load of cardboard, pushing her cart several blocks down Kościuszki from Central Store to a collection center. In retrospect, I'm not sure whether I helped or insulted her. She was certainly surprised, as were folks at the recycling point.

I don't know whether any social disesteem attaches to these jobs, whether they are assignments one got by crossing Party ideologues, or failing college entrance exams, or being fired from too many other jobs, or being stupid or drunk or useless or inept . . . but I empathize strongly with the street workers. I collected garbage one summer during my college years, and I've also worked cleaning streets and parks. I know it's a tough, ill-paid life. These people work harder, under more uncomfortable conditions, at greater risk to their health, than the bureaucrats and the service industry people, and they seem considerably more conscientious. This is certainly not the kind of job most of my students would ever dream of taking, at least not in Poland, although a season or two on the streets would do them good. Maybe it would do me good too: put in some socially useful work for a change, quit talking, forget the insubstantial and inconsequential student essays and conference papers, get off the typewriter and on the shovel. I'm all for intellectuals putting in a few weeks in the potato and rice fields.

I might even one day deliver a lecture at the Institute dressed in the blue or gray uniform of a Polish street worker, offering if an not an example, a statement: "Street workers do a good job with minimal equipment, and their work contributes much to the charm of an otherwise bleak landscape. Can you say the same about yourself?"

Polish Woodstock

"Rock Jarocin 1991" reads the T-shirt, black on white or white on black. It costs $3. Small only, this being the third day of the festival, but the woman does have two XL in a loud shade of peach. I buy two of those (they fit; the smarter black-and-white models will be of no use to anyone over the age of seven), and tuck one into my shirt and give the other to Agnieszka Jabłońska, my companion at this the eleventh annual Polish Rock Festival, and I wish I had brought a few more złotych, because there is a very nice Sting T-shirt for $6 that daughter Kristin would just love, and where in the States can you get a Sting T-shirt for that kind of money, but I blew my wad on tickets—$6 apiece—and ice cream and the train from Poznań to Jarocin, so Sting will have to wait, but I should be happy to have these two peach beauties, and let's get on with the music, and the seeing and being seen, and the scene in general.

It's a small town, Jarocin, and the festival quite overwhelms it. On the ride over, Agnieszka and I worried about finding the music, but amplified sound could be heard even before our train stopped, bouncing off brick and cement walls, emanating vaguely from the far end of town, by the football stadium. Her friends had fretted about thieves and hooligans, but cops are everywhere, beginning at the station, thickening toward the town center, thinning out toward the concert site (maybe they are in plain clothes there). Anyway, you want to get to the music, follow your ears or the line of *policja* away from the tracks, around one corner, into center city past an unmemorable market square festive with "Rock Jarocin 1991" banners, past the truck selling bottled soda pop and cartons of fruit juice, toward the lights, toward the noise. On your way, study the Polish Punkers in their Mohawks, black leather jackets, and torn jeans, a look of studied aggression on their faces, but nothing, really nothing to fear, and in a way mildly amusing: their black boots are still East Bloc soft, and these Bad Dudes walk out of their way at corners to cross at the zebra stripes. The coloring in the hair is a washed out shade of blue or red, nothing like the flames on a British punker's shoulders, and ear rings are limited, usually, to one per ear. One fellow has ripped out both cheeks of his pair of Levi's, and flashes a lot of hairy ass at passers-by, but he's the badest of the bad. Alcohol is forbidden in Jarocin

173

during the three days of festival, and inhale as deeply as I can, I sniff not a trace of Turkish Gold. Jarocin is Woodstock without dope, no threat of Altamont or Brixton. Even the foreigners from Holland, Germany and England are well behaved.

Or maybe they're just a little fagged out. This festival has been going on for two days, building toward a big Saturday finish today: 24-hour music on the rock stage, and the folk stage and jam sessions in odd corners of town. Fans have been crashing in tents or on sleeping bags or just curled up on blankets for a couple of nights, sleeping as best they can, eating what provisions they have brought or care to purchase (very little price gouging, considering the opportunity: I would have thought citizens of Jarocin would squeeze this thing for more than they are apparently getting). Music freaks lie in heaps around the perimeter of the stadium, spaced-out black-and-blue sacks of unconsciousness, their brains trashed by overdoses of heavy metal. Walk carefully. Avoid the fence, which has functioned as a toilet for the past two days. Observe the fans, observe the midde-aged Western observers of the fans, observe the fans observe the middle-aged Westerners, observe the stage, the musicians.

The stage is simple by western standards: two banks of speakers stacked three high, blasting sound against your chest and ears as you walk by, spotlight from raised sound booth a hundred meters to the front, some overhead lighting, but none of the tangled, flashing erector set of tubes and lights and cables that accompanies most Western rock groups, gyrating and pulsating to their music, spinning, revolving, doing everything except count the gate and calculate gross

receipts. For a backdrop, squares of white cloth stretched across wood frames, painted in black with graffiti and silhouettes of the famous: Lech Wałęsa beside Marilyn Monroe, James Dean, Elvis Presley and Charlie Chaplin. "We want to go further and further . . . and to get a Mercedes." In the gathering dusk, a half-naked lead singer impersonates early Mick Jagger as his drummer flails away behind him. If you can't play well, play loud. Vibrations waft through numb ears into aggression-sated skulls which are mostly just resting, at the moment, before 8:00, when the heavies come on and live television coverage begins and this place really cranks up. What the hell—his kid can honestly say he played Jarocin, and nobody will ever ask whether he followed Pink Floyd or strummed an acoustic guitar in the men's can. He's even got a T-shirt to prove he was there.

We've played Jarocin too, Agnieszka and I, and we also have T-shirts to prove it. We've seen the heavy metal stage and all the punkers and their birds, perched like black vultures on the low railing beside the sidewalk entering the exiting the stage area. Noise rattles our ear drums. Threading our way through semi-conscious bodies, we reach the front gate just in time to see an ambulance, accompanied by several police, whisk some burned out hunk of a punker toward recovery in some atmosphere more serene than this stadium. Then we exit with the ambulance through a crowd of late-comers milling around the gate, perhaps hoping to buy a discounted ticket from somebody like ourselves, somebody leaving never to return, a little blue-and-black pass, "Festiwal Muzyki Rockowej/Agencja Rock Corporation," which would admit them cheaply to that big finish. Maybe they intend to crash (seems unlikely: they're pretty chilled out). Maybe they're awaiting some moment late in the evening when the gate opens and music is on the house. Maybe they just want to hear what they can hear from the outside, which would be the Polish thing to do.

We're also outside, headed for the folk stage, down streets lined with cars selling souvenir T-shirts, kiełbasa and ice cream, through a small park strewn with more black-and-blue bodies, past a battered Trabant with one of those plastic hands sticking out of the trunk, attached to a nearly invisible string with which the driver gives it a life-like twitch every thirty seconds or so. Past the old Protestant church where two fans keep candle-lit vigil in front of a makeshift shrine. To the folk stage (free at Jarocin '91) where the amplification system is under control, where the music is, it seems to me, a little better and a little more variegated than what's going on at the main stage.

Where we can sit on a wooden bench under the darkening sky and count the stars and listen to the tunes and talk quietly with each other.

(You know how these things work: the focus of attention is never where it's at. What's really happening goes down in a street corner or on a side stage, enjoyed by only a few . . . who then spread the word, and next year what was out is in, but by then it's not really in, because the focus of attention is usually never where it's really at.)

175

On stage when we arrive are a drummer, a bass, a guitar, and a clarinet. The clarinet works okay, although I've never before heard one in a folk group. Then a second Polish group, this one singing in English and in Polish, doing instrumentals with titles like "The District Attorney Defends Himself" and "The Stockholm Police Chase Each Other Through Sex Shops." Far out! Then a Dutch folksinger, who opens with "the obligatory Dylan" ("The Wicked Messenger") before moving to traditional Irish and British songs, including a mild political statement titled "Fuck the British Army."   A Polish folk group in full mountain costume: balalaika, drums, pipes, recorders, mandolins. One song from the nineteenth century is titled "It's Good in America."   A Polish folk group from Warsaw, extremely professional, playing music from Ecuador. Even their leads are in Spanish: "*uno, dos, tres, cuatros. . . .*"   "This is the music of the future," their leader preaches to the already converted: "*natural* music, nothing electric or synthetic about our instruments."   Video-cameras whirl around the group as it plays, and tape recorders: this bunch is obviously a favorite of organizers and promoters. I don't understand why Poland should go to Ecuador to find the natural music of the future, but the musicians are professional in the extreme, including the single female (her red dress contrasts sharply with the black and grey parkas of the other musicians), whose main job seems to be to swing forward and back in time to the music's syncopations. Ecstatic fans dance in the aisle.

More changes of sets and performers, each change necessitating careful rebalancing of microphones as performers of this natural music demand the most flattering electronic amplification possible. Members of different groups come together in ad hoc performances, singing Polish, Russian, Czech, English. A duo from Britain offers debased Jethro Tull. The Jorgi Quartet appears, a very talented trio (despite the name) of professional musicians working out of Warsaw, their songs long and intricate with syncopations, counter-rhythms, and changes of key, their motifs mostly borrowed from Polish mountain music. Cello, bass, and metal and wood pipes. Guitar and bass are used as often as percussion instruments as as they are bowed, the very epitome of folk-art music, but quite popular here, and in Warsaw, and even in Łódź, where I twice heard them in the Jazz Club 77 on Piotrkowska Street.

Late in the night (or early in the morning) a group from Yugoslavia or Turkey (we are not sure) singing in some tongue neither of us can recognize, the lead singer given to shouting angrily into the microphone at the audience or the band, then returning the mike to its stand to stalk around the stage, even off the stage, like a tall, hunched-over bear, boring into his guitarist or the audience with coal-black eyes, long hair trailing behind him in the breeze, thence to return to his mike for more lyrics spitted angrily into the darkness.

By the time his group has finished, not a hundred fans remain at the folk stage. Not a vibration is heard from the heavy metal stage somewhere in the distance. Moonlight reflects from the polished surfaces of the cobblestones on market square as we return to the train station.

"What I would really like," I confess to Agnieszka, "is one of those cloth banners that reads 'Rock Jarocin 91.' What a tremendous souvenir that would make."

"Maybe if you ran really quickly," she answers dubiously.

Then, quietly, almost to herself, "You Americans are very different from us Poles. . . ."

Well shit—late as it is, cops abound, watchful as ever, and a few punksters straggling toward departure. I don't need me or her or both of us to be packed off to jail, and what the hell, we have the bright peach T-shirts, and photographs as well, and tunes in the head and pictures in the mind, and just a little more insight into the soul of this remarkable people which so loves music of all varieties. It's been a really good evening, one of the fine moments to keep locked away forever in my head. Why wreck it? Who needs a banner anyway?

177

Three Who Made It

It's hard to say what astonished me more: the Polish naiveté regarding fundamentals of capitalism, or the speed with which Poles learned their sometimes painful lessons in free-market economy. For example, the notion that a product's price must exceed its cost of production seemed entirely foreign to their minds. Who could even tell what the cost of production was? Who kept accounts? Who considered consumer demand? Who had heard of a marketing survey? And inflation-deflation? Poles naively assumed that inflation was the sole option: prices only increased, the value of the złoty only decreased. Buy an infinite supply of whatever the market made available while prices were lower than they would become; convert all your money to hard currency, and hide it in a teapot. For their part, producers assumed that the buying public had an almost infinite capacity to absorb whatever goods a merchant could provide, at virtually any price he set, quite independent of such considerations as competing goods and services, the laws of supply and demand, and the general atmosphere of the shop. Everyone assumed that anybody who stooped to go into private business would automatically become wealthy.

But in 1990 Poles learned that the value of the dollar against the złoty could actually drop, and that savings put in złotych accounts at 50% interest outperformed savings stashed in the teapot. That prices might drop as well as rise. That goods could become so plentiful as to make lifetime stashes cumbersome and unnecessary. That the market would not absorb whatever commodities a supplier chose to throw at it, at whatever prices he set. That not all capitalists become rich over night. That an attractive shop offering friendly service might make the difference between success and failure.

That even in a capitalist economy, failure is possible.

Poland's venture into capitalism was far enough along by spring, 1991 that several private shops had already failed. Intermak sticks most prominently in my mind, a multi-roomed, privatized yuppie shop when it opened, complete with red awnings and a row of banners hung from light posts all up and down the sidewalk and a stylized western-style logo. Its clean, bright windows were filled with cartons of pasteurized (French) milk, packaged (German) cakes, tins of

Mövenpick tea.   For a few months it was the talk of downtown Łódź.   But Intermak's location was just a bit out-of-the-way, and soon more conveniently situated shops on Piotrkowska stocked identical products.   The owner apparently tried to leapfrog ahead of his competition with a frozen yogurt machine, but this proved one jump too far for Łódź in winter 1990-91.   So there was a period of brave front, when the shop stayed open and well dressed sales clerks gazed idly out its windows at passing non-customers, and then there was the period of locked doors with a sign on the window, and now Intermak sits quite empty, its fading red banners a potent reminder that all that rises does not necessarily reach the heavens.

But my purpose is not to speak of failures, it is to focus on three commercial successes not in wealthy, cosmopolitan Warsaw, not in touristed Kraków, but in the working-class city of Łódź.   Three cases of entrepreneurs walking, as it were, off the edge of conventional communist economic wisdom, learning a few tough lessons and grasping a few basic principles, and flourishing.   Here are three different businesses, three different stories, three different reasons for success (at least to spring, 1991), each proof that there is money to be had in Poland, even in depressed Łódź, and you do not have to run off to Britain or America to Make It.

The first of these enterprises is perhaps the simplest: a private grocery which opened at the corner of Północna and Mariana Buczka (since 1990, Alexandra Kaminskiego) not 200 steps from our flat.   With all the fanfare of a new coat of paint and steel grills over the windows, this shop opened in the spring of 1990, when many private groceries were opening, including one half way around the block.   It flourished for three simple reasons.

First, it stays open longer on more days of the week than competitors. Michelle and I nicknamed it "The Seven-Eleven Spożywczy" because of its hours.   We, and others in the neighborhood, spent a lot of money there when other shops were closed.

Then the owner struck on two ideas which were to make his fortune: beer and video cassette rental.   At first he sold only one brand of beer, Żywiec, a good Polish beer hard to find in Łódź, which, by driving frequently to the brewery south of Kraków, he managed always to keep in stock.   Neighborhood beer-drinkers drank prodigiously, conditioned by the Polish axiom, "Nothing good lasts very long." Gradually they learned that the beer would always be there, and their appetites abated. Still, this store is the neighborhood beer center

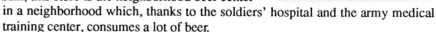

in a neighborhood which, thanks to the soldiers' hospital and the army medical training center, consumes a lot of beer.

The owner's venture into video-rental was equally successful. You walked into the store for a loaf of bread or a few bottles of *piwo,* and on the screen of his TV-VCR you saw *Sesame Street* or the Smurfs or some grade B western, and you just naturally stopped to watch, check out rental fees, and maybe head out the door with a couple of tapes for the wife and kids. Whether the owner conceptualized this combination of groceries and videos himself, or borrowed it from some U.S. Stop-and-Go store, I don't know. However, the combination made his fortune, nearly crowded out all other commodities, allowed him to restrict his hours and let him hire a bunch of clerks to do his work for him. If he advertises at all, it is with a simple board hung on a telephone pole, bearing the single word *PIWO.*

The Golden Duck Restaurant, 79 Piotrkowska, is a different matter entirely: class operation all the way, no drunks hanging out here, wine preferred over beer, although you can order western beer in aluminum cans with dinner. A red awning with rich golden letters—English, Chinese, very small Polish, there on the logo—identifies the establishment, which, being just down the street from the Grand Hotel, attracts a lot of foreign visitors. The Golden Duck today offers a rather extensive menu in Polish, German, and English; waiters in black suits and white shirts who give good service and speak several languages; and take-out service available at a 10% discount. Diners sit on plush red seats, at tables with elegant white tablecloths covered with deep red napkins. The usual Chinese bric-a-brac comprise the interior decor, with black and gold lanterns, live rubber trees, wall paintings. A vase of flowers adorns each table, and a bouncer guards the door.

When first the Golden Duck opened, Michelle and I often dined there alone. Poles were generally unfamiliar with Chinese cooking, and waiters advised customers the pork was going to arrive cut into small bits, not in one large Polish brick. One evening when Michelle was finishing a can of beer, two small boys snuck up to the table, asking if they could have her empty can to collect the deposit. The owner himself chased them off. Seats were plain, the menu was one language only, and as often as not only a couple of "Chinese" dishes were available. We sympathized with the owner's problems in keeping a restaurant functioning given the then-chronic Polish food shortages, and because we were thrilled to have a more or less genuine Chinese restaurant in Łódź—and because dinner at the Golden Duck then cost only a few bucks apiece—we ate there often, bringing friends whenever possible.

When we returned to Poland in the fall of 1990 after summer abroad, the owner had a surprise for us: he had privatized the restaurant. Elegant red-and-black paper napkins had been printed, and gold-and-black business cards. No more boys hustling aluminum cans. Redecorated interior and a new menu. Larger portions and slightly larger prices. Noticeably more customers, as the doors of Łódź continued to open to the West, and German and Austrian businessmen sought alternatives to the heavy Polish cousine at the Grand Hotel. One night I overheard an Austrian tell the waiter, "I have had the duck and the chicken my last two nights here; now I want you to recommend something else." If the Grand Hotel ever wakes up and upgrades its restaurant, the Golden Duck may be in slight trouble, but by then Łódź will be a thriving hub of international commerce. The owner of this restaurant passed a critical threshold somewhere in the fall of 1990, and he appears set for quite some time.

What made the Golden Duck was a combination of its excellent location (coupled with the increased foreign interest in Łódź), the owner's

insistence on quality, and his two years' experience in London at various Chinese restaurants, whose business cards of can be found posted on the front door of the Golden Duck. The man knew his business, bet on a new, western-oriented Łódź, picked his clientele, and won the gamble.

Jet Tours/Rainbow Tours does not sell beer, and its location—up the street from the Grand Hotel and the (once) internationally famous Roszkowski Confectionary—is not entirely convenient. Except for a few turquoise, yellow and lavender flags proclaiming "Jet Tours," you would not know this place exists, frankly, because it's tucked back in one of those court areas off a side street off Piotrkowska. Jet Tours advertising took the form of a large billboard (oil paint on canvas stretched over a steel frame, standard Polish advertising sign) located first at the very busy intersection of Piotrkowska and Piłsudskiego, then at Fabryczna train station. Jet Tours is the house that advertising built . . . with help from the utterly inadequate, state-owned Orbis Travel Agency, and the general opening up of Poland the the West.

Sławek Wiesławski, general manager of Jet Tours, is still technically a fifth-year student at the English Institute, but he, like his colleague Grzegorz, has put his studies on hold to devote full time to the business. I remember vividly the founding of Jet Tours, thinking maybe I should help bankroll this venture in capitalism, hesitating, deciding finally I would support it in the best way I could: by having Sławek handle all my international travel . . . not a difficult decision, really, since I had not once visited the Orbis agency and come away with anything close to satisfaction, let alone tickets for an airplane flight. Pan Am was also arrogant, American Airlines had not yet arrived on the scene, and Lot was just Orbis with another name and bureaucracy. So Jet Tours handled our flight arrangements, and the arrangements of other Fulbrights I recruited, and a very difficult time they had of it in those days.

In the early months customers paid for air tickets in hard currency only. The actual tickets had to be bought in Berlin. Twice each week, Sławek and Grzegorz drove their battered Fiat from Łódź to Berlin and back (ten hours each way, even with a minimal delay at the border), carrying with them several thousands of dollars, returning with airline tickets for their clients. There was no other way. Once I accompanied them, tending the car as they scouted services and connections at Tegel Airport, fending off a German cop who drove up all hot to bust this illegally parked Polish Fiat, then turned polite as pie when I flashed my American passport. That journey remains one of the great epic odysseys of my life, an exercise in improvisation in the teeth of one roadblock after another: hostile border guards, hostile airport officials, hostile cops, hostile Berliners on both sides of the wall. I can't imagine making such a journey twice monthly, let alone twice each week.

And I remember the opening of Rainbow/Jet office, remember thinking how new and pristine everything looked, wondering if this venture was really going to fly.

It's hard to get into the place these days (larger offices are being renovated in a new location just off Piotrkowska). The office looks as if a political campaign was being run out of it: notes everywhere, papers heaped on shelves, desks a mess—business, business, business. S ławek and Grzegorz, of course, no longer drive to Berlin to pick up tickets, and with the newly unified Germany and reconfigurations in airline schedules, it's just as cheap to fly trans-Atlantic out of Warsaw as out of Berlin anyway. Jet Tours has patched into American Airlines' computer network, and can make reservations all over the world. It can book flights on Lot, Delta, American or even Bulgarian Airlines. It can book reservations on the night ferry to England, one of S ławek's coups: "I requested just a few tickets a year ago, but P and O Ferries said they needed some big agency like Orbis. I got nothing. Then a couple of months ago, they phoned me, asking if I was still interested. I asked them about Orbis, and their only response was, 'confidentially, the people at Orbis didn't know what they were doing.' This we already knew. Anyway, they offered me several tickets at quite good terms, really. We use their ferries for the bus trips to England."

The bus trips—the Rainbow Tours end of the operation—are this office's greatest success: 30 hours by bus, direct from Łódź to London. $125 round trip, which for Poles is quite cheap, and easy access for trading or work. All my students from the English Institute book their summer transportation to England at Rainbow Tours. "It helped when Germany reunified and we had only one border to cross," Grzegorz tells me. "And then we had a big upsurge in business when Germany allowed Poles in visa-free."

"If England ever allows Poles visa-free entrance, this operation is going to be a gold mine," I observe.

"It already is," he tells me confidentially; "in July we are sending eleven buses to London in one week." Multiply that out, at 52 seats per bus, and you will understand where Sławek found the money for a new flat and a new car, why he and Grzegorz are content to shelve their English studies, why Sławek's wife Agata is pleased as piwo to work her tail off here, why the couple has not had a prolonged holiday in over a year.

Something in me takes great vicarious pleasure in the successes of these enterprises, each so close in its own way to my life in Poland. I cannot really claim to have played any role in their success, except to applaud from the sidelines. However, I also sense a loss of that Old Poland that at once enchanted and maddened, the loss of Difficulty and Inscrutability, the loss of my status as Special, the loss of innocence. Something's gone and something's gained, as Joni Mitchell once sang.

But in balance I am more than happy for the New Poland, and for the small part played in it by three entrepreneurs in Łódź who have made it.

184

Cityscape: Poznań

The Great Romanesque buildings of the old Kaiser's palace hunker heavily on St. Martin Street, just outside of Poznań Głowny railroad station, their gray stone walls now blackened by auto and bus exhaust. The black accentuates their squat, stubby, square towers capped by low pyramids, the heavy, low arches framing small windows, the broad, horizontal stairway leading to what is now a cinema. Across the street, more heavy neo-Norman architecture: the Wielkopolski Bank Kredytowy. Behind, the Berliner heaviness of the Poznań Opera rises in neoclassical simplicity, either side of the entrance flanked with a large lion. (The interior is lighter, mostly gold and crystal reflected in mirrored walls and marble floors.) Across a small square, the neo-Renaissance buildings of Adam Mickiewicz University, dark as everything else in the neighborhood: the Aula and Collegium Minus, with a splendid baroque meeting hall upstairs. In the middle of the square, a typically heavy East Bloc monument: two thick crosses, one bearing the date 1956 in memory of the Poznań riots of that year, the other bearing the dates 1956, 1968 (student demonstrations, mostly in Warsaw), 1970 (demonstrations at Gdańsk), 1976 (Radom), 1980 (Solidarność), and 1981 (martial law).

Poznań is a heavy city, old German heavy, roof lines red or black with tile, whose sharp peaks bubble at intervals to incorporate the low half-oval window of Berlin roofs. In some older buildings, you still see a lot of German timber ornamentation, especially along the upper stories and under the eaves. There are several brick and half-timber buildings reminiscent of Bavarian architecture; some of the side walls rise on the top story in a scrolled steps common in northern Germany. Elsewhere around Poznań, more Berliner neoclassical or Jugendstyl, stucco over brick, painted, once, a yellow or orange or dull gray, darkened now to diesel-fume black.

An old, German, heavy city with broad streets and a bustling populace and—for Poland—a thriving economy. Smudged exteriors aside, a tidy city: "You can always tell when you're in a part of Poland that once belonged to Germany," a Pole once told me. "The cities are cleaner, the people more industrious. Poles do not like to admit it, but that's just a fact. Maybe there are

185

Polish people living in these places today, but they behave as if they were Germans. Perhaps geography conditions people more than ethnicity."

Poznań is a city largely in possession of its soul: it lacks Warsaw's pretension, Kraków's self-consciousness, Gdańsk's aggressive working-class mentality. Ship engines are built here: the technology is a little higher. The Poznań English Institute is acclaimed throughout Poland as *the* best for English philology (it's Łódź, of course, for literature). In the presidential elections of 1990, former Prime Minister Tadeusz Mazowiecki, the intellectual, received a greater plurality from Poznań, his home town, than from any other part of Poland. Poznań hosts the annual International Trade Fair, biggest trade fair in Poland. The Poznań consulate is infinitely more pleasant than the American Embassy in Warsaw, or certainly was when Tom and June Carmichael were there. Situated directly on the train line between Berlin and Warsaw (with Moscow to the distant east), Poznań owes its considerable sophistication in part to the presence of Westerners. In town for an conference in the spring of 1991, who should I run into but my old friend Brother Leo Ryan, Dean of Commerce at DePaul University, come to Poznań to finalize arrangements for a seminar in Western business theory and practice. Things like that happen in Poznań.

Poznań contains two zoological gardens, one nearly in center city, the other at a quiet remove from downtown confusion.

Poznań contains a number of old churches, and on Sunday morning you open your windows to the sound of church bells.

Poznań contains two, almost three large lakes, where Poles swim, sunbathe, jog, picnic, play sports.

Poznań offers a greater variety of Western goods than any other major Polish city, including Warsaw. It was in Poznań that Michelle and I were finally able to buy an electric toaster in spring, 1990.

Poznań, which goes back even to Piast Poland, has preserved its past: on the far side of the river remain fragments some Gothic chapels and a rebuilt cathedral.

Food is good in Poznań. Poland's best bakery is the Merkury Bakery, and the Merkury restaurant is not bad either. Downtown, any number of small, absolutely acceptable eateries, including a little café operated by an Iraqi immigrant who likes to play his own ethnic music for visiting Americans during the late hours; and the ice cream parlor with the white grand piano on the far corner of market square; and the Restaurant Club Elite, in the middle of square, in the building next to the watering trough with the bronze statue of the little girl. Here, in Poznań's prime location, $8 buys you cutlet stuffed with liver paté, boiled potatoes, cauliflower in cheese sauce, cabbage salad, and a non-alcoholic drink. Try the Lithuanian beet root soup too, while you're at it. Fresh carpet on the floors, newly painted beamed ceiling, attentive waitresses, leaded glass windows looking out onto the square, and a fresh rose floating in a brandy snifter on each table. Beer available, always.

Poznań is Berlin of 1960 available in 1992, at German prices of 1970.

Poznań is a city of museums, none of them particularly crowded. Most popular is the Old Garrison Museum and Cemetery, the museum filled with World War II memorabilia; the museum grounds filled with tanks, air planes, trucks, and artillery; the cemetery filled with graves British (narrow), Polish (equally narrow) and Russian (spacious). Drive toward downtown Poznań, then follow the signs, some of which are in English. If the gate to the Museum grounds is locked, an attendant will give you the key to the padlock: let yourself in and browse to your heart's content. A museum of musical instruments on the perimeter of old town square houses instruments from all over the world, made from brass and wood and shells and skins, instruments fashioned from turtles and deer skulls, from animal horns and tree trunks. Two glass harmonicas. One of Chopin's (apparently numerous) pianos. A heap of regimental snare drums from the early 1800s. Several "dudy" (a bagpipe-like instrument made from the stomach of a cow, with a horn shaped to resemble a goat or ram).

The military museum's collection of pikes, armor, sabers, and other weaponry approaches the Tower of London display. There is the City Museum, with a display relating to the Uprising of 1956: photographs, a list of citizen-martyrs (many mere teenagers), artifacts, the shirt of one victim, blood-ringed bullet hole directly over the heart. There is a very fine branch of the national art gallery, its exterior a monument itself, all heavy with mosaics and nineteenth-century ornamentation, its interior rich with works by Dutch and French painters as well as Poles, especially Malczewski. The mediaeval and Renaissance

187

paintings are especially well restored, few, carefully chosen, high in quality.

There is an ethnographic museum with a wonderful collection of folk wood carvings. There is the old town hall, restored, with a celebrated goat clock (overly celebrated, methinks: I've visited Munich), commemorating the Goat that Saved Poznań by escaping one market day to the top of the tower, whence his owner followed him, from which vantage point he observed a fire which might have destroyed the city. The tower was burned during World War II from the second floor up, but the Renaissance Hall on the first floor is genuine and well worth seeing. The exterior style reflects the Italian influence common throughout Poland: despite the copper dragon-shaped downspouts, the building takes a visitor immediately to Renaissance Padua or Verona.

There is, more than any other museum, the old town square itself, everything rebuilt, of course, but quite as charming as the squares in Gdańsk or Warsaw, and not nearly as touristed.

For people who would rather buy than look, Poznań is full of antique shops with prices quite more reasonable than Poland's big three cities, where genuine Russian icons go for $300-$500 each, and a nice second-hand book shop on the corner of the square, where $150 will buy you a vellum-bound treatise in Latin printed in the sixteenth century.

On Ślusarska Street, between the town square and the Warta River, there used to be a crazy little cabaret, not often open, a refugee from pre-War Paris: cozy, decadent, small stage for cabaret singer, seating for maybe fifteen, drinks and meals available.

On the square's perimeter is a jazz café right out of America in the late fifties: Sarp, originally the Architects' Club. Espresso coffee or beer, taped period jazz (no rock-n-roll), Polski beats (middle twenties) in black clothing nursing inexpensive drinks through endless hours of political and intellectual analysis.

Off a side street, through one of the darkened doorways, a staircase with lovely art nouveau railings and newel posts. On one of the back streets of old town, a real violin-maker's shop. On another, an art glass shop. Several shops sell silver and amber, and one features what I believe are the finest amber pieces in all Poland: cleaner, modern cuts instead of traditional Victorian elaborations found in places like Gdańsk and Warsaw.

A shop for making picture frames.

Any number of gateways and entrances and side streets that transport one immediately into Normandy, Berlin, Kraków, Italy. Wrought iron gates and cobblestone streets. What remains of the old royal castle, of the Jesuit complex.

Poznań, even old town, even high season, is not yet killed with tourism. Across the cobblestones of market square, a father walking with his daughter hand-in-hand, the only people in sight. An old woman with a market basket passing along a low-vaulted colonnade out of some mediaeval monastery. One of those achingly beautiful Polish women, dressed to kill in a black-and-white skirt eight inches above her knees, setting out a doormat and plastic bushes in front of her dress shop.

Down Swietoslawska Street, the old Jesuit Church, Fara Poznańska. The approach to the church, through a narrow street with stucco walls painted now in a dirty rose color, smacks of northern Italy, Padua or Ferrara. The church itself is a baroque magnificence built between 1651 and 1701 on the site, of course, of an earlier Gothic structure, a church which at "150 elbows in length and 70 elbows in width" had been "one of the largest in Europe at the time." The cruciform building is paved with white and pink marble, mainly neoclassical in appearance, with enormous fluted Corinthian half-columns set in the walls, reaching to a ceiling divided and subdivided by arches and windows into elaborate patterns of square, triangle, rectangle and octagon, each component further elaborated in high relief plaster: scrolls, foliage, reliefs, Cupids, angels. Umber, red, peach, orange, and pink predominate. A baroque high altar, flanked by two huge white statues, was designed by Pompeo Ferrari. Around the perimeter of the side aisles, a series of altars, also baroque, flush with seraphim and cherubim, angels and spiraled columns. All confessionals and pews are carved: there's not a right angle in the building.

Despite its baroque elegance, Fara Poznańska is, like Poznań, a working church: there are no tours, and those responsible for its maintenance go about their daily business with matter-of-fact directness. Parishioners enter to kneel and pray. A custodian sweeps the imitation oriental rugs with an electric vacuum cleaner. Somewhere in a back room, a choir practices songs and chants.

189

The organist practices on the 1875 pipe organ. A nun climbs up onto the high altar, there beside the gold and silver facing, to put fresh gladiola in the flower vases. Another nun crosses the transept, kneels, crosses herself, hurries out a side exit. A knot of German tourists mutters in surprise at having stumbled upon this treasure in the old city of Posen.

This building served as a German magazine during the War. It was vandalized but not severely damaged, so restoration was relatively easy, and finished shortly after 1945. By now a patina of heavy dust makes the building look much as it would have in the 1930s: dirt darkens the laps of cherubs and angels nearly to black, removes the shine from gold and silver. Several paintings are blackened nearly indistinguishable; they hang loosely in their huge gilded frames in the dark recesses of the nave. Cobwebs fill the crevices between altars and behind the free-standing columns. These new layers of grime smudge to invisibility the seams between restoration and original surfaces.

Fara Poznańska is an old, elaborate, quiet, and complex building, a metaphor for the city of Poznań, for the country of Poland. An exterior which is basically quite simple conceals an incredibly complex interior, not a straight line in the place, now a rich mix of old and new, distinctions rendered by time and history incoherent and indistinguishable even to those who might want to draw distinctions. Here is an odd mixture of genuine marble and plaster imitation, cleverly decorated and almost as good as the real thing. Here is a good deal or serenity and solitude, among the most luxurious of surroundings, a vaguely hidden quality. Here is a great deal of beauty, and a great deal of dirt and apparent neglect. Here is something very substantial, very compelling.

I have spent a great deal of time in this church, and in Poznań, and in Poland, and I barely begin to penetrate below the surface. It's that kind of a church. That kind of a city. That kind of a country.

Car Ownership in Poland, Joys of

"Modern Poland's problems are rooted in symbols," a friend meditated aloud one afternoon shortly before I left Łódź. "The old symbols are dead. All our lives it's been the Party or the Church, but neither works any more. The red flag, however illegitimate its authority, however illusory its promises, however corrupt its method was in its time a very a compelling symbol. Solidarność, which would like to supplant the red flag, is too ad-hoc to be an effective counter-symbol. A symbol springs almost unsummoned from the psychic depths of a people—neither the red-and-white flag nor the Solidarność logo springs from those deep roots.

"Our other symbol was the Virgin. She defined Poland for centuries. She endured longer in Poland than elsewhere, but secretly we all know this is romantic self-delusion. Today not even the virgin works."

"American symbols too are bankrupt," I suggested. "Only in the Heartland do you find any real faith in flag, the cross, or the Statue of Liberty. I suspect we were never strong on the flag or the cross, and wildly extended claims to racial and gender entitlement have stretched faith in Liberty pretty much to snap."

My companion laughed. "The defining symbol of America is not the flag, and not the Statue of Liberty and certainly not the cross. The symbol of America is the car. Poland envies America not its Statue of Liberty, but its car. The whole world wants your car, but it is the wrong symbol for other peoples, even Europeans. It might work, one day, in Russia, which is immense, like America. Poland? The car can never mean in Poland what it means in America."

Well, she is right. America is the land of the automobile, and most Americans—even those who live in cities, even those who protest loudly to the contrary—love their cars, rely on their cars, believe in their cars as do no other people on earth. The Germans have adapted well to car culture, building fine autobahns and engineering fine machines. The British have adapted less well, muddling cars the way they muddle everything else, unable even to figure out which side of the road to drive on. The French? The Italians? French and—for

191

all their nervous stylishness—Italian cars are silly. The clever Japanese learned the superficialities of car culture from Americans and Germans, but Japan, a small island better served with trains, missed the soul connection. (Which may explain the attraction of Japanese vehicles for soul-less yuppies.)

The Poles? Another case of the general idea. . . .

Car ownership in Poland is not easy, even in the New Poland. The roads stink. Gasoline stations are few and hard to find. Insurance is a nightmare. Repair is next to impossible, and honest mechanics are even scarcer than in the States. Road hazards are everywhere, especially other Polish drivers, who are *the* worst, worse than the mad Italians, worse than the befuddled Brits, worse than the spaced-out Mexicans. Theft and vandalism are common. Police checks are common and arbitrary. Buying, selling, and registration are confusing even to natives.

Besides, trains and buses will take you everywhere you want to go: who in his right mind owns a car in Poland?

Well, me for one, after days spent in pursuit of international train tickets, after lugging that damned TV/VCR back and forth from flat to Institute on the trams twenty-odd times, after spending one weekend in Gdańsk with Allen Weltzien, who had bought a small Fiat, and another weekend in Poznań with Steve Nagle, who had bought a Czech Skoda. After spending an hour and a half getting to Agnieszka Salska's house in the suburbs, using a sequence of trams and buses, and waiting fifteen minutes in the cold for each. After hauling 200 copies of the *Norton Anthology of American Literature* from Warsaw to Łódź on the train. "A car would be a really great thing," I told myself on the five-hour train ride from Łódź to Poznań, departure at some owl-blinking hour of the morning, leave the flat an hour before departure to catch the tram to Kaliska station, could have been driven easily in three hours. "A really fine thing."

By the end of my first year in Poland I had convinced myself a car could even be a wise investment: inflation would let me sell it for more than I paid for it, have one year's free use, travel to Austria and Germany, England and Hungary, not to mention out-of-the-way hamlets in Poland, at my own convenience, explore the Polish countryside as I went, visit the real Poland that most tourists never see. I would skip across borders in a quarter of the time it took trains full of Polish peddlers to clear customs. "Just get the liability insurance," Nagle advised me. "You can't collect on the collision, and there's no way to get body work done anyway. Collision-theft insurance is expensive. Regular insurance is cheap, eight to ten dollars a month."

It was Steve's mud-brown Skoda I bought. Allan's Fiat had a bad rep: two accidents—one with a tram, no less—and overheating problems. Also, the Skoda looked to be—no, it was—a fine automobile, a 130, top of the line, built for export. It had plenty of pep for Polish roads, although in the West, Steve warned, you got squeezed between the BMWs and the Mercedes blasting up the left lanes, and the little East Bloc cars—Trabants, Fiats, Ladas—chugging down

192

the right lanes. All in all, it served me well: I paid $1800 in the spring of 1990, sold it 40,000 kilometers later in the spring of 1991 for $1650, having spent about $200 on maintenance, repairs and tires, and $100 on insurance. Thus transportation for the year cost me $450 plus gas, which is cheap in any country's book.

Everyone offered advice when I bought the car, beginning with what car to buy. Some held for a Western car, as they were at the time difficult to import into Poland, and here was a good way to get one more older Mercedes or Volkswagen across the border. "You will have no trouble selling a Western vehicle," folks assured me. "You will have great difficulty selling any East Bloc car."

Others held for something local, a Lada or a small Fiat: "You will have no trouble finding parts when it breaks down," they assured me.

The Skoda had a good reputation, even among my German friends, best built among East Bloc cars, a Czech factory bought out, finally, by Volkswagen in the fall of 1990. A Skoda offered the best of both blocs.

Setting a price was another matter. There is no such thing as a Polish blue book, in spring of 1990 ads for used cars were as scarce as Polish autobahn, and insurance valuations were meaningless. Finally Steve and I visited the Poznań car market, looked at more or less comparable vehicles, and settled on a figure, a little lower than the going rate for friendship's sake and because, as Steve said, "These are four bad Czech tires which ought to be replaced as soon as possible. The one thing I haven't been able to get is good tires."

I brought the vehicle home to more conflicting opinions: "You paid way too much," Jules Zonn told me. (Jules drives a Mercedes.) "They will never believe you paid only $1800 when you go to pay your sales tax. You'd better say at least $2,000," Łukasz Salski told me. Łukasz drives a Syrena, with a two-stroke engine that generates maybe forty-five horsepower.

When I sold the Skoda, the same difference of opinion: "You did very well for a vehicle with 79,000 kilometers." "For a Skoda 130, you should have asked much more." Who really knows the Polish car market?

By the spring of 1991, a brand new Ford Escort in the window on Piotrkowska sold for $14,000. American cars were flooding Poland, mostly used, bought in the States and delivered by ocean freighter, all shipping charges and a handsome profit folded into the selling price. They came with U.S. license plates: Minnesota, Iowa, California, New York. A shop on Piotrkowska sold old U.S. plates, probably from such vehicles, for $10 each. The road from Frankfurt am Oder to Poznań was lined with used car lots, and every time we crossed the German-Polish border spring of 1991, we saw private car traders bringing in a small trailer with two or three used Western machines. I paid what I paid, and I got what I got, and I had many adventures between.

Just registering the car was an adventure. Nagle told me, I thought, that he had paid insurance through the end of the year, so I held off changing registration from his name to mine until after Christmas. "If the insurance is paid, don't change the registration," I was told repeatedly. "No Pole would." It was not, however, insurance he had paid; it was road tax. I drove uninsured from September through December . . . through Poland, Germany, Czechoslovakia, Hungary, Yugoslavia, Greece, and Austria.

In January, friend Łukasz and I set out to complete the sales agreement—Steve had left it signed, blank, and undated—and get new registration and new plates. The registration bureau is just down the street from Poznański's palace on Zachodnia, so Łukasz and I agreed to meet there at 10:00 one Tuesday morning. Of course the line stretched out a bureau door and around a corner, and of course we both had noon classes, so we agreed to meet again, same place, one hour earlier, on Wednesday.

Which we did, waiting our turn, fingering our sales agreement, anticipating angles and eventualities. When we got to the window, the bureaucrat in charge asked the question we had not anticipated: had I paid my sales tax?

Well no, I had not.

Well, sir, that sales tax will have to be paid before this vehicle can be registered. The bureau for paying sales tax is in another building, three tram stops from here. Then bring the receipt for paid tax back here, and we'll continue.

(Stop me if you've heard this one before.)

Łukasz and I betook ourselves to the sales tax office, killing the time spent waiting in line anticipating further eventualities. We covered all possibilities, I thought, except the one problem which actually arose: "Do you have a document with your address on it?" this bureaucrat wanted to know. "How do we know that you live where you claim to live? There is no address on either your *legitymacja* or your passport."

Perhaps the university's rector's office could prepare such a document?

It could indeed. "Then you must take that document to the city registration office at the police station, where the law required that you registered within two days of entering this country, and they will give you a document that says you live where you live, and then come back here. . . ."

(You see how things work in Poland?)

To condense a long story, I let Łukasz go his way and walked the papers through myself. I am very proud of that fact, since it involved finding my way through four major league Polish bureaucracies: the rector's office, the police station, the tax office, and the motor vehicle registration office. I lost a day in the process when somebody—I think the city registration bureau—closed just as I arrived. I almost came away with a set of genuine black Polish license plates, but I was discovered as a foreigner at the very last second, with the result that the woman had to write out a whole new vehicle registration, and give me *green* plates starting with the code ILD, the plates used to identify foreign-owned cars (diplomats get blue plates). When I went to affix my plates back at the flat, I discovered that the holes in the plates matched neither the original holes in the Skoda's rear bumper nor the new set of holes Steve had drilled because his Poznań plates didn't match the original holes either. Two days later I borrowed a drill, punched a couple of holes into the plates (plastic, would you believe?), bolted them, slightly askew, to front and rear bumpers, and had myself at last an officially registered, legal, A-okay, uninsured Skoda.

Ewa helped me with insurance two days later at yet another bureau, this only two doors removed from the Institute. Originally the bureaucrat wanted to ship me off to Piotrkowska because of the green plates, but Ewa insisted that foreigners could buy insurance at this office, and the woman did some checking, and wasn't Ewa correct? Three months of regular insurance cost me 500,000 złotych for coverage I knew I could never use. (When I returned to pay for a second quarter of insurance, I spent half an hour convincing them that my policy was indeed registered in this building, not on Piotrkowska, an argument which was repeated three months after that.)

My insurance was not valid for travel outside the former East Bloc, and whenever I wanted to travel to Austria, Germany or Greece, I had to buy additional insurance at the Warta agency. Four times I purchased Warta, or green-card insurance, and never did it go the same way twice. The first time, Ewa and Michelle and I walked to a small agency on Kościuszki, paid 180,000 złotych for two weeks, collected our papers, and walked out. In December I was sent to the office for foreigners, where they completed a form, collected 240,000 złotych for one week . . . well, two weeks really, because two weeks was the minimum period allowed, and even though I'd be away only six days, I'd have to pay for fourteen, very sorry, but those are the regulations. For a longer April excursion, I returned to the Piotrkowska, filled out forms, and was sent to pay, in dollars, at the Central Bank of Łódź: a very time-consuming process.

For my fourth trip outside of Poland, I faked the whole thing. It was just a weekend visit to Berlin, and I rebelled at the thought of paying two weeks' premium for three days of coverage on a trip exactly 100 kilometers into the West. Against Michelle's advice, I took an old card, converted the 04 in the month column into an 05, and took off for the Hauptstadt.

Don't you know, the only thing the German border guard asked about was insurance? Nothing about passports, nothing about gold, pornography, dope, vodka, or Russian icons. Not even vehicle registration. Just green card insurance. "You got your insurance?" he wanted to know.

"Ja, ja," I assured him, flashing a stack of car papers with the green card insurance right on the top.

"Ist es gültig?" he wanted to know.

"Ja, ja. Natürlich."

He studied the card for a long while. Then he announced matter-of-factly, "This five used to be a four."

What could I say? In the back of my mind, I kept hearing the phrase, "Any Pole would have done it. And any East German too." But what could I say, caught red-handed?

Then the German border guard, undoubtedly a rehabilitated DDR Saxon, an East German hard-ass, worse even than the Soviets, one of those Terrors of the East who so intimidated all of us one short year ego, just waved us through and told us to have a good time.

Welcome to the New Germany!

Paper is not, however, the real problem with car ownership in Poland. The real problems are roads, service, gasoline and road hazards. "It's a nightmare, little Tommy."

Poland boasts few superhighways, and what passes for superhighway is nowhere close to American standard. Remember the old West Virginia Turnpike, or that old stretch of I-70 between New Stanton and Wheeling? That's East Bloc superhighway: crumbling concrete, sometimes even cobblestone, potholes ready to swallow whole a juicy BMW or Honda Civic. No superhighway at all between Warsaw and Gdańsk, a relatively good road from Warsaw to Kraków, one stretch of so-so road between Warsaw and Poznań, an 80-kilometer run you're on before you know it and off before you know it, dumped right in the middle of downtown Poznań. Security in Old Poland prohibited superhighway within sixty kilometers of any border, so once you pass Kraków headed south, Wrocław headed southwest, Poznań going west, or Warsaw east, it's two-lane backroad all the way.

The two-trackers lead you right through the center of every village on the route. Some routes circumscribe large cities, not with I-495 superhighway by-passes, but with a series of side streets. Directions are usually poorer than the roads; it's usually safer to go right into town, and out the other side. All that saves a motor trip in Poland from real chronological disaster is the fact that traffic remains light, except on that road from Frankfurt/Oder through Poznań and Warsaw to Russia, across which passes all the international truck traffic bearing trade and food relief to the old Soviet Union, and all the used Western cars headed for Poznań and Warsaw, and all the . . . well, that is the Mother of all Roads.

So most of your trip is spent snaking around small Polish villages and not-so-small Polish cities. Depending on time of day, you could be following horse-drawn wagons hauling potatoes, straw, turnips, or hogs; Polish trucks hauling milk, coal, potatoes, or hogs; tractors hauling nothing at all; bicyclists, drunk or sober; buses local and long-distance. Syrenas, small Fiats and Trabants putter along at 70 kilometers per hour and lack power to pass anything except small Fiats, Syrenas, and Trabants. Polish trucks are dark, slow and virtually unlit: 40-watt headlights in front, (maybe) a reflector or a ten-watt taillight behind.

On the up side, standard Polish driving etiquette requires slow-moving traffic to move onto the shoulder of a two-lane road to facilitate passing, thereby allowing you to pass even in the face of on-coming vehicles, which will probably also drift to their left shoulder to accommodate you. This practice

197

could be profitably incorporated into American rules of the road.

On the down side, it is also common Polish driving practice to stop a car for whatever reason in the middle of a traffic lane, not necessarily on the shoulder or on a side street, so you'll be blitzing along at 80 or 90, and suddenly there's a truck parked in the road ahead of you while the driver checks his engine or changes a tire. How I drove for eleven months without killing somebody, I can't say. It certainly wasn't defensive driving skills of the Poles; they seem lost in the fog of their own anxieties, muddling along the roadways, speeding up, slowing down, swerving in or out without warning, stopping, starting, cutting in, cutting off, worse than the Italians, and slower than the East Germans. When, after 1990, Poles in significant numbers began driving Western cars—all that technology and horsepower they don't know how to handle, and nobody to teach them proper control, and roads as twisted and dilapidated and hazard-strewn as ever—the number of serious accidents rose dramatically. It will only increase in the foreseeable future.

Theft and vandalism are another problem. My Skoda survived, because it was parked day and night right in front of the Police Hospital across from our flat. The only damage I sustained was a couple of banged up doors, whapped by the doors of cars owned by careless or drunk hospital visitors. A small price to pay in a town where Sławek's Fiat was completely vandalized one night, and Łukasz's Mickey-Mouse Syrena was actually stolen while parked in front of Kaliska Station. (To everyone's surprise, and his great disappointment, Łódź police actually recovered the car, not much the worse for having been seduced and abandoned, a month later . . . just after Łukasz had filed an insurance claim.) "The most important thing about your Skoda," said the car dealer who finally bought it from me in 1991, "is that it not be stolen. So many cars in Poland are stolen vehicles, especially the big, powerful ones that came from the West."

Rafał Pniewski remembers driving to Warsaw one day and noticing a loose connection in the radio. It proved to be a defective jack, so upon reaching the city he stopped at an electronics store to buy a replacement. Then he returned to his Fiat Polonaise, unlocked the front door on the driver's side, and crawled across the seat, back down, face up, twisting himself around back of the radio. While working on the radio, he kept hearing a kind of rattling, a wrenching sound, and felt the car moving. "It wasn't me making the noise or the movement, I was certain. When I straightened up to look, I found a street thief removing my rear tire.

"'What do you think you're doing there?' I demanded of the fellow.

"'No problem,' this guy tells me. 'You take the radio, and I take the tire. . . .'"

(At the Poznań car market with Steve Nagle, Michelle and I picked up new door molding for Rafał to replace the original, stolen while the Polonaise was parked in a Łódź hospital parking lot.)

On the whole, I was lucky with my car in a land where big cars need watched lots and alarm systems, and even small cars are in constant danger of losing radios, tires, parts.

I was less fortunate on maintenance and repair. We nearly blew one bad tire on the trip to Greece, did not, pushed our luck, and by the time we reached Salzburg (our second major trip), the tire was humping so badly I thought it would wreck the shock absorbers. A two-day conference left me no time to shop, but Michelle somehow found, in expensive Austria, a good used Western tire which some Austrian lad at a Salzburg gasoline station—fascinated, no doubt, by this attractive American girl driving a Skoda with Polish plates and a ruined Czech rubber band tire—sold, balanced and mounted for $18. "That tire will last longer than the car," Dr. Dorota Steiner told us before we headed back to Poland.

A second tire blew thirty kilometers outside of Berlin late one Sunday afternoon when most businesses were very closed. Hitching a ride into town, we phoned Gabriele Jones, who soon rode to our rescue. We stopped at a Shell station, but it stocked nothing in our size. "Used to have them, but I guess we sold them all," said the proprietor, giving us the address of another Shell station guaranteed to be open and guaranteed to have what we needed. "Guaranteed. Buy it there and bring it back here and I will mount it for you." This station was open, but it too was out of our size. "165-13? Used to have them," the owner told us. We had just about resigned ourselves to staying overnight, when a fellow who had stopped for a pack of cigarettes overheard us talking. "I have a 165-13 radial in the back of my car," he said.

And he did. Half an hour later, we were on the road again with a new used German tire: 25 marks, or $15. "That tire will last longer than the car," Gabriele told us as we drove away.

The third bad Czech tire went as we approached York, England in June. We stopped at, of all places, a Skoda dealership and were directed up the road to a new/used tyre shop, where we found another Western tyre for 8 pounds, $14. "This tire will last longer than the car," Michelle quipped as we drove off to Jack Donovan's house.

The fourth tire I never did replace. "This car has three good Western tires, and one bad Czech tire," I told the fellow who bought it from me. "The Czech tire ought to be replaced as soon as possible."

My major problem with the Skoda was overheating, which tempered during the winter, became a problem again with spring. Regularly we boiled off a liter of antifreeze, so that we took to driving with a five-gallon tank of water in the luggage compartment under the hood. I had it looked into once or twice at one of two Łódź Skoda shops, but the advice of their mechanic confirmed an axiom I had already formulated in the States: "Drive it until it breaks; then you will know for sure what the problem is, and we can fix it."

It broke when Jim Hartzel borrowed the Skoda to fetch his visiting parents from Kutno railroad station, a week ahead of our trip to Berlin. The temperature gauge went all the way to red, steam hissed out the coolant reservoir, the engine was hotter than a fire-cracker. "We had to leave it just outside of Ozorków," he told me apologetically. "We can go get it tomorrow."

Next day we refilled the radiator and started driving the thirty kilometers to Łódź, only to have the thing blow at Zgierz, ten kilometers from town. "I'll let it cool, come back with more water, fetch it later," I told Jim. "Have a good time with your folks, and don't feel guilty."

Next day Łukasz Salski, I and Michelle nursed the Skoda into the nearest Skoda repair shop, shutting the engine off at every stoplight to minimize heat build-up. I let Łukasz explain the problem to the mechanic.

"Can't do a thing," the mechanic told him in language I understood even without translation. Michelle and I looked at our broken toy, shrugged our shoulders in silent resignation, and turned to leave. But Łukasz, who understood the situation perfectly, kept talking, and after ten minutes of negotiations, the mechanic motioned for us to push the car over the pit in the garage. Then he inspected the engine from above and below.

When he climbed back out of the pit, he told Łukasz, "I can't tell anything right now. This may be a split hose, or it may be in the engine. If it is an engine problem, I can't do anything. Come back tomorrow and I will tell you what is the matter."

Again Michelle and I moved vaguely toward the gate, but Łukasz was not ready to leave. Another ten minutes of talk, and the mechanic began tearing the head off the engine. Half an hour later, he was holding the head gasket in his hand. "See here, where oil and fumes have been passing from one cylinder to another? This causes water to back up into the reservoir, and the engine overheats. You need a new head gasket. Unfortunately, this is a Skoda 130. They were made only for export. I do not have a head gasket for this kind of engine. There is nothing I can do."

"I don't think there's much to be done now," I told Michelle.

Łukasz kept on talking.

"We'll take a train to Berlin. Maybe we can get a gasket there," Michelle suggested.

But not so quick; the mechanic was saying something to Łukasz. Seemed he had a friend who might be able to help. "My friend is not here right now, but come back tomorrow morning, and maybe my friend will have what you need."

Then Łukasz stopped talking at last, and we all left.

Next morning, the news was not so good: the mechanic's friend did not have such a head gasket, and probably there was not such a head gasket in all of Poland.

Michelle and Dave looked glum. Łukasz jez kept talkin'.

"But there is a factory in Katowice which could manufacture a head gasket. . . ."

Given enough time, even the dullest Westerner gets the picture. Later

200

that afternoon I returned to the Skoda shop with two bottles of fine *Wódka Wyborowa*. The following morning a head gasket had appeared. The day after that, the car was ready to drive to Berlin (on the doctored green card insurance).

More or less. We picked up the Skoda the afternoon before our departure to Berlin, drove to the home of a friend on the south side of town, and don't you know it, the car overheated, just as it had before being fixed. "That's $150 in hard currency we're talking here," Michelle observed as I broiled hotter than the engine.

"It will be in there 8:00 a.m. tomorrow," I promised.

It was.

My mechanic was nowhere to be found. "Vacation," somebody said. Nothing for it but to explain the problem to this new mechanic: "We had this car in here to be fixed, here's the receipt, here's the guarantee, same problem, radiator fluid leaking all over the place, see the trail of drops where I drove in?"

The second mechanic examined the engine. "You have a split hose," he said finally. "At the end there: the water leaks from the hose and drains down the exhaust pipe. I can fix that easily. Oh, and by the way, the bottom bolt on the alternator was not replaced. See there?"

I looked in disbelief, but he was indeed correct: the alternator was missing a bolt. Also, the plastic housing covering some electronic gadget on the side of the engine compartment was gone.

Nothing that another hour of labor (and another ten bucks) couldn't fix. *Then* we were off to Berlin, and a fine old weekend among friends, until Sunday of our departure, when we turned the key in the ignition and nothing happened.

No grind, no click, no ignition. No headlights and no dome light either. Gabriele shook her head. Michelle wrung her hands. I steamed.

I raised the hood and opened the battery compartment to have a look, to find a disconnected battery cable. How we started the car in Poland, or when it came loose, I couldn't image. Part of the mystery of East Bloc machines, I suppose. I fixed it easily with a few twists of the wrench, then shut the hood and turned the key. The engine roared, and we were off down the autobahn on our way back to Poland.

And that's when the second Czech tire blew.

General Motors

WANTED

DEAD or ALIVE
1.000.000. $

Z PARTYJNY
POZDROWIENIE

BIG CYC

Polish Jokes Real Poles Tell

A cop stops a farmer in a wagon, wanting to know what he is carrying.
"It's hay," the terrified farmer whispers; "just hay."
"If it's only hay, why are you whispering?" the cop wants to know.
"I don't want the horse to hear," the farmer answers.

＊   ＊   ＊

A Russian has finally saved enough rubles to buy a new Lada, so he
takes them to the proper bureau and purchases the new vehicle.
"Your production number is 5,394,238," he is told. "The car will be
delivered on July 16, 1998."
"In the morning or the afternoon?" the Russian wants to know.
"1998 is eight years from now," the clerk points out. "What difference
does it make, morning or afternoon?"
"That's the day the refrigerator repair man is supposed to come," the
Russian answers.

＊   ＊   ＊

A high school zoology teacher is giving his class an oral final. He
calls in the first student, holds up a stuffed rabbit, and asks the student, "What is
this?"
The student looks at him blankly, coughs a couple of times, finally
stammers, "I don't know."
"You flunk," the teacher tells him. "Send in the next one."
The second student comes into the room. The teacher again holds up
the rabbit and asks, "What is this animal called?" The second student looks at
him blankly, shuffles his feet, finally admits, "I don't know."
"You flunk," the teacher says. "Send in the next one."
The third student enters the room, the teacher holds up the stuffed
rabbit. "What is this named?" he wants to know. The third student looks at

him as blankly as the previous two. "I don't know."

This is more than the exasperated teacher can take. "What the hell do you mean you don't know?" he shouts. "What have we been talking about all year?"

The student's eyes brighten. "This is Karl Marx," he says confidently.

*   *   *

A reporter working on a television story about the world meat crisis flies with cameraman and crew to Rumania. He approaches a Rumanian on the street and asks, "Pardon me, sir, what do you think of the world meat shortage?"

The Rumanian looks puzzled, scratches his head. "Meat?" he wants to know. "What do you mean by this word *meat?*"

So the reporter flies to America, asks an American in the street, "Pardon me, sir, what do you think of the world meat shortage?"

The puzzled American scratches his head. "Shortage?" he wants to know. What do you mean *shortage?*"

So the reporter flies to Warsaw, sets up his camera, stops the first Pole walking out of the Palace of Culture: "Excuse me, sir, what do you think of the world meat shortage?"

The Pole looks puzzled, scratches his head. "Think?" he wants to know. "What do you mean by this word *think?*"

Undaunted, the reporter flies to Frankfurt, sets up one more time, asks the first German he sees the same question: "Pardon me, sir, what do you think of the world meat shortage?"

The German, genuinely puzzled, scratches his head: "Pardon me? What is meant by these words *pardon me?*"

*   *   *

A Polish cop gets off work and hurries home to help his wife with her name day party. "Is there anything I can do to help, honey?" he wants to know.

"Yes," his wife tells him. "If you want, maybe you could write my name on this cake I bought. That would be a help."

The cop wanders off with the cake, fumbles about in the next room for ten minutes, finally returns. "I don't think this is going to work," he reports; "I can't get the cake in the typewriter."

*   *   *

The Little Devil is out collecting his due. He pops through the ground in Leningrad in front of a startled Russian. "I am a Little Devil," he announces. "Here is my pitchfork and here is my pail, and I am come to collect my due."

204

The Russian looks at him in disgust. "You stupid," he says. "Is here nothing to collect. Go to America, there is plenty of things."

So the Little Devil is off to America, pops through a sidewalk in downtown Dallas, right in front of a six-foot-four-inch Texan. "I am a Little Devil," he announces, "and this is my pitchfork and here is my pail. I have come to collect my due."

"Whoa, there boy," the Texan tells him. "You go stealin' stuff around here, you gonna end up dead or in jail. Go over to Poland; they're a little more relaxed than folks in these parts."

So the Little Devil goes off to Kraków, pops up right in the middle of the Old Market Place close to St. Mary's cathedral. "I am a Little Devil," he announces to the first Pole he sees." "This is my pitchfork and this . . . now what became of that pail?"

*   *   *

Early in 1989, when the Communist Party began losing support, one card-carrier suggested a membership drive. His colleagues thought this a good idea, and the following proposal was adopted: any member who brought in a new member would receive an award of 1,000,000 złotych. Any member who brought in two new members would receive an award of 2,000,000 złotych and he would have his own membership in the Party canceled. Any member who brought in three new members would receive a reward of 3,000,000 złotych, would have his own membership canceled, and would receive a letter from the precinct chairman saying that he had never belonged to the Party.

*   *   *

Three men—a Pole, a Puerto-Rican, and an American—fall out of the twelfth story window at the same time. Which one hits the ground first?

The American.

The Puerto-Rican stops to spray graffiti on the walls on the way down. And the Pole has to go back three times to ask directions.

*   *   *

One engine on a trans-Atlantic jetliner dies and, despite the pilot's best efforts, the plane starts losing altitude. The crew jettisons meals, equipment, finally even luggage, but still the plane drops toward the water. Passengers and crew unbolt seats and bulkheads, unload them, and still the plane loses altitude. Finally the group decides there is only one thing left to do: some passengers will have to go. The passenger list is inspected, and four names are drawn, representing each of the four nationalities on board.

205

"For God and the Queen," the crew tells the Brit.

"For God and the Queen," shouts the Brit as he jumps out the door.

"For the Red Army," they tell the Russian.

"For the Red Army," shouts the Russian as he jumps out the door.

"Everybody's doing it," they tell the Frenchman. "It's the fashion."

Then comes the Pole. They try everything on the Pole: God, country, the Polish army, his moral duty. He will have none of it, and still the airplane has not leveled off.

"It's no use," the steward tells the pilot. "This guy will never do it."

"Oh yeah?" cries the Pole. "Who says? . . ."

*   *   *

The same jetliner is in the same trouble, and the crew settles on the same solution. "For God and the Queen," shouts a Brit as he jumps. "For the Lone Star State," shouts a Texan and jumps. "For the Polish Republic," shouts a Pole, pushing a Russian out the door.

*   *   *

Did you know Lech Wałęsa will be president only until the end of September?"

Yeah? Why?

Because school begins in October.

*   *   *

Former communist premier Edward Gierek, visiting Silesia on a good will tour, meets a worker and his family in their home. In front of the television cameras he talks with the family's small boy. "So, little boy, do you have a nice flat to live in?"

"Yes, sir," replies the boy; "We have a lovely flat with nice furniture."

"Do you have a nice television to watch?"

"We have a television set and we watch it all the time."

"And does your daddy have a nice car?"

"My daddy has a Fiat Polonaise and takes us driving every Sunday."

"Well you know, little boy," the premier says, as much to the camera as to the child, "I am the man who makes all of these good things possible."

The kid runs excitedly into the kitchen yelling, "Mommie! Daddie! Uncle Wolfgang is here!"

*   *   *

Gierek is visiting another little boy, this one less advantaged than the first. He asks him, "If you could have anything in the world, anything at all, what would you want?

The kid asks for a television set with windshield wipers.

"Why the wipers?" Gierek wants to know.

"Because every time my dad is watching TV and your face appears on the screen, he spits at it," answers the boy.

*   *   *

Two brothers are separated in 1939, one sent to Siberia, the other to Germany. After the war, the German prisoner is repatriated to Poland, but the other remains in Siberia. Then, in 1987, somebody at Polish television gets wind of the story, and he knows somebody at Russian television headquarters, and they track down the missing brother, now living in Minsk. A joyous reunion is arranged in Moscow, in Red Square, before television cameras.

The Polish brother flies in with a Polish television crew, and a whole bunch of dignitaries. The brother from Minsk comes also to Moscow with an even larger entourage of dignitaries. Across the great square, all decorated with red banners and roses, the illustrious Polish delegation approaches an equally illustrious array of Soviet dignitaries. Television cameras record the historic moment. With the delegations still at a great distance, the man from Poland rushes to one man in the crowd of Russians, throws his arms around him, and kisses his long-lost brother.

"This is amazing," somebody from television says. "How did you know it was him in such a great crowd, at such a great distance, after so many years?"

"Easy," says the Polish brother. "I recognized the coat he is wearing."

*   *   *

A bear, a fox, and a wolf are playing cards. After half an hour, the bear announces, "Someone is cheating, and I will not embarrass the red-furred one by naming him."

*   *   *

What's black and white and runs away when called?
A Polish waiter.

*   *   *

A mother-in-law, testing the loyalty of her three sons-in-law, invites them individually to visit the family cottage in the Polish Lake District. The oldest daughter and her husband come first. The mother prepares a great dinner and, after all is finished, walks to the end of the dock and throws herself into the lake. "Help me!" she shouts. "Help me, my dear son, I can't swim."

The son-in-law rushes out the door, runs to the end of the dock, jumps in the water and rescues the woman. Next morning the young couple awakens to find a brand new white Fiat Polonaise 127 parked in the driveway. On the windshield is a note: "Thank you, my dear son. I know now you love me. Signed, your loving mother-in-law."

Then the woman invites her second oldest daughter and her husband. Once again after dinner she throws herself in the lake, and is rescued once again by her son-in-law. The couple awakens the next morning to find a new red Polski Fiat 126 parked in the driveway with a note on the windshield: "Thank you, thank you, my dear son. I know now that you love me. Signed, your loving mother-in-law."

Finally the woman invites her youngest daughter and her husband. After a huge evening meal, she walks to the end of the dock and throws herself in the water. "Help me, help me, my dear son," she shouts. "I can't swim." The husband of her youngest daughter hears the noise, walks to the door and listens carefully. Then he slams the door and returns to drinking vodka with his father-in-law.

The next morning the couple awakens to find a brand new Mercedes 200 in the driveway with a note on the windshield: "Thank you, thank you, my dear son. I now know you love me. Signed, your loving father-in-law."

A Soviet soldier and a Polish soldier on border patrol near Brest get to talking things over. "It's a hard life, comrade," complains the Soviet soldier.

"A hard life indeed," the Pole replies.

"They treating you okay?" the Soviet want to know.

"Not so bad," the Pole replies. "And you?"

"Okay," the Soviet answers. "You got warm clothes this freezing winter?"

"Yeah, we got new coats this winter, so it's not so bad. How about you?"

"Well, I'm warm enough," says the Soviet. "And boots?"

"Not the best, but they keep my feet warm. We were issued new boots this winter, and they are holding up. How about you?"

"They are not the best either, but my feet will survive until spring. You eating okay?"

"I'm okay on food," says the Pole. "We get our 2,500 calories a day."

"Comrade," replies the startled Soviet, "do not make up stories. No man can eat 50 pounds of potatoes in one day!"

*   *   *

A Pole worried about his health visits the doctor. "So how long do I have?" he wants to know.

"You smoke cigarettes?" the doctor wants to know.

"Never," the man replies.

"You drink much vodka?" the doctor asks.

"Never touch the stuff."

"You chase around with many women?"

"No, I never chase women."

"What do you care how long you live?"

*   *   *

A man returns early in the morning to a bar in which he'd spent the previous night. "Is it true I drank 100,000 złotych worth of vodka here last night?" he wants to know.

"You did in fact drink 100,000 złotych worth of vodka last night," the bartender assures him.

"Thank god," the man says, greatly relieved. "I was afraid I'd lost that money!"

A Polish monk is transported in a vision to deepest Hell. It is something out of Dante, exactly what he always pictured: insufferable red heat, a constant din of lamentation, enormous caldrons filled with grotesque distortions of the human form, stews of suffering sinners kept in perpetual boil by flames below. Using iron pitchforks, grotesque demons with leathery wings and scabby tails toss those who would escape their caldrons back into the bubbling oil.

Upon close examination, the monk notes that the caldrons are segregated by nationality: Germans in one, Italians in another, Russians in a third. He also notes that one caldron is entirely unguarded, although it boils as intensely as the others.

"How is it," he asks his guide, "that no demons guard this caldron, yet no man or woman escapes?"

"These are Poles," he is told. "We need no guards here. Should anyone climb only a few feet above the surface of suffering, his neighbors will pull him back down."

        *   *   *

A man sits down in a Polish restaurant, orders red borscht, pork cutlet, potatoes, cabbage salad. The waiter brings him his soup, and it's not red borscht, but chicken with noodles. The man complains: "I ordered red borscht, but you brought me chicken broth."

"Look, friend," the waiter tells him, "soup is soup, okay?"

The man thinks to himself, "What the hell, these are hard times. I've had a lot of chicken soup in my life. Soup is soup."

When his dinner arrives, it is not pork but chicken. "I ordered pork," the man complains to the waiter; "but you brought me chicken."

"Look, friend," the waiter replies, "meat is meat. We're out of pork, okay? Meat is meat. This is a good dinner."

The man thinks to himself, "What the hell—I like chicken. Meat is meat."

The man finishes his meal, asks for his check. The bill is 12,000 złotych (this is an old joke). The man takes out a 1,000 złotych note, leaves it and the bill on the plate, and heads for the door.

The waiter is on him in a flash. "Hey, the bill was 12,000 and you left only 1,000!"

"Look, friend," the customer tells him, "money is money, you know?"

On the Road, Part IV: Leningrad, the Final Frontier

Ewa Bednarowicz looks out the tram window at the long queue of women in front of the milk store. "This trip is a journey into Polish history," she says.

*   *   *

This nine-day excursion to Leningrad is costing Michelle, Ewa, Neil and me 850,000 złotych each, plus $50 spending money, plus $40 hard currency for tourist visas. At the June 1991 rate of exchange, 850,000 złotych amounts to $70.83 . . . $70.83 each for second-class train travel Warsaw to Leningrad to Łódź—two entire days and one night each way—plus six days at a comfortable and quite modern hotel, double occupancy, with toilet and shower in the room, three meals a day, Polish guide for the entire trip and Intourist guides and buses to monuments and museums in and around the city. The souvenir money buys meals on the train at fifty cents a dinner, sheets and blankets for the bunks at eight cents a night, and Soviet champagne at one dollar a bottle. And souvenirs: T-shirts that read (in Russian) "Hard Rock Café, Leningrad," several art books, Soviet army and navy gear, matrioshka dolls, hand-decorated wooden boxes, a six-poster poster of Lenin, a watercolor of the Neva River.

*   *   *

St. Isaac's Cathedral is one of many surprises in Soviet Russia—a surprise that it's still standing, a surprise that, like churches in Poland, it's being carefully restored. Apparently religion is not dead in Russia either. St. Isaac's took 500,000 workers forty years to build. Half of them died during its construction. Enormous columns of dark red granite on the outside, gorgeous intricacies of marble, lapis, malachite, and gold leaf inside. The oil paintings, now flaking, are being converted into mosaics at the rate of one square meter per worker per year. A cruciform with four symmetrical and very abbreviated axes,

211

St. Isaac's lacks the long nave characteristic of Western churches. St. Isaac's couldn't accommodate 15,000 workers, let along 500,000. St. Isaac's is a monument for the nobility.

"During the siege of Leningrad, St. Isaac's was closed but not vandalized," our guide tells us. "You cannot eat gold. After the War, vandalism became a problem."

She does not say at what expense this church has been restored.

*   *   *

On the evening of the longest day of the year, Ewa, Michelle, Neil and I gather a few bottles of Soviet champaign and head for the number 3 electric bus, intent on spending a white night beside the Neva, talking, drinking, watching ships, open to whatever adventure comes our way. As the bus makes its labored way through the cratered streets, Ewa falls into conversation with two middle-aged Russian women, both curious about the foreigners, both a little blitzed on vodka or cognac. Not ten minutes into our quest for adventure, we have been invited to midsummer night's revels in the flat of two private Soviet citizens . . . well, at Sasha's flat, but Vera will take us there while Sasha runs to fix maybe a bit of food with friends in the neighborhood. "You accept, comrades, our invitation?"

Accepting, we hop off the bus at the next stop and follow Vera to Sasha's apartment, where she fumbles for ten minutes with the key—some kind of screw device foreign to us and, apparently, to Vera—until Sasha returns, half a dozen bagels in hand, and opens the door.

The fourth-floor flat is small: kitchen, living room, bath. The kitchen contains a sink and stove, on which Sasha sets to work immediately creating some kind of egg and tomato dish, with a couple of cans of fish-in-tomato-sauce served on the side. As she works, Vera entertains the guests in the living room-bedroom-dining room, seated around the small table or reclined on the bed in front of the color television, on which plays a Soviet version of *Wheel of Fortune*. This room—divided almost entirely in half by the refrigerator, wardrobe and vanity—is decorated only with Soviet girlie calendars (legs only, no bare breasts or behinds), and a team photo of some hockey squad. One shelf holds plastic lead soldiers and a few books, in Russian. Vera, half drunk, is pressing a little close to me, but I shift onto the bed, using Michelle as a screen, and she redirects her interest to Neil. The Wheel of Soviet Fortune spins, Soviet Vanna White poses, and the Soviet audience applauds politely. Sasha calls Vera to the kitchen, sends her back with a bottle of vodka, a real treasure since Gorbachev curtailed production (one reason he's out of favor these days). The bottle is opened, drinks are poured, toasts are raised. Rejected by Neil, Vera returns to me, maneuvering around Michelle. "Russian men are hot and fat," she says. A man from Leningrad wins the Wheel of Fortune competition and is

212

eligible to win final grand prize if he can identify a famous work of art by a Renaissance Italian painter. I move away from Vera. Ewa translates English to Russian, Russian to English, her fluency increasing with each shot of vodka. The man on the television selects the letters A and O, but they are not enough to allow him to identify Da Vinci's "Madonna d'Litta." The smile fades from his face as he sees his chance for the grand prize (a toaster oven) washing down the river. Sasha appears with supper. "He should have known it; it's in the Hermitage Museum." Sasha changes into a better dress for dinner.

Both women are divorced. Sasha has two children, "away at summer camp" right now. Camp, Ewa explains, might mean communist youth Pioneer Camp, or might just mean a summer cottage. Vera has no children, will never have children, a minor sin in the CCCP, which promotes Family almost as strongly as the Catholic Church. In her childlessness, she feels obviously inadequate and incomplete. For her there is no hope: short, dumpy, middle-aged, round-faced, no children, no man, only one vacation in her life, Bulgaria this summer, her first trip out of the country after nineteen years of work . . . ahead of her now only the downward slope of life after 40. Recently Soviet women have taken to advertising in the West: photos and resumés to magazines and newspapers, marriage brokers and underground networking, even expensive video-taped self-promotions aired on Western television stations. But Vera has no money, no looks, no youth. No possibilities.

Her affections fixate on Michelle. "I like you the best. I cannot say why. People just have tastes. I love you the best. . . ."

For Sasha, perhaps more hope: she is slender, she has children, she is a boss in some factory in the city. She holds her vodka better. She worries about her guests, about what they will say about her, about her city once they leave. "Have you had enough to eat? Would you like some potato and fish soup? Please do not tell anyone how poor we are here. Tell them this is a beautiful city." She circulates a photo of herself and her children.

Michelle deflecting Vera with toasts of vodka. Sasha telling Ewa about her job, her children, her ex-husband. Vera coming unraveled. On the television, some Soviet big band. Sasha obviously in the mood to dance, but both males ignoring her signals. A toast to peace, "the most important thing." Vera in the kitchen, drunk and desperate for affection. Sasha knowing Vera is crumbling. Her guests beating a panicky retreat. "Things getting out of hand here." "Who knows where we are, what could happen." "Want to watch the police." An exchange of addresses, promises to write—in English? in Russian?—and then four Westerners stumbling out the door, past the small winter coat of one of Sasha's boys, quick, quick, quick down the steps, toward the street, Vera and Sasha waving from the window, shouting in English "We love you," and the four of us waving back even as we run toward the tram, quick, quick, quick onto the tram, away from that dark Russian desperation, toward the chartered banks of the Neva, there to swill champaign beside the broad, accepting waters, and watch the bridges rise, and the freighters parade through, in a scene off some tourist painting or an Aurora Publishers postcard.

*   *   *

"Have you noticed," I point out, "there is not a single banana or orange or grapefruit or lemon for sale anywhere in this city." In Poland, bananas were the first fruits of the new capitalism. You found them everywhere after the country opened up, and people eating them everywhere. Exactly one banana's distance from every street market, you found a trash can overflowing with peels.

But that was Poland.

"I don't know how they live or what they eat," says Ewa. "No salad, no cauliflower, not even cabbage and onions. Only cucumbers. Vera told me that tomatoes cost 10 rubles a kilo, which is unbelievable for these people."

Meat, even sausage and ground meat, is scarce and bad. Cucumbers are indeed the only vegetable in plentiful supply. Lunch and dinner, every meal of our visit, it's cucumbers, cucumbers, cucumbers. Our last day in Leningrad brings to the street market what appears to be the first hint of this year's strawberry crop: maybe ten quarts. Long queues at the milk store. Empty shelves in the food stores—not even fruit juices, apart from strawberry juice concentrate. And certainly no kiosks on the corner selling *hamburgery* or *hot doggy.* Only ice cream on a stick, and coin-operated drink machines: deposit 15 kopeks, and get a glass full of watered-down sugar water. Leave the glass for the

next customer, comrade.

The Russians are handsome and well formed, especially the males, but I don't know how they live or what they eat.

*   *   *

Among "Things to Do During Free Time," a sign in our hotel lobby lists theater, ballet, boat rides on the Neva, and souvenir stands at the semi-privatized, semi-policed Ostrovosky Square Market.

"Be careful," the sign warns.

I have spent long hours among Russian traders in Warsaw and Łódź, in street markets from Białystok to Kraków to Berlin. I have found Russians to be more or less honest traders (occasionally they'll slip you a half-empty jar of caviar or a dead watch, but keep your eyes open and your hand on your money, and you'll be okay). I have seen interesting things for sale at this market. Also, we'd like to try our hand at trading some Western goods for Soviet souvenirs, especially a couple of shirts and blue jeans brought for that very purpose. So the morning of our fourth day in Leningrad, we are off to the market with a bag full of trading goods and a head full of plans.

And by golly, this works! First try, we trade a pair of just slightly worn American blue jeans for an English language souvenir book on Leningrad I had been wanting since we hit town, published probably at $2 or $3, but $20 the asking price all over Leningrad. For $20, I can get a brand new pair of jeans

215

at Poor Borsch's back in Minnesota, so this is a good trade.

Then we trade three Southwest State University T-shirts (the old logo, and that the reason the bookstore had marked them down to a couple of bucks apiece, but the Soviets neither know nor care) for a super hockey jersey, bright red, number 9, CCCP across the front, KPUTOV in yellow letters across the back. Michelle very pleased, and I as well.

Fending off peddlers of watches we don't want and matrioshka dolls we already have, I move toward a display of lead soldiers, hand painted, for friend John Nemo and perhaps a few for myself. I've got a brand new pair of 501s, label still on, direct from the U.S.A., and how many soldiers you going to give me for this pair of Levi's?

The lad looks them over, noting the stitching and location of the seam, the tag, the size. Then he offers me eight soldiers for the jeans.

Fifteen, I suggest.

Ten.

Ten soldiers and one of those ceramic pipes there, for Michelle. Ten soldiers and one pipe.

While he ponders my last offer, a couple of other boys come up behind us, offering hard cash for the jeans. I indicate I want soldiers, not cash, and return to bargaining with the vendor. The boys say something to him in Russian, but I can't understand. "Ten soldiers and one pipe for the jeans."

"I will sell soldiers only for money," the toy soldier man announces. "Three dollars each soldier."

I turn to the boys who want to buy the jeans. "How much?" I ask.

"Twenty dollars."

"How many soldiers will you give me for twenty dollars?"

"Sell us the jeans, Mister. We give you twenty-five."

"Ten soldiers and one pipe for $25?" I ask the vendor. He agrees.

"I'll take your $25," I tell the boys, "and give them to this fellow for the soldiers and pipe." They count two tens and five ones into my hand, I give them the jeans, and turn to the vendor.

But my hand contains only five one-dollar bills. The two tens have vanished.

Michelle and I look at each other and say the same thing simultaneously: "Rip-off!"

"You go this way, I'll go that," I tell her. I'm off running, looking for a pair of band new Levi 501s, a couple of young boys on the run, finding not a thing, stopping, angry, perplexed, feeling stupid and gulled, pushing ahead, knowing the chase is up and the hunt futile, hesitating, pressing ahead, returning, hesitating, angry, foolish.

Half way around the market square I meet Michelle.

Who has the jeans in her shaking American hands.

"Out of the corner of my eye, I saw them duck behind one of the vendor's stands, and I followed them. One began to run, but the other just walked along He had the jeans. I caught up and grabbed them. I think they're the same ones."

What a tough Western girl I have! "Son of a bitch!" I keep repeating over and over again. "You got the jeans."

"We gotta get out of here," she repeats over and over again.

Now it's our turn: quick down Nevsky Prospect. Melt into the crowds. "We'll take these jeans to the store that buys Western clothes," I tell Michelle the Bold, sell them, and use the money to buy soldiers and a pipe."

Alas, we're not quick enough. A tug at my sleeve and a voice in my ear: "Hey, mister, how about my five dollars back?"

"What?"

"You have your jeans. Please give me my five dollars."

"For two years I live in Poland," I lecture the lad, two fingers raised for emphasis, knowing the old Russian-Polish animosities, "and for two years I have never been cheated by a Pole. I am three days in Leningrad, and already somebody tries to steal from me."

"Please, mister, my five dollars?"

"Well, you've learned a lesson: don't fuck with Americans, and especially don't fuck with tough western American girls. Now get lost before I call a cop."

At the Passage Store we negotiate a price of 500 rubles for the jeans. A Godfather type peels five one-hundred-ruble notes off his bankroll and hands them to me. This is another scam: fifty- and hundred-ruble notes, repudiated over a month ago, are no longer legal tender. "Nyet," I tell the Godfather. No hundreds. Twenty-five ruble notes only. He chuckles amicably as he counts out 20 twenty-five ruble notes.

"Man, you can't trust these Ruskies," Michelle says.

Returning to Nevsky Prospect, we encounter Neil and Ewa, tell them the story of Michelle, Scourge of Market Pirates, share a good laugh, and send them off to the market to buy as many soldiers as 500 rubles will buy.

Which turns out to be sixteen. "Sixteen lead soldiers for the pair of jeans," I tell Michelle the Avenger.

"Plus the hockey shirt, plus the book," she reminds me. "Plus we have five dollars from those nice Russian boys."

*   *   *

The museums and churches and palaces of Leningrad are impressive, as is the old brick building along the Neva where Stalin interred those who disagreed with or threatened him, as are the canals and the river itself—but the most impressive things in Leningrad are its monuments to those who died in the 900-day blockade of World War II: the Memorial to the Heroic Defenders of

217

Leningrad on Victory Square, and the mass graves of the Piskarev Cemetery.

Especially the cemetery, where 470,000 soldiers and workers lie buried in mass graves, rectilinear mounds arranged in long rows, each headed by a stone bearing the year in which these people died, the number of the mound, and a star for soldiers, a hammer and sickle for workers. The mounds number over 200, and the grass grows lush on each of them. An eternal flame burns at one end of the cemetery, a stone memorial rises at the other.

Most of our company is too hung-over for cemeteries, but Ewa and I want to see this place. Our visit coincides with the fiftieth anniversary of the start of the Nazi blockade, an occasion for parades and a wreath-laying ceremony. Ewa and I stall until noon, chatting with our Intourist guide and one of her older comrades, a medal-encrusted survivor of 78 who claims to have co-founded the Pioneer camp to which every East Bloc teenager aspired. Our guide's deference and respect suggest his story is legitimate, as do his medals: row upon row, more medals than stars or hammer and sickles on grave mounds. The old Russian affection for medals never died.

Just before noon, he excuses himself to join the parade of mourners marching down the central aisle between the green mounds. First, surviving veterans and children of the blockade. Next, representatives of political organizations, followed by military organizations, party representatives, foreign representatives—China, France, even Germany . . . but not the U.S.A. A dozen Orthodox priests with a large white wreath. Then the people, anybody, everybody, people with a single red rose or a red carnation, for the mounds, for

218

the memorial, for trees near some of the graves. A great river of people. The amazing capacity of the Slavic people to sustain suffering, the great anonymous masses of the Russian folk.

To one side, a demonstrator with a hand-lettered sign: "I did not die during the blockade. I am dying a little bit at a time now."

*   *   *

I spent most of the train trip through Poland toward the Soviet border trying to figure a good place to hide my illegally purchased rubles, settling finally for a pocket hollowed out in the end of my couchette mattress, where the cover had been ripped, probably by somebody else making a pocket in which to stash illegal rubles. I improved on his plan slightly, twisting the cover off to one side and making a second pocket, in which I deposited my 1,000 rubles, then twisting it back into shape, so the old pocket would act as a decoy . . . then turning the mattress upside down in its sleeve, tearing a new hole and making yet another dummy pocket . . . all of which proved needless precaution, as the customs agent searched neither mattress or luggage, asked only about gold and pornography.

Most of the return trip I spend worrying about customs agents confiscating the champagne and vodka we are bringing with us, anxious lest I lose the Soviet sailor's cap and army belt I've bought as souvenirs for Ensign Stephen Pichaske, wondering whether I should have bought that $150 nineteenth-century icon at Ostrovsky Square. And talking and drinking and eating with Ewa and Neil and Michelle. And looking out the window at the potatoes, more potatoes, and yet more potatoes grown in small private garden patches along the railroad tracks. And drinking tea made from water heated at the coal-fired boiler at the end of our sleeping car.

On the return trip, we fall in briefly with a young soldier from Kazakhstan en route to assignment in Dresden. He speaks no English, of course, but is quite taken with one of the Polish girls on the tour (also with Michelle and Ewa) and by the idea of being among Americans and Brits. We offer him some champagne, which he drinks without enthusiasm. "True Soviets do not drink champagne," he informs us. "True Soviets drink vodka. Would you like to drink some Russian vodka?"

Ewa and Michelle, old hands at vodka drinking, accept enthusiastically, but our soldier has no vodka to drink. He can find some, however, and off he goes, up and down the entire length of the train, searching for good Russian vodka for his Western acquaintances, who meanwhile suck away at their good Russian champagne, becoming in the process increasingly drunk and just a little loud. One passenger complains, is offered a cup of champagne, and turns us down cold: "Soviets do not drink champagne," he informs us gruffly.

Around 12:30 the soldier returns with a bottle, which he presents to us.

219

We open it, pour some in a cup, and drink, not tossing shots properly, just passing the cup around. But our soldier refuses his turn, and his refusal fuels our paranoia. So does our guide's warning: "Be careful. Something is up."

We consider our position: four Westerners alone in the amplitudes of the CCCP, suitcases loaded with souvenirs and Western clothing, purses and billfolds still thick with hard currency. The Soviet sleeping car has no proper compartments, no doors to lock before falling asleep, only a whole car full of ostensibly snoozing Soviets, some possibly playing bird-in-bunk, just waiting for us to get good and drunk so they can pull some slick stuff. Possibly the soldier himself is a Merry Prankster.

Our suspicions grow when he ducks back to his own bunk, then returns with a bag full of what smell like drug-laden balls of this or that, offers them around, again with vodka, again refusing to partake himself. "Be careful. Something is up."

The upshot of the whole paranoia trip is that we refuse to either eat or drink, at which the disappointed soldier returns to his bunk and sleeps soundly, as we do not, until dawn. Daylight reveals the drug balls to be goat cheese. The vodka was a good-faith offer, we decide.

To restore Soviet-America relations, I offer him a T-shirt in English—"World Fencing Championship, Denver Colorado, 1989"—before we leave the train at Brest.

*   *   *

Crossing the Soviet-Polish border is the all-time slickest thing I have ever seen, a stroke of genius on the Polish guide's part, and—like the tour itself—a fortuitious conjunction of strategy and the blind luck of catching the CCCP at the confused moment of its collapse. Half a year earlier, the entire tour would have been impossible, or, if possible, would have been tightly controlled and closely guided. Half a year later, the tour would have cost ten times the price we paid, and been twice as dangerous. Sometimes you get lucky. A month earlier our egress from the CCCP would have been an agonizing twelve- or twenty-four- or forty-eight-hour nightmare peopled with huddled, smelly, hostile masses and surly, truculent guards. Sarah, Jim, others at the Institute had tales to tell. A few months later—who knows? Maybe easier, maybe tougher. Maybe duties and inspections. Maybe confiscations. Maybe delays. We have none of them. We have seized a moment, and it is ours.

Russian-Polish border crossings, everyone in Łódź understood, take so long that trains generally rolled out of Brest without their passengers, who disembark, squeeze into a large and crowded customs hall, ooze ever so slowly through inspections, emerge after eight or ten or fifteen hours on the other side of the fence, to meet the next train to Warsaw. Thus, while trains from Moscow are usually only an hour or two delayed, passengers arrive in Warsaw twelve to twenty-four hours delayed, and on a train different from the one on which they left Moscow. The crises at the crossings are a direct result of new Soviet freedom of travel—more people going in and out—and the arrival of The West at Russia's very doorstep. No longer insulated by Poland and East Germany, Russia now shoulders alone the burden of policing East-West trade and traffic. And she's hopelessly unprepared.

The resultant crush of traders and tourists overloads the system, producing legendary waits: five days in some cases, many kilometers of trucks, cars, and buses at the motor vehicle crossings, which number only six.

Mindful of this, our tour guide has formulated a plan: take the train to Brest, take a taxi to the crossing point, walk across the border, and meet a Polish tour bus on the other side of the line.

Which is exactly what we do. Outside the Brest train station, we hire six Soviet taxis to carry us to the actual border crossing, past 2.5 kilometers of waiting tour buses and trucks and automobiles, as close to the gate as the drivers dare to come. We pay them, shoulder our luggage, and walk a hundred meters past more cars and buses toward a gate in a cyclone fence. Our Polish guide explains that we were on foot, and the gate opens. We pass through, carrying our luggage, arriving half a kilometer (and hundreds of additional cars and buses) down the road at a second gate. Here our guide speaks to another Russian guard, and again the gate opens, and again we walk west, another 200 meters, past more cars and buses. To yet another gate.

At the third gate a problem develops. This guard orders us to queue with others: members of other tours, car owners, Russians in vehicles loaded with trading goods. No special treatment here. As we are well within sight of a large customs hall and the actual border, most of us would be more than willing to congratulate ourselves on having jumped perhaps four kilometers of people and wait out turn. But our Polish guide is not satisfied. She returns to the second gate, brings her man to the third gate, and passes with the second and third guard into the customs building. I study the people around me: Russians camping out in tents, families cooking dinner in a stew pot over a fire made of cardboard boxes, people in various states of distress, anger, boredom, despair. Not a single west-bound vehicle passes through, although several east-bound vehicles exit, headed for Brest and Moscow.

Eventually our guide returns, and collects our passports (those of the Westerners on top, please), handing them to a guard who disappears into the building. We are permitted to pass through the third gate, walking our luggage past more cars and buses, to the front of the building. There we wait, barred from the twisting gravel road through Russian-Polish no-man's-land only by a couple of young army guards with light arms. We speak loudly in English and glance nervously at our watches: the guide's story is that the Americans have to catch an international flight out of Warsaw.

After half an hour, two Belgian cars pass the auto inspection on our right—which includes driving over a grease pit from which guards can inspect the underside of vehicles—and speed down the gravel road to Poland. A tour group from New Zealand comes up beside us. Their bus crosses the grease pit. They climb inside. "Could you hold the bus for us?" our Polish guide asks; "We're going only to Polish customs." Scorning us peasants on foot, they zoom off the road toward Mother Poland and the West. Our guide asks one of the soldiers about renting a bus to take us to the Polish station. 80 rubles we could pay. No, he thinks, this would not be possible. We will have to walk.

"How far?" somebody asks in Polish.

"One kilometer," the soldier answers in Russian.

"One kilometer?" I repeat in English, thinking I have misunderstood. "Only one—not two, not three?"

"One kilometer."

"Then we will run," I say in English. The soldier smiles.

Still we wait, an hour, the New Zealanders gone ahead of us, and the Belgians. Finally our guide calls one of the soldiers over, goes with him into the customs house.

Ten minutes later, she returns, with guard, with passports, with permission to move on. "We go now," she says brusquely, and quickly enough the whole group hoists their luggage, walks gingerly past the bemused soldier, and heads down the winding gravel road to Poland. Goddam! We are out of Russia, and nobody but nobody has once examined our luggage. I could be hauling five icons. I could be hauling ten kilos of Soviet gold, fifteen kilos of Ukrainian Red. Anything. Everything. Nobody even looked.

Michelle and I rifle our passports looking for a red "CCCP" egress stamp. Nothing. "Westerners don't get stamped," Ewa tells us. "You didn't get stamped coming in, either."

"Unfair," Michelle objects. "Let's go back and demand our stamp."

"Keep walking," I suggest tersely. The toy soldiers and the books are heavy, and the sun warm.

Around the first bend in the gravel road, a curious sight: cars and buses backed up, as outside gates one and two and three.

"Nothing is moving here," Michelle whispers. "Something's going on at the Polish border too."

The Polish word for "strike" passes back and forth among members of the group, but we just keep walking, past cars and buses, more of them now, past the Belgians, past the New Zealanders in their comfortable bus, to the Bug river, to an armed guard in front of a red and white striped crossing barrier.

"Passports," he demands as we approach.

I hand him mine.

"No stamp," he points out.

"Americans are not given stamps," I tell him. Unsure of himself and certainly unwilling to assume responsibility for a decision of this magnitude, he

confers with a colleague in the sentry box. "Westerners are not given stamps," his colleague confirms. The guard phones his superiors. Finally he shrugs his shoulder, raises the gate, and the whole tour group goes trip, trip, tripping over the bridge, toward a Polish guard on the other side of the Bug.

"Polska Tour," our guide smiles. With a wave of his hand, the Polish guard motions us through his barrier, examining not a single passport, not a single piece of luggage. Past more parked vehicles we walk, toward the Polish customs shed, where, after a ten-minute pause (apparently the Polish guards are on strike), we walk on through, past cars, past buses, to the back of the building. Where waits—yes!—the bus from Łódź.

And that is the story of the Polish tour group that just walked across the border at Brest—three hours flat, ahead of all the queues of Russian cars, Soviet citizens, Intourist tours, New Zealanders, Belgians. They are waiting there still, for all I know. A happy bunch indeed, of Polish and American and British tourists, headed back to Sweet Home Łódź with disco tape blaring over the bus loudspeaker.

"Once at the German border last year, a friend and I waited two days," a Pole tells me. "It's good we had Westerners with us."

"It was good at the Polish border that we had Poles along," I responded.

"The line of cars to get into the Soviet Union is 17 kilometers long," the bus driver announces on the loud speaker.

Then a second announcement: "We will pick up a group of traders headed for Łódź. I met them earlier today and negotiated with them for a ride.

223

Thirty-five people. Please, everyone on this tour sit in front of the bus."

Well, why carry sixteen when you can carry fifty-one and make extra złotych on the side?

At the train station we meet the Russians and their guide, loaded with suitcases, tired, anxious, having endured heaven knows what to get this far, delighted with this bus which will bring them to the Promised Land, wary of Poles and Americans, confronting, most for the first time in their lives, The West, here, now, on this bus, a little sooner than they had expected.

Carefully they load their bags, press watchfully into the rear seats, stare forward at us. They are tired, but also alert to possibilities. Not two kilometers on the road one member of our tour has bought a Zenith camera for seventy Deutschmarks, hard currency. Other Russians offer watches, sweatshirts. One girl shows me a silver and gold bracelet: "Twenty dollars," she says in English. Michelle holds up the hockey jersey: "Does anyone have one of these?" (She wants one more for John Nemo, Dean of the College of St. Thomas, a former player himself, a peewee coach, and in fact the Minneapolis-St. Paul coach of the year.)

No hockey jerseys. The lead soldiers will have to suffice.

A "Perestroika" watch?

None: perestroika is history, and so are perestroika watches.

There is bartering all up and down the bus, and later off the bus when it pauses in Warsaw for kiełbasa and beer. One Russian has already sold his chainsaw, and the girl with the silver bracelet is approaching everyone in sight. I feel a curious adopted national pride, showing Poland off to in-coming Russians, an emotion apparent as well in the other Poles. Welcome, comrades, to the West, land of plenty, bananas in the streets and all the good beer you can drink. Even easy conversion into hard currency.

I buy the bracelet for $10 American.

This is indeed what the Soviets have come for. "They get only one chance usually," their guide says, "and they have unbelievable trouble: trouble getting visas, trouble at the borders, trouble on the trains, trouble in Poland. Poles and Russians do not like each other, as you know. Each knows a truth about the other which neither admits, not even among themselves. These people get cheated and robbed in Poland, by customers and by the host families they stay with. None speak Polish. They don't even know the currency. They have only themselves to help each other, and they are all afraid. But the hard currency they bring home will pay half a year of expenses in the Soviet Union."

"This sounds just like Poles only a year ago," says Michelle to Ewa.

"How Poland has changed," Ewa exclaimed. "This trip has been a journey back in time."

224

Home

29 Żrodłowa was a middle-range Polish flat, biege cement walls on the outside, biege cement on the inside, not as modern and airy as the suburban residences some Poles have managed to construct for themselves around the perimeters of Łódź, not as high-ceilinged elegant as flats in surviving pre-war urban bloks, but larger and quieter than the apartments most Poles wait decades to acquire and more comfortable by far than the dorm rooms assigned to some foreign faculty and most visitors. It was "the Fubright flat," maintained by the University for Fulbrighters and British Council appointees, inhabited by my predecessors and my successors. Michelle and I assumed a proprietary attitude to which we were not entirely entitled, buying furniture and kitchen utensils (we stopped short of repainting the walls). I still remember 29 Żrodłowa as home, residence for two of my fifty years on this planet, an important address on my list of addresses: 911 Delaware Road, 555 Delaware Road, 540 LeHann Circle, 930 N. Fountain, 700A East State Street, 245 Briargate, 2724 N. North Street, R.R. 1 Minneota, 29 Żrodłowa, R.R. 2 Granite Falls.

The flat was on the first floor of a three-story building built after the war on a triangular plot of ground in a quiet part of Łódź, on the edge of the former ghetto. It fronted on a dead-end alley, entrance to which was restricted to residents. On one side was the Military Hospital; on another was a larger, higher and less attractive blok of flats; on the third side ran Żrodłowa itself, a quiet and spacious boulevard leading from Strykowska past a public park (once the private estate of some long-forgotten industrialist; a flight of neglected cement stairs led from his crumbling fountain to the site of his long-gone mansion), past the bed of a dried up river, to the terminus of bus 57. Our livingroom window looked out on the hospital, on the hospital balcony, where patients and visitors came to smoke cigarettes at all hours of the day and night, on the small parking lot beside the hospital, where I parked my Skoda that second year in Poland. The window of my study looked out across a well tended rose garden at the tan wall of the adjacent blok, where most afternoons of the fall and spring a young girl from upstairs played skip-rope games with her friends. We called her the "Good Morning Girl," after her greeting to us Americans,

225

which was the same morning, afternoon, and night, and probably the only English she knew. The kitchen window of our flat overlooked Żródłowa to the gardens beyond, eighty or a hundred contiguous plots, 30 by 50 feet, surrounded by a gate and hedge, privately owned, cultivated each weekend (and many weekdays) of the year by urbanites desperate for the country.

The outside walls of the brick and cement building were thick enough for Michelle to sit in the window bays on a long winter afternoon while blowing soulfully on a tenor saxophone (made in Elkhart, Indiana) we bought for $100 in a Kraków second-hand store. The iron bars which protected our first-floor flat from intruders also enhanced radio reception, and by holding my boombox close to the window I could, very late at night and sometimes just barely, pick up baseball, football, or NCAA tournament basketball games on AFN out of Berlin—the sounds of fairytale America left lightyears away. Those thick walls, the first-floor location, and drafty windows made the flat a chilly home, even in the summers, and especially in October, before the government turned our heat on for the winter. Michelle and I spent whole days sequestered behind the closed door of the kitchen, warmed by the lighted stove, eating, reading, drinking, playing a few games of rummy before scampering to the bedroom, ducking under multiple blankets, and shivering ourselves to sleep. Heat improved the place considerably (as it arrived late, it lasted long, so as October was overcold, May was overwarm), but even closing inside doors and drawing the thick tapestry cloth drapes could not cut drafts, which I tamed finally by stuffing rolls of newspaper into the cracks above and below windows, then covering the seams with duct tape. It didn't help that the outside pane on the livingroom window was broken—it was broken when we arrived in September 1989, and it remained broken until we departed in August of 1991, a low priority item, apparently, on a long list of Things That Need Fixing in Łódź.

Still, I am thankful for those tall double windows, opening to the inside and painted bright white enamel (it was the multiple layers of paint, I think, which prevented them from shutting tightly): opened in the late spring, with the drapes thrown aside and the breeze drifting through white lace undercurtains, they admitted the sounds and smells of Old World Łódź, and hinted at the elegance of older European flats, the ones with huge rooms, elaborate plaster ceilings, parquet floors, oriental rugs, and antique cupboards, wardrobes, dining tables.

Our flat consisted of four rooms plus a bathroom, all opening off an entrance foyer which itself contained a closet and a bookshelf and might legitimately have been considered a fifth room. On the top shelf of the closet—buried beneath the cardboard boxes, string, tape, and wrapping paper we scavanged at every opportunity, I tucked a plastic travelers' checks wallet with the $5,000 in U.S. currency ($100s, $50s, $20s, and, for gratuities, fifty dollars in $1s) we brought in September, 1989. The closet was probably the first place a thief would have looked . . . if ever a thief had had opportunity to ransack the

flat, which no thief ever did. In the closet we stored the electrical vacuum cleaner. In the closet I hung my denim Dylan jacket with the USNA patch on the right shoulder and the Sgt. Pepper patch on the breast pocket; then the brown cloth winter coat I bought in Warsaw for $4; then the suede coat I found in a Cepelia for $60; and finally the dark blue USNA pea jacket Steve gave me, which, with a black Russian fur hat, comprised my *Hunt for Red October* outfit.

The smallest room I claimed as a study; it contained a sofabed, a desk, and two sets of shelves. The shelves I filled with artifacts for use in American Culture lectures: a Sears catalog, two Southwest State catalogs containing fall and winter 1989-90 course listings, an *Information Please Almanac*, several Dr. Seuss books, two styrofoam Big Mac containers, a whiffle ball and bat, a genuine horsehide baseball, and a stack of Minnesota Twins plastic Coke cups with pictures of Kirby Puckett and Kent Hrbek. On the desk I set the manual typewriter I was lucky enough to find in a second-hand shop for $50 in October of 1989, and a stack of letters from home to the left, teaching materials and syllabuses to the right. The walls I papered with pictures of son, daughter, and friends. A large map of "Illinois Authors" and a calendar-poster promoting the Minnesota State University System constituted necessary ties to the States. This room was our guest bedroom, in which slept Ken and Robyn Luebbering, Wolfgang Drexelbauer, Norb Blei, Gabriele Jones, daughter Kristin, and Michelle and I while vacating the main bedroom for visiting parents. I'd give a great deal of money right now to be back in this room, pecking away on a letter to Steve or Kristin, on a lecture or syllabus, on a paper or talk for Poznań, Wrocław, Warsaw, Salzburg, München, York (England), Rach im Hochgebirge

227

(Austria), or sunny Szeged (Hungary).

The bedroom was spacious, a good fifteen feet square, although the bed itself was a narrow double or wide single which sagged slightly in the middle. The room was furnished with a small bureau and two large wardrobes, both blonde wood or particle board. Otherwise it was mostly space, taken up initially by the trunk in which we brought our electronic equipment and audio and video tapes, later by two Soviet three-speed bicycles (heavy as steel tanks, they will endure to Judgment Day), a child's rocking horse I bought in Central for $20 one otherwise unmemorable afternoon, and after March, 1990, by a large birch desk I bought for $80 in a Cepelia on Piotrkowska. Michelle had long wanted a desk of her own, but even used furniture was scarce in Poland. I bought the desk as soon as I saw it, having no idea, really, how to get it home. Bus and tram were out of the question, although Poles are not too embarassed to haul automobile fenders, television sets, and large children's rocking horses on a tram. Łukasz Salski volunteered his Syrena, but the desk would have crushed it, I'm sure. Owners of larger vehicles were wisely silent. Folks around the Institute thought I could hire a "taxi truck," but nobody had any idea how to get hold of one. I wasted the better part of an hour guestimating the time it would take for Michelle and me to carry the thing, perhaps 200 yards at a leg, up Piotrkowska (or some back street) and down Nowotki, knowing this would never work, realizing that even if it did, Michelle would be most uncomfortable with the stir it created.

Finally, in response to the obvious question directly posed—"Where to find a truck in Łódź, in this moment of street markets all over the city?"—the obvious solution presented itself, and betaking myself to Supersam Magda I approached a peddler who appeared to have just sold out of flour, or bread, or whatever he'd been selling. Would he, I asked in very broken Polish, take me and his truck to Cepelia, pick up this desk, and haul me and it to 29 Żrodłowa? The $10 I gave him was probably more than he'd cleared all day, even after he paid the traffic ticket he received for illegally driving, at my instruction, several blocks up Piotrkowska to Nowotki. Within half an hour we were unloading said desk in front of a very pleased Michelle, and he had a good story to tell friends and family.

The bathroom was spacious and relatively clean: tiled floor and some tiles around the sink (a previous tenant, probably true Brit, had applied decals of violets and ducks and swans to the yellow tiles around the mirror; I never took the time to remove them), large white bathtub, clotheslines for indoor drying, hot water heater, trash basket, and cabinet for towels, sheets, soap and toilet paper if you had any. Michelle rearranged and reinforced the clothlines to support a shower enclosure made of two American shower curtains clothespinned together, and we added a large metal pail used mainly for a laundry basket, but also to store drinking and cooking water whenever water service to the flat was shut off, which was about every third month. I saw enough flats around Łódź,

228

around Poland, to appreciate the size of this bathroom: in post-war flats, the bathroom is basically a toilet: back in and you can exit forward, but enter face first and you'll have to back out. Ewa Bednarowicz claims (and her assertion is corroborated by considerable other testimony) that most modern Polish girls lose their virginity in the bathroom, it being the only private place in flats or dorms. Accomplishing this in most Polish flats must require real agility, and can't do much for the experience. Ours would have been positively luxurious, maybe even kinky fun . . . although no virginity was lost there, to my knowledge, during our stay in Poland.

The kitchen was small and inadequate, except perhaps for someone accustomed to New York or Los Angeles efficiency apartments. It measured five feet by twelve feet, with a low counter running length-wise along the long, exterior wall, and the sink, the garbage pail, the oven, and the refrigerator taking up the other long wall. At the far end was a clothes washer (ours was the only Fulbright flat in Poland to come with a clothes washer), which connected to the water faucet and drained into the sink when in use. At the near end stood a small table, useful only for preparing food: the room was far too small for chairs.

The sink was metal and often-painted, Midwest farmhouse circa 1920. There was no trap in the drain, and the sliding wood doors on cabinet underneath, painted moldy cream, had long ago rotted around the bottom. A plastic rack above the sink served for air-drying dishes. The sink was the most deficient feature of the flat, and we used it two or three times a day. The gas stove was perhaps 20 years old, its oven caked with years of grease. The refrigerator was

small but modern, and even contained a tiny freeezer compartment: American college dorm, 1983. A storage cabinet above the clothes washer had ripped loose before we came, its presence marked by a few mollybolt holes in the wall. Storage shelves, limited to the area below the window wall counters, were rendered largely inaccessible by the narrowness of the kitchen and the presence of the table and washer, so Michelle and I bought a new unpainted birch cabinet which we set atop the counter next to the window. In it we stored popular food items, glasses and dishes (more of which we also purchased, heavy dinner plates hand-painted in a floral pattern, imported from Vietnam), leaving the lower cabinets for bulk food items and for pots and pans. Eating utensils we kept in a tray set literally on the windowsill, next to the cookbook and a jar (later a "Kuwaiti [evaporated] Milk" tin) which held the cooking utensils.

In this less than ideal kitchen, Michelle and I learned to cook. This had not been our intent before entering Poland: looking at the generous exchange rate and knowing our hectic lives in America, I'd dismissed the problem of eating rather airily: "We'll just eat out," I told a number of people before we left. When we heard that Sara Sanders and Steve Nagle on the night of their arrival in Warsaw dined on roast duck, delivered with all the trimmings to their hotel room, for $1 apiece, Michelle and I were ready for ten months of fine dining. "Łódź has to be even cheaper than Warsaw," I told Michelle, "and they ate in a four-star hotel. When I worked that summer in Neuwied, Germany, I used to reward myself on Saturdays I worked overtime with a steak dinner at the best restaurant in town. Steak, fries, salad, desert was 4 marks, one thin buck, served by a waiter with a white towel draped over his arm. Man, those were the days."

We ate in one restaurant, I believe, our first week in Łódź, a two-bit greasy dive of an East Bloc joint which was the only place still serving food at 7:30 p.m. on September 28, 1989, haunted by drunks and pan-handlers. The food was fatty pork and cold potatoes, the dishes were dirty, the service was almost self-serve. The following evening we tried the Grand Hotel (four stars) dining room at 5:00, but the entire facility, a waiter indicated, had been booked for some "occasion" (a word for "party" does not exist in Polish). We poked our noses into the dining room of another hotel, but left without dinner. Don Morrill had once mentioned a lovely little restaurant "on the outskirts of Łódź," directions to which I still believe he left intentionally vague. We discovered the little Esperanto Café long after we learned to cook, about the time we finally figured out that Poles take their big meal early in the afternoon.

Even when we found them, even when open, even in Poland's second largest city, restaurants were not offering much to eat that fall of 1989. I remember dining one Sunday with Krzysztof Andrzejczak in a restaurant at Żelazowa Wola, site of Chopin's villa, now a lovely museum and a major tourist attraction. The waiter pointed to two items on a long list of entrées and said, "We have this and this, the pork and the chicken [naturally]; and we have only one serving of chicken." To Michelle's dismay, Kris ordered the chicken; to her further dismay, when it arrived, he declared it badly prepared and returned it to the kitchen uneaten.

We ate a lot of toast and jam, and more than once were reduced to making a meal on "frytki" (greasy French fries) and "zapiekanki" (tomato sauce, cheese and mushrooms on an elongated slab of bread, warmed—not quite baked—in a dirty toaster oven) at a train or bus station. We saw stands advertising fish, but they were permanently closed. For the record, the first hamburgers in Łódź were sold from a small window at number 56 Piotrkowska street. It opened in the spring of 1990.

It became quickly apparent that we would not simply "take our meals out," that we had better stock our little refrigerator and pack our little cupboards and learn to fix something with which to repay those colleagues generous enough to host us at dinner during our first few weeks in Łódź.

Much of our food came from the American Embassy commisary, to which Fulbrighters were given access during 1989-90, owing to shortages on the Polish market. Michelle and I made almost weekly trips to Warsaw to shop, visit with Elizabeth Corwin, take a beer and some TV at the Eagle Club, and catch up on newspaper reading (for the record, English language newspapers, three days to a week old, arrived at Łódź newsstands in the fall of 1990, about the time five minutes of CNN headline news began appearing on Polish television). We were temperate, I think, in our use of commisary and check-cashing privileges (how else get money into Poland?), unlike some Fulbright colleagues and many of the embassy personnel. Mostly we bought sugar, rice, tomato paste, wine and beer, spices, scouring pads, cleansers, paper napkins, spaghetti, and such characteristically American luxuries as brown sugar, chocolate chips, cheddar cheese, salad dressing, Oreo cookies, maple syrup, breakfast cereal, popcorn. For meat, vegetables, and cheese we relied on the local economy, especially a little 10x10 grocery on Nowotki run by two older women. This Little Old Ladies' Store managed to stock lettuce, carrots, onions, potatoes, apples and bananas, butter, kraut, eggs, flour, other fruits and vegetables in season, and fresh chicken through the difficult winter of 1989-90.

Chicken was our specialty: in our grease-coated oven, in a grease-coated pan we roasted a chicken every fourth day, inviting guests if guests were to be had, indulging ourselves if there were none. One chicken made one meal, with a wing and a breast left over for lunch. The bones I boiled for soup: a little rice, carrots, a few onions, spices as available. Other evenings we did spaghetti (grinding our own beef in those early days) with salad and Wishbone Italian dressing. Some evenings we ate pancakes; others, omelets. Michelle learned to make lasagna noodles from eggs and flour, and thus her own lasagna. In the same deep pan we used for roasting chicken, I baked apple pies, using real butter for the crust. Of course there was always Polish sausage, and roast pork (a favorite of our British colleagues, although once a large and especially promising roast proved to be mostly bone, much to my embarassment and our guests'

231

disappointment). Sometimes we ate bacon or ham, although good Polish ham proved to be something of a luxury in Poland, being mostly for export.

I have very fond memories of cooking in that little kitchen, of time spent preparing and eating food, of the luxury of having the time to spend preparing and cooking food. Of the anticipation of a good meal with good friends, and good wine and good talk, of the luxury of having plenty of time to entertain good friends with good food. The kitchen, and the dinner table in the living room, were part of the magic of Poland. And for all the eggs, cheese, and meat, my cholesterol level was lower when I returned from Poland than when I left the U.S.

Even during the October chills, the living room was the center of our flat, of our home life in Poland. The outside wall was hung with Jan Filipski paintings of old Bałuty, dangling on strings from curtain tracks. On another wall hung the landscape Michelle and I bought instead of a Christmas tree (which we could not find) in December of 1989, something under which to place our small gifts to each other. Below it was the green sofa-bed with a bad leg. Against the Żródłowa wall a shelf filled with books, and the dining room table, on which sat the short-wave radio which in 1991, brought hourly reports from Voice of America and BBC on the war in the Gulf. Along the fourth wall, a phone stand, a table supporting the Polish television and the American TV-VCR (with the Embassy's voltage converter) and a cabinet containing audio and video tapes. A raggy black-and-white needle-punched carpet covered a stained parquet floor. Early in my first year I considered buying a new, large, colorful, machine-made but still all-wool oriental rug I saw in Central for $100, but discarded the idea as too gorgeous for a one-year stay. By the time we'd elected a second year in Poland, the carpet's price had risen 300% and its size diminished by 50%. Had I foreseen the inflation of antique prices over two years, and my car ownership second year, and relaxed export restrictions and inspections, I would have bought half a dozen oriental rugs, and refurnished the living room in antiques from the Komis on Piotrkowska . . . another notion I toyed with in the fall of 1989, when antiques could be had for a song but could not, of course, be exported. Hindsight is so 20-20.

I remember our living room for the guests and dinners, of course, and for the tremendous party we threw to celebrate Kristin's visit, a party to end all parties, Brie cheese and Diet Pepsi courtesy the New Poland, champagne and caviar courtesy the Old Russia, sound system by Sony, couples into and out of the bedroom, people from all over the world, I ducking out for fresh air around 2:00 a.m., returning 2:15 with a City of Łódź flag liberated from the hospital, Kristin astonished at "a whole new you, dad, I never knew existed."

But I remember the living room mostly for long hours spent there with Michelle, watching a videotape, listening to an audiotape, reading books, playing double solitaire, working crossword puzzles, studying the almanac, listening to the radio, or dialing away at the telephone lines to Gabriele in

Berlin. Or waiting for the phone to ring. Or discussing what we might do with a long, chilly winter evening. At such moments I was a child again, with enormous stretches of time to kill, and nothing much to kill them with. Łódź was in that regard a genuine sabbatical rest.

During our stay, everything in our flat broke at least once. Water was a constant problem: every other month, it seemed, a water main would break, and blue-uniformed workers would pry up the paving stones of the sidewalk on Żrodłowa, shovel out the sand beneath, drop in a new section of pipe. The city would park a truck of drinking water beside the job site, from which inhabitants of effected flats would fill jugs, buckets, pots and pans. The first repair caught us short of containers, but we wised up, bought the galvanized bucket-clothes basket, and had no problem during ensuing repairs.

The gas water heater went twice; once it was fixed, the second time it was replaced. We heated water on the stove, and took baths instead of showers. The clothes washer went once, due clearly to a previous tenant's abuse. The repairman fished from its rubber hoses and mangled pump a variety of articles, none of them ours, one a warped comb that had penetrated right through a weak hose. The doorbell ceased to work and was never repaired. The screen of the Polish black-and-white television set went blank early in 1990. I reported its demise to officials at the Institute, indicating that I personally didn't much need a television, although a subsequent Fulbright might want one. In fall of 1989, Polish TV offered little beyond stale travel films, flat soccer games, and "talking heads" shows. By fall of 1990 Polish television had become more interesting, but the University had already sprung for a water heater and a refrigerator, and I didn't want to be a greedy. The refrigerator broke late in the spring of 1990, a failed compressor, probably overworked from being next to the stove. When we left Łódź for the summer, it was still dead as a brick, but Tom Bednarowicz promised to monitor the situation. A replacement arrived, finally, in September after Tom told University officials, "The Americans are coming back next week, and they're going to be awfully pissed if there's no refrigerator in their flat when they return."

The phone died winter of our second year: no dial tone on out-going calls, no buzz on in-coming calls, no nothing. We reported its demise immediately and were put on a list of people awaiting phone repair. Estimates in January were a month to six weeks, since we ranked behind important facilities like hospitals, hotels, and government bureaus (probably ahead of most individual Poles, except those who dropped a few bucks on the list-makers), but we waited, finally, three months for the phone's resuscitation. Crises domestic and foreign disappeared as if by magic: we were genuinely inaccessible except by mail, which was running about two weeks for an airmail letter between Łódź and the States, a month total for question and reply.   At least we no longer sat around waiting for the telephone to ring.

I was naturally impatient with the delay, until one afternoon while

walking along Kościuszki Street I happened upon an open manhole in which a man was working on telephone repair. Beside him was a cable probably a foot in diameter, spun of thousands of tiny colored telephone wires, which he was checking, one at a time, connecting one after the other to a strand he held in his left hand, then dialing up some number on a phone beside him, waiting for a reaction, breaking the connection and trying another wire, and then another wire. I don't know just what he was trying to do, but I understood why re-establishing phone service to 29 Żrodłowa could take forever. I also understood how enormously difficult it was going to be to build a modern telecommunications network, the foundation of modern commerce, in Poland.

In retrospect, the dead phone becomes less irritating than it was at the time, a kind of emblem for our comfortable isolation. For years in my office at Bradley Polytech hung a poster of a man walking through the woods with his daughter, captioned simply, "Take Time." It hung right over my desk with the Dylan poster, the *Easy Rider* poster, and the photos of Martin Luther King, Jr. and Jack Kennedy. Of course I believed in the idea of taking time, as I believed in King and Kennedy, and Steve, Kris and I took time, whenever I could, for walks in the woods at Jubilee Park. But I never really *took time* in the hustling seventies, and I certainly never took time during the scrambling eighties. Lost time with my children is the great regret of my life.

In Poland, finally, of necessity, I took time. Time to walk the mile and a half to the Institute. Time to wander through street markets, to explore the alleys and parks of Łódź, to ride the rails and drive the Polish back roads to cities and towns and hamlets I never knew existed. Time to queue, time to think. Time to become involved, as I had been in the late sixties and early seventies, in the lives of my students. Time to cook my own dinner, to talk civilly and at length to friends. Time to play solitaire and read books and listen to tapes with Michelle. Time to do not much of anything. Time to take things "easy, easy."

Taking time is really the core of any return to the past, and taking time is at the heart of nostalgia. It's more than merely finding hours and weeks to remember and return, although return and memory do require time enough; it's a matter of shucking the time-driven sense of urgency we picked up somewhere in our early teems. Our loss of innocence came precisely at that moment when we become aware of time's iron grip on our lives; prerequisite to any return to innocence, however temporary, is some loosening of the reigns, a willed stilling of the false clock that ticks our our days.

Learning in Poland to take time probably added a decade to my life and five pounds of sugar to my disposition.

Taking time was, finally, what 29 Żrodłowa meant to me, why it so easily became for me, why it will always remain for me, Home.

A Postscript: January 1993

I entered Poland in September of 1989, and returned to the United States in August of 1991. During that two-year period Łódź—and the rest of Poland, and the rest of the old East Bloc—was transformed and retransformed three or four times over. Change continued after 1991, and change continues today. 'Tis not, sir, the same country with which I fell in love . . . although it was, and remains a place I love and, in some small measure, know.

The meditations of this book reflect the Poland Michelle and I knew: inflation, political chaos, economic reform, the shifting face of Piotrkowska Street. Throughout 1992 and 1993 Polish friends provided periodic updates: letters, phone calls, visits. For longer or shorter stays, Michelle and I hosted both Tom and Ewa Bednarowicz, Agnieszka Salska, Agnieszka and Grzegorz Siewko, Agnieszka Leńko, Anna Kępa, Ella Tarnówska, and Ewa Ziołańska. We drank a lot of vodka, talked a lot of stories, ate a lot of crabs' legs.

I returned to Łódź in December of 1991 and, most recently, in December of 1992. My habit has been to land in Berlin, then take a train from Berlin to Łódź. A round-trip flight Berlin-Warsaw adds one to two hundred dollars to the cost of an international ticket, several times the price of a second-class train seat . . . and the Berlin lay-over allows time for a bottle of wine with Gabriele.

The Berlin Wall is a thing of the past in December, 1992, little more than a long and winding path through the heart of the city, used at some points as a park, at some points as a garbage dump. Michelle thinks it would make an ideal bike path, but land in this city is too precious. Already Siemens and Sony plan a huge joint-venture building on Berlin Wall no-man's-land near Brandenburger Tor, and despite all that newly added emptiness in eastern Berlin, other sections of the no-man's-land will inevitably be developed. The crossing at Friederichstrasse, where Michelle and I and several thousand other people stood like impatient cattle in 1989, is a museum these days, and both S-bahn and U-bahn run smoothly east to west, north to south, along the tracks of a unified city. I saw the Wall go up, and I saw the Wall come down, I reflect in early December 1992 on a river walk between the arrival of my airplane from

237

Minneapolis and the departure of my train for Warsaw. I remember Kennedy's speech and the Berlin Airlift. I am becoming one of the Old Ones, and Gabriele too. *Sic Transit* whatever.

At Hauptbahnhof I buy a train ticket from Berlin to Kutno: $25 one-way, second class . . . still cheaper than plane fare, but I can't help feeling nostalgic for that first round-trip ticket Michelle and I bought in 1989 for a couple of bucks total. One corner of the station, on the lower level by the mostly vandalized lockers, retains the old ticket windows for eastern destinations, signs in Russian still, washed out photos of Soviet landmarks on the wall, even a dead tourist bureau behind one open door. The old yellow East Bloc furniture, the old yellow East Bloc wall paneling. Tales of things past, of things passing.

$25 isn't the end of the ticket business, however. My train to Kutno (junction with the north-south Polish rail which will take me down a short leg of the triangle to Łódź) is some kind of new Berlin-Warsaw super-express. It has a proper name and number—the *Berolina*, EC #43—and proper printed schedules lie on each seat. The carriages are brand new in all acceptable yuppie colors: teal, beige, plum. The lavatories are clean and toilet-paper equipped, the train includes a dining car and refreshment carts, and we are On Time right down the line. Formalities of the Polish-German border crossing are accomplished, most graciously, with the train in motion by officials who board in Frankfurt/Oder and leave the train at Rzepin, its first stop in Poland. A survey, printed in four languages and collected somewhere around Poznań, solicits suggestions for further improvements in service and equipment. During the five-hour ride, at least half a dozen service personnel enter my humble second-class compartment: purveyors of refreshments, passport inspectors, collectors of survey responses, conductors German and Polish.

Such service requires reservation and a surcharge as well, collected en route in marks and złotych. My Berlin-Kutno train ticket costs, finally, about $40. Second class, one way.

"Welcome to the new New Poland," I think, wondering if maybe I should not have flown directly to Warsaw.

At Kutno I have exactly sixty seconds to get myself and my suitcases off the Berlin-Warsaw express. The Berolina arrives and departs almost before I disembark, nearly blows me right off the platform as it hustles on down the line. At the Kutno ticket window I request a one-way, second-class fare to Łódź, a distance of maybe fifty kilometers, offering in payment a 10,000 złotych bill, about one dollar. "No, no, sir," says the clerk; "not enough these days." She shows me the ticket: 11,200 złotych, second class, one-way.

Well lackaday: this slo-mo ride on a battered double-decker used to cost mere pennies, kopecks, groszy, centimes. Used to be, used to be: the days of riding PKP rails are gone for good. Those were the days, my friend. . . . You may be back in Poland, but it's 1992.

Notes on the new New Poland? How about Casino Łódź for starters, main floor of the Centrum Hotel opposite Fabryczna Station: mirrored walls and potted (plastic) plants, a couple of bars, slots, blackjack, piped-in disco music and strobe lights, dealers in black tuxedos with white ruffled shirts, the loveliest of long-legged Polish lovelies skating across the smart black-and-white expanses, glitz and glitter, noise, flash, cash, bash . . . virtually empty. "It's losing money like crazy," confides a student who works there; "it attracts almost no foreigners. But for the moment, the wages are very good."

Seriously now, would you trust a Polish gambling operation?

Along Piotrkowska Street, more polish than ever. Part of the street is a walking mall finally, and dressed to the nines this December for Christmas. Colored lights and plastic trees. The bedraggled Santa Claus in a dirty red suit and scuzzy white beard handing out trinkets in Central wouldn't fool my dog Bear. New ownership at Hortex translates roughly to same delicious ice cream, same deluxe service, double the price. Mercedes and BMWs line the streets around the Grand Hotel. Rooms cost $100 a night (when you wake up in the morning, you're still in Łódź), the restaurant and café are full of foreign businessmen sweet-talking smart, young Polish women. For a dollar and a half, one of those young boys outside will hand wash the Polish mud off your car while you linger inside.

The Golden Duck is packed; you need reservations to get in, and even reservations are no guarantee. "When first the Golden Duck opened, Michelle and I often dined there alone. . . ." Rainbow Tours, now in swanky new offices,

239

is also packed; Grzegorz, Sławek, and Agata have no time to talk now. The frozen foods store, where you could always, even in the darkest days, get packages of frozen strawberries and frozen cauliflower for fifty cents a kilo, has become a new restaurant, one of a dozen along this street, all British-American cheap and cheerful: tile floors, plastic tables and counter in red and black and white, clean plate glass windows, microwaved burgers, gyros, fish and fries. The hamburger window at 56 is just another window, no burgers and no commemorative marker. Fashion stores are everywhere, and jewelry shops. Piccadilly and Argentum. Leather skirts and jackets in Central now run 75% of American prices, maybe 100%. Bargains in crystal, cloisonné and porcelain, on anything imported from Russia or China. Łódź is still the best shopping in Poland, in terms of goods and prices. But Łódź is no longer free. Not on Piotrkowska, not on the side streets and parallel streets. Not anywhere.

Two years ago Bob Jones and I walked down Piotrkowska one afternoon. "In four years, we won't be able to afford this street," he told me.

Tram service has been further reduced, the price of tram tickets is up another notch. A Łódź-to-Warsaw, second class train ticket costs now nearly four dollars. Seventeen cents round-trip when I came to Poland. The 50% discounts for state employees will end soon. Automobile and truck traffic is a problem during peak morning and evening periods: rush minute traffic in Łódź. Things will get worse before they get better.

In the book stores, translations of Harlequin romances side-by-side with Dostoevsky and Hemingway. "I just finished translating a biography of Michael Jordan," one fifth-year male at the Institute tells me. "It was terrific!" The

hottest book going is a kiss-and-tell exposé written by a French journalist who balled her way through the whole Polish legislature before doing a strip-tease in print.

I visit the bread store: same as ever. Some things are forever. The public market is more structured but lively as ever; seeing the boxes of puppies I hear again the voice of Michelle: "Somebody's got to save these puppies."

Agnieszka and Piotr Salski have found a new Chinese restaurant in Łódź, better than the Golden Duck, somewhat removed from Piotrkowska Street, but quiet and clean and nicely decorated with a goldfish pond and oriental graphics. Mario's pizza in the Polonia Hotel still serves the best pizza in Łódź, in the most authentic American fifties pizza restaurant atmosphere.

Hamburgers? Anywhere. Everywhere.

Agnieszka Salska and I make a one-day excursion to Warsaw: small business at the Fulbright office, mostly chat. Coffee and cake in the subdued elegance of the old Victoria Hotel Café, Berlin of 1958. The Russian street peddlers have been evicted from the square around the Palace of Culture, relocated "elsewhere" in the city. There's nothing here now but a small village of permanent wooden sheds—Polish-owned and licensed and selling mostly clothing—and a more or less permanent carnival. The old Party Headquarters on Jerozolimskie now houses the Centrum Bankowo Finansowe. Why not? Ground floor of the Palace of Culture had been converted into an indoor shopping mall long before Michelle and I left. In one bank, a cash machine.

In Old town Warsaw, tourist and prices approach levels of London, Berlin and Paris. No art bargains here, or even souvenir bargains. Wood carvings, prints, paintings, woven wall hangings, amber, silver, greeting cards made of dried flowers: so many lovely things. I buy nothing, grieve inwardly for the old days of solitude and low prices. Even the churches are crowded. On the steps of the old cathedral a Western tourist in pleated slacks is stopped by a native, who objects to his ice cream cone: "No food in the church. You may not enter this place eating ice cream." In a thick New Jersey accent, the tourist shouts ahead to his wife: "Go on ahead, Shirley; I'm sick of all these goddam churches anyway."

During lunch at the Bong Sen, a British pop vocalist complains to her agent about the Polish royalty offer. Two Austrian businessmen talk joint ventures with one Polish colleague. A can of Canada Dry tonic water costs a dollar. Lunch for two runs nearly twenty dollars, and not as much food, methinks, as in the old days when Michelle and I ate here together, two bucks the pair of us, including two bottles of generic Polish tonic.

Warsaw now has car dealerships for Ford, Chevrolet, Porsche and BMW. In Warsáw every hour is rush hour.

Agnieszka Salska, Roman Catholic, hard-core Solidarity member with a Ph. D. in American literature, mourns the "westernization" of New Poland, the new materialism, the harsh economic bottom-lining, decline of "old values, old

241

culture, old traditions." She frets aloud over church incursions into state, especially on the areas of education and abortion rights. She worries about the old folks, about Łukasz now in Poznań, and about growing old herself. "When your parents start to go, you realize you're next on the edge." There is little joy in watching one's self become, gradually, inexorably, one of the Old Ones.

I visit Poznań, hosted by Łukasz Salski and Iwona Kozlowiec. Łukasz treats me to the opera, Iwona to a student party in a fifth-floor downtown loft. Knock at the door, tell them Marek sent you. Tall windows set below tall ceilings, white lace curtains, white paint on the walls, mattresses on the floor, the only real furniture a stereo system and speakers. Wine, vodka, and my bottle of Lithuanian champagne. This used to be "Soviet Champagne"; the very label is a cultural artifact. We sit on the floor propped against a wall. The music is mostly cool jazz. Tobacco and marijuana. Couples disappear into the recesses of the flat, reappear after five or ten minutes. American beat, 1962. Iwona, a fifth-year student at the Philological Institute, is writing her thesis on Henry Miller.

Łukasz still drives a Syrena. His flat is decorated with kerosene lanterns. He makes me a present of two all-metal model cars, produced in Russia, the good ones, two models I did not have, including the big black stretch limos beloved of old party bureaucrats. "A friend from Russia stays with me when he comes to Poland to peddle these," he explains. "He will not mind if I give you two."

One afternoon on the way to her flat, Iwona announces that we must detour to the "school" where she "teaches": the European Correspondence School of Foreign Languages, a few offices in one of the upper stories of an old Poznań factory. Its operational center is a room perhaps forty feet square, two walls of which are taken up by shelves supporting 120 or 130 cardboard boxes, each bearing a name, each filled with envelopes. The names on the boxes are the correspondence students' teachers—*Kozlowiec* reads one box—who read their weekly assignments, correct and grade them, add a personal comment or two, seal them in self-addressed stamped envelopes, which return to this office for counting, certification and mailing. Iwona does not know what students pay for their correspondence work in English; she receives 3,000 złotych, about twenty cents, per lesson corrected. Each course consists of 32 lessons, and there are many levels and courses. The correspondence package includes workbook, exercises, a tape, and "your own personal tutor." Iwona is personal tutor to maybe five hundred correspondence students.

"This is a terrible way to learn English," Iwona admits. "The lessons are simple translation or substitution exercises: 'Change the verb to the present tense.' 'Make the singular subject plural.' 'Substitute the correct form of *you* for *me*.' Nobody ever checks pronunciation. This is no way to learn English.

"But it's a very good way to make money. I earn about a hundred dollars a month. It's useful at Christmas, and for buying books."

This more than anything else strikes me about Poland, 1992: English

is everywhere. It's the smart language. Everyone wants English, everyone needs English . . . and people who can teach English are in great demand. My former students, despite their complaints, lead good lives these days. Anna 22, newly married to a medical student, complains in her new flat—fresh paint, parquet floors, floor-to-ceiling bookshelves filled floor-to-ceiling with books—about needing a new car. Agnieszka and Grzegorz, 23, newly married, complain about his inability to find work outside of their clothing-manufacturing business, and about living still in a dorm. About having traded the newer car for an older model . . . to underwrite their three-month trip to through the States last summer. On their TV, we watch several hours of videotape, taken with their own camcorder. At the moment, Agnieszka is making big bucks giving private English lessons at the school where she teaches: classes she organizes, which she teaches, for which she collects. She's grumpy that once these classes approached the $200-a-month level, the school raised their room rent.

Magda, 22, complains about a job offer somewhere in the east of Poland: the flat which comes with the job is attached to the school, a part of the school, not a separate building or a flat in some separate blok. "It would be too noisy," she thinks. Her starting salary would be substantially more than that of an experienced biology teacher, who pays for his own flat, because she teaches English and the school needs English.

Beata is unhappy because translation contracts pay so little and the work is so long. "Ink is where you find it," I tell her, thinking back to my early twenties dining on rice and chicken wings in a frosty graduate school apartment I shared with two other guys, $25 apiece a month, a now-demolished hovel behind the Maple Shade Inn across the street from the Athens, Ohio Airport.

Who do these kids think they are, anyway?

1993 America students, I guess. "We're not supporting education these days," our university financial aid officer once told me; "we're supporting lifestyles."

Or perhaps they're just Poles, pessimistic and insecure as always. "Nobody expects this to last," Agnieszka tells me. "I have plenty of work now, but tomorrow—who knows? Nothing has ever lasted very long in this country. You get what you can while you can."

Okay. Things change, and things do not change. Some things survive all change. Sometimes the more things change, the more they stay the same. In Poland as in the rest of life.

"What do you think of the New Poland?" everyone wants to know. In two weeks, I am asked the same question a hundred times, and at the end of two weeks, I still have no answer. This country has aged a decade in slightly over a year.

So what do you tell your former lover, meeting her again ten years after the great affair?

"You look great, haven't changed a bit. Same old you, same old me. Nothing could ever change, could it?"

Is that what you tell her?

"I'm happy for you, pleased things worked out so well for you. I wish I could have been part of your new prosperity."

Is that what you say?

Do you play her a song? Ray Charles, "I Can't Stop Loving You"? Dire Straits, "Romeo and Juliet"? Sinatra, "Thanks for the Memories"? Bob Dylan, "A Simple Twist of Fate"?

Is that what you do?

I guess. Mostly, I think, you thank her for the good times neither of you ever expected to last, for the good times locked safely away in both your hearts and in the vault of time-space eternally present. For the silly, irrelevant, insignificant scenes which, for whatever silly and irrelevant reason, have come to rest comfortably on the cupboard of your mind, polished to a platinum luster by the buffing cloth of time. For sanctifying a place, to which you can return, by time-struck gifts you cannot reclaim.

You thank her mostly, and bless her, and praise her ripeness, and promise she will stay forever young.

Well. She was very beautiful, graceful as a willow and fine-featured. She was dressed stylishly in black and white. She smiled when I waved, but turned her back quickly as I raised the camera. Then she disappeared into a blok of flats.

Photo Credits

All photographs by David R. Pichaske or Michelle Payne Pichaske. Dates and locations as follow: (x) park scene, Łódź, 1991; (2) street scene, Łódź, 1990; (3) statues removed from Staromiejski Park, Łódź, 1990; (4) street scene, Łódź, 1989 (7) near village of Novy Świat; (10) student group, Poznań, summer 1991); (11) graffiti, Łódź, spring 1990; (12) Sienkiewicza Park, Łódź; (14) countryside north of Łódź; (15) courtyard off Narutowicza St., Łódź; (21) Kaliska market, Łódź, fall 1989; (23) Pabianicka market, Łódź, 1990; (26, 27) Zgierska market, Łódź, 1990; (29) town market, Gdańsk, 1990; (33, 35, 37) Jewish Cemetery, Łódź, 1990; (38) café, Kraków; (40) barbican, Kraków; (41) ul. Kanonicza, Kraków, 1989; (44) courtyard, Collegium Maius, Kraków, 1990; (46) bakery, Nowotki near Kili ńskiego St., Łódź; (49) bread store, Nowotki at Mariana Buczka St., Łódź; (50) ice cream stand, Gdańsk, 1990; (53, 54) paintings, Jan Filipski; (58) Poznański factory, Ogrodowa St., Łódź; (60) rear of workers' flats near Poznański factory; (62) Fako workers, 1991; (68) Warsaw Central Station, 1990; (70) chimneysweep, Torun, 1990; (73) Piotrkowska St., Łódź, 1990; (78, 80, 81) Łódź street scenes, 1990; (82) Gdańsk Shipyard Monument, 1990; (84) Mariacka St., Gdańsk; (88) Gdańsk Shipyards; (90, top) gate at Auschwitz; (90, bottom) doorway, Łódź, 1990; (95) train yard, Łódź Fabryczna; (97) detail, Gdańsk Shipyard Monument; (98, top) kitchen workers, Poznań, summer 1991; (98 bottom) street sweeper, Łódź, 1990; (101) Łódź skyline; (106) souvenirs of Poland, 1990; (109) Łódź alley, 1990; (118) graffito, Łódź, 1989; (121) Łódź Cathedral; (122) drawing by Andrzeja Mieczki; (124) Russian market in front of Palace of Culture, Warsaw, 1990; (126) sleeping bum in Warsaw Central Station, 1990; (129) queue at Central Store, Łódź, 1991; (136) Gdańsk Shipyard memorial; (140) Popiełuszko memorial, Jesuit Church, Łódź; (142) building façade, Łódź; (144, 145) Poznański Palace, Łódź; (147) Moniuszki St., Łódź, 1990; (148) Credit Society of Łódź, 21 Pomorska St., 1990; (150) Michelle and Wojtek; (153) Hotel Iwa dining room; (155, 158, 160) Białowieża countryside, 1990; (162, 163) Łódź street scenes, 1990; (168 top) Łódź street sweeper, 1990; (168 bottom) Poznań street worker, 1991; (170) building façade, Narutowicza St., Łódź; (172) along Nowotki St., Łódź, 1990); (174, 176) Jarocin, 1991; (178) Jet/Rainbow Tours, old location, 1990; (180) beer advertisement, 1990; (181) "Seven-Eleven Spożywczy," 1990; (182) The Golden Duck, Łódź; (187, 188) Poznań city square; (193) Nowotki and Kościuszki streets, Łódź, 1990; (196) Łódź street scene, 1990; (202) assorted Polish posters, 1990; (207) Łódź graffiti, 1989; (213) Russian train, 1989; (215, 218) Leningrad, 1991; (223) Leningrad tour group, June 1991; (227) Żrodłowa 29; (229) Restaurant Europa, Kościuszki St., Łódź, 1989; (234) painting by Jan Filipski (235) street scene in Bałuty, Łódź, 1990; (236) alley off Piotrkowska St., 1992; (238) Berlin Wall, December 1989; (240) Central Store, Łódź, Christmas, 1992; (243) Piccadilly Delicatessen, Piotrkowska St., Łódź, 1990; (245) alley off Piotrkowska St. near Łódź Cathedral, 1989 (printed also on front cover). Cover: alley off Piotrkowska St. and poster remembering the German Occupation of 1939-45, defaced to indicate Soviet "Occupation," 1945-89, Kraków, 1989.